The Quest for Meaning

The Quest for Meaning

Friends of Wisdom from Plato to Levinas

ADRIAAN T. PEPERZAK

Fordham University Press
New York
2003

Library of Congress Cataloging-in-Publication Data

Peperzak, Adriaan Theodoor, 1929–
    The quest for meaning : friends of wisdom from Plato to Levinas /
Adriaan Peperzak. — 1st ed.
        p. cm.
Includes bibliographical references and index.
    ISBN 0-8232-2277-2 (alk. paper) — ISBN 0-8232-2278-0 (pbk. : alk. paper)
    1. Meaning (Philosophy)—History. I. Title.
B105.M4P46   2003
190—dc22   2003016057

Printed in the United States of America
07 06 05 04 03   5 4 3 2 1
First edition

CONTENTS

PREFACE

To become a philosopher, one needs guides. Skillful teachers are not enough; we want experienced thinkers whose lifelong search for meaning has opened ways to wisdom. Who would not delight in being guided by the greatest of them? In fact, you are welcome at the university in which they teach. Their lessons are available for everyone who knows how to read the texts they left. True, they do not address all your questions, but are their central questions no longer yours? How many of our important questions are really new? In any case, the thoroughness of their struggles with truth are exemplary; even if you cannot agree with all they say, they might inspire your own attempts to make sense of humanly living in this world and time.

Alas! you may object, posthumous words can only be the beginning of a dialogue: their authors no longer participate in discussions. They neither change their writings, nor do they even explain the most difficult passages. Indeed, they need interpreters to speak in their name or, from a distance, about their work. Sure, no interpreter can replace the author, who thus generates a plurality of second hand philosophies. But what would become of our own responsibility for thoughtful experience and experienced thought, if the masters did not refuse to answer all our questions?

Plato, Plotinus, some theologians of early Christianity, Anselm, Bonaventure, Descartes, Pascal, Leibniz, Hegel, and Levinas have been guides for me, as they have been for many other lovers of Sophia. This book offers some reports about their guidance, in the hope that you, in your way, might profit from it. Do not expect a synthesis that transforms these classics into parts of one overall system. Wisdom cannot be condensed into a theory, even if arguments and meditation belong to the search. The quest for meaning is greater than a doctrine, because it encompasses entire lives of unique individuals on the way to something greater and more profound than thought.

But why *this* selection of guides? Many others could have been chosen, but one life is too short to study with all of them. The Platonic inspiration of the philosophers represented here and the Christian roots of the reporter are obvious. The combination of different personalities with Western classics generates various affinities, and affinities are important; they should not be avoided as too subjective for philosophy.

ACKNOWLEDGMENTS

Many friends have again cooperated to produce this book, too many to be thanked by name. I do, however, want to express my deep gratitude to Catriona Hanley, Ryan Madison, and Laurel Madison for their generous dedication in translating early versions of several chapters from French into English, and for ameliorating the English of all the chapters.

The first versions of chapter 1 and 7 were published in *Faith and Philosophy* 14 (1997) and 15 (1998). The first version of chapter 3 and French papers that were transformed into chapters 4, 5, and 10 were presented at the biannual "Colloquium Castelli" organized by Marco M. Olivetti, who also accepted them for publication in the Proceedings published by CEDAM (Padova): *Incarnation* (1999), *Ebraismo Ellenismo Christianesimo* II (1985); *L'argumento ontologico* (1990), and *Theodicea Oggi?* (1988). Chapter 6 is a revised version of my contribution to the Festschrift for Louis Dupré: *Christian Spirituality and the Culture of Modernity*, edited by Peter J. Casarella and George P. Schner and published by Eerdmans in Grand Rapids (1998). The first version of chapter 8 was published in *History of Philosophy Quarterly* 12 (1995). A Dutch version of chapter 9 was my inaugural address at the University of Amsterdam and part of my *Zoeken naar Zin* (Kampen: Kok Agora, 1991). The French article that was used in chapter 11 appeared in the *Revue Philosophique de Louvain* 84 (1986). Chapter 12 is a new English version of a German text published in *Verantwortung für den Anderen und die Frage nach Gott* (ed. H. H. Henrix, Aachen: Einhard, 1984); see also the translation into English by Gregory Renner in Jeffrey Bloechl, ed., *The Face of the Other and the Trace of God* (New York: Fordham University Press, 2000).

I thank the publishers and editors for permission to use the texts enumerated above for their transformation into chapters of this book.

ADRIAAN PEPERZAK
Chicago-Wilmette
Christmas 2002

INSTEAD OF AN INTRODUCTION

—Human beings seek meaning.

—Isn't that a bit vague for a definition?

—Perhaps; but vagueness is inevitable at the beginning of a search, and a definition is the conclusion of an investigation, rather than its first premise.

—Why then do we not seek our point of departure from a well-established definition that has been accepted for centuries: *homo est animal rationale* ("a human being is a rational animal")?

—Do you find this expression clear? Have we not become suspicious about its components? Do we even know what we mean by "homo," "animal," and "rational"; do we understand how the union of animality with rationality produces humanity? In America we have banned the overarching meaning of "man" by splitting it into "men and women." What "animal," or its predecessor "*zōion*," means, has become obscure: should we correctly translate it by "a living being" or give in to scientist pressure by preferring "animal"? If we accept the latter, "rational" seems misplaced; if we stick to the generic meaning of "being alive," then the meaning of "rational" ("having *ratio*" or the Greek *logon echon*) bears the entire burden of characterizing what kind of life is at stake in our existence. Can we capture the essence of *logos* or *ratio* by "reason" and how do we explain what reason enables us to do, feel, desire, create, be, and think?

—Apparently you do not expect much help from the sciences. However, they could teach you precision in your endeavor to define what typifies human lives.

—I do respect the sciences and thank them for all that they have been able to teach us. I also share your respect for formulas that have been proved by a long tradition from the ancient Greeks to our times; but I have the impression that "seeking meaning" can be recognized by innumerable people as an expression of something that they and all others in fact are doing, albeit implicitly.

—To save your proposal, you now appeal to a distinction between explicit and implicit behavior. But what could the latter be? Do you hint at some sort of unconscious search for meaning? Should we not be even more suspicious about all appeals to the unconscious than about an appeal to reason with its scientific definitions and arguments?

—What I appeal to is what a very long tradition—longer and more universal than the one you evoked—has understood as a quest for wisdom. We do not (yet) know precisely to what extent un- or sub- or preconscious motivations play a role in this quest, but you will agree that the very living of a life, though not a privilege of philosophers, can make us wiser and a life more meaningful than before.

—Your move demonstrates precisely the need for my earlier warning. Instead of pursuing a scholarly investigation, you appeal to existential adventures and heartfelt experiences, while neglecting scientific or philosophical expertise. What sort of "philosophy" can emerge from such material?

—The separation between scholarship and the experience of lives-in-search-of-meaning (their own and "the meaning of it all") is one of the causes of philosophy's gradual turn towards irrelevance. The great philosophers did not buy into such a separation. If they had, their logical refinement would not fascinate us as anything more than skillful precision work. In reading their writings, we recognize that the meaning of our existence is at stake, even if it is not treated explicitly as the focus of their discussions.

—I do not separate life and philosophy, but I want to protect philosophy from the subjectivism that infests all kinds of individual experience and evaluation, which you are pleased to call wisdom.

—Excuse me, my friend, I do not contest your suspicions, but I contend that there are other, more profound kinds of experience and reflection than those that take center stage in theories that systematically exclude the existential search for truth.

—I know the kind of argument you are pursuing, but how can you protect yourself against a takeover of philosophy by arbitrary beliefs, moods, impressions, judgments, and decisions?

—We all know that reason cannot prove its own beginnings. At least some beliefs, perceptions, and feelings must be accepted before we can begin arguing. In order to avoid arbitrariness, we must find out which basics, instead of being "subjective" in the subjectivistic sense of this word, are so fundamental that they deserve a high degree of respect and even trust.

—Are you pleading for a restoration of faith in philosophy? I consider the separation of faith and reason to be as much a definitive conquest as the separation of Church and State.

—I see both separations as two sides of a modern myth that never has been realized. However, let us leave the political question for another time and concentrate for now on the relation of philosophical reason to faith.

—Back to the Middle Ages?

—Not to the Middle Ages alone. And not back, but forward with gratitude. At the ending of modernity, our perspective on the four or five centuries in which it flourished might be less biased than the one that dominated its participants. Looking back to 2,600 years of philosophy, we might argue that the modern period represents an intermission between the Greek and Roman, Jewish, Muslim, and Christian tradition that lasted more than 2,000 years and the scattered, still undecided time in which we happen to live. So long as the modern conception of reason and theory triumphed, the epoch between Greek *epistēmē* and modern autonomy (that is, the period from Augustine to Descartes) was interpreted as an interruption that separated two enlightened periods: the "Greek" period, which lasted more than one thousand years, and the modern period, which lasted four of five centuries. During the "Middle Ages," the autonomy of human thought was betrayed by those who submitted their thought to Jewish, Christian, and Muslim myths, or so the story went. Today, however, nobody can forbid us to see modernity as an experiment that interrupted the longstanding tradition of contemplation that we call the premodern history of philosophy. If the latter view is correct, it implies a task: we must retrieve the premodern tradition in a transformative way, without, however, losing the discoveries of modernity and postmodernity.

—How can you want to reintroduce medieval faith into the philosophical life of a pluralistic world? Don't you see the danger of Jewish,

Christian, Muslim, Hindu, Buddhist, and other fundamentalisms that will tear philosophy (and not only philosophy) apart?!

—Not so fast! From a philosophical perspective, the question of reason's relation to the faith that rules a human life should not immediately focus on this or that confession, as it is practiced and preached in a religious or quasi-religious organization, but rather on a more universal and neutral concept of faith. By faith I mean the basic stance, including trust and conviction, from which reason emerges as a kind of light that makes explicative and evaluative reflection possible. I want to defend the hypothesis that reason is rooted in trust (or, if you prefer Pascal, in "the heart") and that its orientation originates in a desire that draws its overall interpretation from a certain faith. In fact, there are many of such basic interpretations, but all of them show a certain affinity insofar as they concretize the same fundamental desire: the human desire for meaning. No philosopher can escape this desire. When we were initiated into philosophy, we were already betting on a certain faith and no professional philosophy can fully demonstrate or refute this or another faith, although it may help us in critically altering it. According to the modern myth, philosophy is autonomous, but none of the modern or postmodern philosophers have been able to accomplish this ideal. All philosophers, including atheist, agnostic, and skeptical ones, translate a basic stance into conceptual language, without ever being able to reduce its depth and height and length and breadth into a fully demonstrative theory.

—Are you suggesting that all attempts at philosophizing produce no more than cryptotheologies?

—That would be the case if all philosophers necessarily believed in God, even while denying it.

—Do you then claim that all philosophers who affirm the existence of God cannot produce anything other than an overt or masked profession of faith? Such a fideism seems to oppose you to your own tradition, according to which theology thinks about God's revelation, whereas philosophy is the practice of "natural" reason, which finds its evidence in empirical data and self-evident principles.

—Neither fideism, nor rationalism, or empiricism are appropriate points of departure if we wish to have a fresh look at the relations that distinguish and connect faith and reason. Here and now we cannot discuss the huge questions that assail us as soon as we seriously consider all their ins and outs.

—At least we should maintain the universality of human reason and its autonomy with regard to all religious faiths; for how could we otherwise prevent a wave of philosophical (and quasi-theological) fundamentalisms? How can reason serve peace, if it cannot guarantee well-established convictions and practices? I am afraid that, in your view, philosophy, if it's more than a frivolous game, cannot escape a return to totalitarian claims and institutions.

—That would be the case only if the various philosophies were to replace the various religions, *and* if their fundamental faith did not imply tolerance toward other faiths. The discussion itself must show to what extent certain philosophies can fulfill the same function as the world religions, while at the same time remaining tolerant and hospitable toward one another.

—I doubt whether your hypotheses allow for such a demonstration. If you abandon the distinction between a universal dimension of understanding and the various faiths that add particular beliefs to it, you will end up with a biased conception of the universal truth.

—I do not want to abandon the distinction you mention, but for me every faith is a concrete but never perfect version of the truth rather than an addition to it. The idea that a universal dimension of truth, as the domain of "natural reason," can be isolated from its concretizations has become doubtful for me. Plato's philosophy, for instance, does not consist of two parts: a part of universally valid truth and a separable part composed of typically Greek, Athenian, Platonic opinions. The whole "Plato" expresses a Platonic approach to the universal (but perspectival and contaminated) truth, which simultaneously speaks and hides in it. We recognize this approach as a way of access to the truth and experience at least some affinity in studying its characteristic detail, while also experiencing distance from its historical and individual strangeness. Though I doubt whether we can delineate a basic theory that is valid for all humans in all times and places (the truth of "natural reason"), I hope that all truth-loving philosophies, in spite of or due to their particular "biases," converge in a kind of understanding that cannot be fully captured in its verbal and conceptual expressions, although such versions are necessary as preparatory exercises.

—To convince me, you need to present more evidence than your—still rather vague—indications. For our next meeting you should offer a more elaborate theory about all the notions you have used today.

—I agree. But allow me to begin by presenting some illustrations of the postulates that I still have to justify. In emphasizing striking aspects of a few famous thinkers, I would like to show how much their work is motivated and shaped by underlying faiths that cannot be reduced to logical skills or empirical evidence.

1

Philosophia

For Giovanni Ferretti

THE RELATION between philosophy and theology is no longer a hotly debated question among Christians, and yet it is constitutive for the framework in which their thinking develops. Their schools seem to have found a *modus vivendi* for the coexistence of both disciplines, but as far as I know, this coexistence is not supported by a generally accepted metatheory and "philosophico-theological" methodology. In this chapter I would like to challenge a powerful conception of the way in which philosophy and theology are and should be related and to propose a different conception. I will focus here on these disciplines insofar as they are practiced by Christians, and, more precisely, by Catholics. The question is fundamental and consequently difficult, as are all questions regarding the transcendental conditions of basic practices and theories. A skillful solution presupposes not only competence in both philosophy and theology, and especially in their methodological and metatheoretical parts; it also demands that Christians who practice these disciplines have a genuine, practical as well as emotional, experience of their faith and that they be aware of this experience while reflecting on their faith. It is, thus, neither enough to have studied all of Greek or modern philosophy, nor to be a professional theologian, unless the latter also participates in the ongoing philosophy. Since I myself have spent more time doing philosophy than theology, my approach will show a certain one-sidedness. I hope, therefore, that professional theologians, from their perspective, will correct my errors and lack of sensitivity. Another wish is that philosophers and theologians join their skills to discuss the assumptions this chapter states only in a programmatic way.[1]

---

1. Throughout this volume, references to publications without an author's name refer to the author's publications listed in the Works Cited section.

The Question

The format of a chapter does not permit me to begin with an accurate description of the situation of philosophical and theological studies in most Catholic universities. Neither can I summarize here some of the splendid and highly relevant studies on the historical genesis of this situation, from Henri De Lubac's *Surnaturel* (1946) to Michael Buckley's *The Origins of Modern Atheism* (1987) and Louis Dupré's *Passage to Modernity* (1993). Instead of a diagnosis, I will limit myself to a few obvious reminders. Let me begin with the trivial observation that, like almost everywhere in academia, most Catholic universities have separated philosophical and theological studies by offering them in different departments. Most departments of philosophy do not tolerate theological interference, while many theology departments do not care for philosophy. If we had enough time to discuss the explicit and implicit beliefs and assumptions underlying this division, it would probably stir up critical amazement among the discussants and, I hope, convince some of them that our question is an urgent one. Let me immediately pass instead to a more constructive observation, sketching some elements that we should take into account if we want to practice philosophy and theology according to their most rigorous demands.

Philosophia

Since Pythagoras, who perhaps invented the word, *philosophia* has been practiced in many ways. A history of its meanings and modes occupies more than 300 dense columns in the excellent *Historisches Wörterbuch der Philosophie*.[2] It reminds us of the fact that the typically modern definition of philosophy as a purely theoretical result of autonomous reason and common experience is only one of the varieties that have developed in Western culture. Between philosophy as, for example, Gregory of Nyssa saw it exemplified in the holy life of his sister Macrina, and the ideal of a universal and fundamental science, which has haunted modern thinkers, many possibilities of doing philosophy have been tried out. Many distinctions should be made when we talk about the definition and the method or the history of philosophy. I

---

2. *Historisches Wörterbuch der Philosophie, vol. 7* (Basel: Schwabe, 1971), c. 572–911.

cannot even start doing this here, but I need to make at least one important distinction: that between philosophy as an existential involvement on the way to truth and philosophy in a less committed sense. Doing philosophy can be a game, like chess-playing; it can be done as a science, pursued out of curiosity, or performed as a job from nine to five. However, in the following considerations, I will focus on the kind of philosophy that is practiced as a decisive element of a human life in search of wisdom. If we may affirm that human life as such desires wisdom, and that this desideratum involves insight, philosophy can be seen and practiced as the reflective and methodical stylization of the human quest for insight and wisdom. This is philosophy as practiced by the great philosophers from Parmenides to Wittgenstein and Heidegger. For them, philosophy was a way of life; some of them even praised it as the only possibility of leading a happy life. They didn't separate it as a purely theoretical discipline from the practical and emotional elements of human existence but insisted on their unity. However, it is characteristic of the Greco-European tradition that it has stressed the role of thinking and *theoria* in the pursuit of happiness.

As a quest for insight on the way to wisdom, philosophy was more radical than any science, *epistēmē*, or mere theory; it emerged from the most radical desire *(erōs, desiderium)* of human existence and remained rooted in what some have called "the heart." As a search for wisdom, philosophy was careful not to cut its conceptuality off from the experiences of humanly growing lives. Reason and rationality were celebrated and refined, but neither isolated nor seen as self-sufficient principles for the discovery of truth. Even Hegel demanded that his students bring a faith to his lectures: "faith in reason" *(Glaube an die Vernunft)* was necessary to follow the master in his showing how reason—and reason alone—could bring to light the truth and meaning of all things.[3]

---

3. Cf. the following emphasized passage of the discourse with which Hegel began lecturing at the University of Heidelberg on October 28, 1816: *"To begin with, I may not appeal to anything else than that, first of all, you come only with trust in science and trust in yourselves. The courage to truth, faith in the power of spirit, is the first condition of philosophy"* (*Gesammelte Werke*. Hamburg: Meiner, 1968, vol. 18, p. 6). Almost the same sentences are pronounced in Hegel's inaugural lecture at the University of Berlin on October 22, 1818: "To begin with, I may not appeal to anything else than that you come with trust in *science, faith in reason, trust and faith in yourselves. The courage to truth, faith in the power of spirit,* is the first condition of *philosophical study"* (p. 18).

I cannot fully justify here the thesis I am advancing, namely that every seriously committed philosophy necessarily involves a basic faith, but I hope that my readers already agree with me on this, or at least consider it plausible. Nobody can philosophize without some unproven but spontaneous or postulated conviction that has the character of trust. A basic moment of such a conviction is the trust that reality, human existence, the universe, and being as such cannot be utterly senseless; they must have (a) meaning (or, at least, under certain conditions they will have meaning). *"Omne esse est intelligible"* is one of the expressions for this faith; *"ens et bonum convertuntur"* is another.[4]

The faith of a philosopher does not stop at this basic trust, however. As soon as it expresses itself in a concrete way of life and thought, it takes a form in which cultural, historical, and personal moments are recognizable. A careful study of any great philosophy can discover prerational elements that have coalesced into a typical stance and orientation. The rationality of modern philosophy was not autarkic enough to shape by its own force alone the basic movement and discoveries of a human life. Reason comes too late for this, although its critical reflections play a role (but only one) in the (re)direction and the (re)adjustment of a philosopher's existence. A human life has taken its basic form before it discovers the possibilities of what we now, in modern contexts, call "philosophy."

The faith of a philosopher realizes itself in a basic mode of experiencing, sensing, accepting, and approaching life and the world. This mode is expressed in a certain mood, a specific way of being attuned (in bitterness, resignation, melancholy, enjoyment, gratitude . . .), of welcoming (or excluding) phenomena, and of participating in the history of human praxis.

Philosophy as Participation in History

Here I must insert another analysis, though again too briefly: an analysis of the historical aspect of all philosophical activity.[5] If philosophy is an activity that cannot be practiced unless it has been learned, participation in philosophical discussions presupposes that I have been

---

4. "All being is understandable"; "being and goodness are interchangeable."

5. Cf. Adriaan T. Peperzak, *System and History in Philosophy* (Albany: State University of New York Press, 1986), pp. 47–60.

initiated and have acquired at least some experience in it. When I philosophize, I am already set in my ways, although I can still change partially or even undergo some kind of conversion. Other philosophers must have trained me in an activity that has been going on before I became a student, even before I or we or America were born. I was introduced into philosophy not by *Logos, Reason,* or *Empeiria,* but by professors so and so and by the texts they recommended as instructive, worthwhile, or exemplary. There is no way to begin autonomously; as a student, I cannot avoid accepting the authority of certain teachers and texts and taking for granted—at least provisionally—that what they do is philosophy. Later, I might discover that *that* was only a particular style within a varied field, that there are other good or better teachers who recommend different texts and argue in a different vein, and that modern philosophy is only a fragment from a history of philosophical activity that stretches over a period more than six times longer than the period from Hobbes and Descartes to our days. By that point, however, it is too late for starting all over again. In the meantime, I have been formed in a specific style of philosophizing on the basis of particular assumptions that were never proven but have been generally accepted for some time. In discovering the relativity of the philosophical position to which I have adjusted, I can start working on a critical reform or conversion of that position, but if it is true that reason is not autarkic, the new position I will adopt will again be a particular one, and— if my thinking has some originality—an individual one.

CHRISTIANS WHO PHILOSOPHIZE

Faith

After these metaphilosophical preliminaries, we can direct our attention to the distinctive character of thinking as practiced by Christians who are also philosophers. Let us suppose that some Christian has been introduced to philosophy by getting acquainted with analytic and/or continental philosophy as practiced in most American universities. Most courses such a person took did not touch on religious questions. The impression was probably given that, in philosophy, everybody could find out the same truths on every topic. Even if the program contained some philosophy of religion, it probably would not have included theological explanations of Christian faith. Yet as a Christian you cannot do without theology, for you are committed to a community of faith with a life and thought of its own. You have been initiated and confirmed in the faith, the beliefs, the rituals, and the ethos of this community, and for most Christians, this has happened long before they studied philosophy. Your faith consists not in the affirmation of propositions, and even less in a theory; fundamentally, it is trust in God as revealed in the life, death, and resurrection of Jesus Christ. This trust orients and mobilizes your entire existence; it permeates all your possibilities and provides your participation in human history with its ultimate meaning. Your faith has a memory and an ultimate perspective: it expects an *eschaton*. This makes you feel grateful for God's work of creation and redemption, and it confirms your hope. It inspires you with love and compassion, natural responses to God's spirit of grace. Faith is neither an opinion *(doxa)* about God, nor a superscience; it is neither Kant's *Fürwahrhalten*, nor Hume's belief. It does not compete with any philosophy, if philosophy is no more than theory. *Pistis, fides*, faith, is the most radical and total confidence that supports all behavior, feeling, and thought of a Christian. It constitutes the basic stance and dynamism of a Christian life and determines its final meaning. It thus sets the meaning of all behavior and thinking in which Christians express their concerns. This does not mean that we can deduce from faith what the full content and method of behavior, ethos, politics, art, science, and philosophy in our time should be, but it does involve an orientation, a certain style, a certain "music."

Culture

Besides being members of a religious community, Christians are children of a particular epoch and *culture*. As such, we spontaneously share many tastes, conceptions, and uses with non-Christians. Some of the prevailing assumptions might be un-Christian or anti-Christian; church authorities or saints might warn us that we should not share these assumptions, but some of the existing practices and institutions are so powerful that we cannot avoid participating in them. The capitalistic organization of the world economy is an example. Church leaders may condemn this system, but if we want to survive, we cannot stop sharing its functioning. We seem to be in a bind, as Saint Paul was in a bind when he sent Philemon's slave back to his master. Another example is the modern institutionalization of massive violence and the widespread nationalism that again and again proves stronger than solidarity with fellow humans and fellow Christians.

These examples might convince us that Christians not only participate in the noble and beautiful aspects of civilization, but just as much in the "sins of the world." A similar remark can be made vis-à-vis the theoretical elements of the culture. It is not always clear to what extent the beliefs of an epoch spontaneously assimilated by Christians are compatible with their faith or form a stumbling block to their endeavor to understand who and how they are.

The Philosophy of Christians

Christians who practice philosophy are committed to an historical process in which universities, journals, books, libraries, conferences, courses, and standard schedules play key roles. Educated in selected styles and schools with a profound reverence for particular authorities and traditions, we participate in discussions on privileged topics according to certain fashions; we prefer certain authors and texts and neglect or despise others, but we continue to talk about "philosophy" and "*the* history of philosophy" as if we knew them in their entirety. In any case, we exercise this activity by participating in "what is going on in philosophy." Even if we are very original, we continue a history that has been developing for 2,600 years, becoming ourselves links in a complicated network of chains.

As philosophers, we began by sharing unproven beliefs and explicit or hidden assumptions; much of the time thereafter was spent in trying to find out to what extent those assumptions are justifiable, but we have not yet arrived at a complete proof for all of them. Awareness of this leads us to the well-known problem of the "beginning," the "*archē*," the *principia*, and the "ground" of philosophy. The main current of modern philosophy (from Hobbes and Descartes to Hegel) has been dominated by the belief that, through common experience and universal reason, it is possible to establish an unshakable foundation on which the system of truth can be built. The attempt to realize this possibility has failed and led to a situation of relativism and skepticism on the one side, while on the other side there is a growing conviction that the empirical and rational moments of philosophy are rooted in deeper levels of existence with a stringency of their own. Some have pointed toward a "logic of the heart," others to our prepredicative familiarity with things as a form of understanding inherent to the practice of human life itself. Above I have identified every philosopher's basic faith as the soil and source of his thinking. Spinoza's or Kant's philosophies, no less than medieval or Greek philosophies, were rooted in and inspired by prephilosophical commitments. Without any faith, no philosopher is genuine, if philosophy is more serious than a scientific specialty at juggling hypotheses according to formal skills.

Theology

Christians are established on a rock: Jesus Christ. The expression of their faith is heavily dependent on the cultural history in which they participate, however. It is thus a combination of that faith and the transitory elements of a specific culture.

In a civilization where philosophical reflection plays an important role, the concrete forms in which Christian faith is formulated contain philosophical elements. The ensemble of its expressions, insofar as they reflect this faith in the language of conceptuality, constitutes Christian theology.

A Christian who has become a philosopher shares a world of arguments with other philosophers, Christian as well as non-Christian. As a philosopher, one must be at home in the ongoing ways of argumentation, possess expertise in the skills that are required or in vogue, have experiences similar to those of others, and look at things from comparable perspectives. At the same time, a Christian is at home in a community of faith that does not belong to any specific period of time, culture, language, race, or country. This community is not an abstraction, however; on the contrary, it is the most fundamental and encompassing, and thus the most concrete, community of all. Grace, faith, hope, and gratitude pervade the entire life of Christians from top to bottom and vice-versa, uniting them in one *communio*, even if their authenticity and innocence is hampered or damaged by the difficulties of human life.

Our question can now be reformulated in the following terms: How can Christians, in their lives and thoughts, combine membership in an historical community of faith and salvation—which at the same time transcends all epochs *and* is culturally concrete—with a real participation in the republic of philosophy, where they practice solidarity with colleagues who are supported by other faiths?

If philosophy were no more than mastery in skills and tools, there would be no problem. Purely formal elements of philosophy—if these exist—can be shared by everyone, like those of mathematics or chemistry. Their universality is paid for by a very reduced relevance with regard to the decisive questions of human existence. A serious or involved philosopher is engaged in orientations and wagers that cannot be justified by formal techniques alone. Once involved, one is already on a specific way, guided by a basic trust that it will lead to more truth.

Why is it that many Christians who are involved in philosophy try to maintain a strict separation between their philosophical work and their reflection on the Christian meaning of the lives they live in their Christian community? Do they want to convince their non-Christian colleagues that their method and findings are as authentically philosophical (rational, empirically justified, universally valid, and so on) as those of agnostic, atheist, or skeptical thinkers? Is there anything in the philosophy they share with the latter that makes a wholehearted adherence to the Christian community difficult? Do they suffer from a conflict between two loyalties? This would be the case if the content, the orientation, the approach, or the spirit of the philosophical practice in which they engage were hostile to the spirit of Christianity. But how would such be possible, since both faith and philosophy are committed to the quest for truth?

To acquire some clarity in these questions, a Christian cannot rely on philosophy alone. As philosophers, we must, of course, research the sources to which we owe our perspectives and convictions, including the philosophical faith that is expressed in our particular and individual modes of philosophical and Christian involvement. But what and how we are insofar as we are Christians is not revealed by reflection alone; faith itself gives a more adequate interpretation of this fact; and faith is a gift of the Spirit, a grace. Christians cannot ignore the way in which their own faith illuminates their experiences of world and history; neither can they simply neglect the reflective self-interpretation of the religious community to which they belong. This statement does not require that a Christian should deny the difference between faith itself and its epochal expressions in typically Greco-European forms of reflexivity; it does mean, however, that we, as philosophizing Christians, cannot refrain from engaging in theological reflection on the relevance of Christian faith for our commitment to philosophy. The issue of the relation between philosophy and faith involves thus two series of questions:

1. questions concerning the relations between the faiths that underlie
    actually existing forms of philosophy on the one hand and Christian
    faith on the other, and

2. questions about the relation between the typically philosophical
    mode of explanation and the theological approach.

Our question appears to involve us in a *theological* question, at least to
some extent.

In fact, every Christian who is not utterly naïve has been initiated in
some form of theology. Catechisms, for example, are full of popularized
theology. They also contain philosophical elements, however, which
most often pertain to a recent or less recent past. Thus, when I was six
years old, I learned that the ultimate meaning of human life lies in union
with God, while at the same time, I was initiated into a Platonizing theory about the separability of our eternal soul and a mortal body.

The "Spirit" of Philosophy

If philosophy were only a technique, having its own fixed and subordinate place and function within the economy of human life, there
would not be any reason to notice the differences between Christian
and other philosophers. If, however, "philosophy" is the name of a way
of life, a profoundly committed involvement in an historical quest for
wisdom, it cannot be separated from the personal and communal faith
to which it owes its motivation. A Christian who enters the realm of
philosophy by getting acquainted with Descartes, Hume, Kant, Hegel,
Nietzsche, Wittgenstein, Heidegger, and so on is confronted with
worlds of thought that express particular modes of faith. If we take
"experience" in its widest sense, as the global and pretheoretical way
in which the unfolding of a human life in space and time is experienced, we can also use the word "experience" here to point at the personal history of events and experiments from which philosophical
thought emerges. The experience of a life shows a certain spirit: the
spirit in which it is accepted and risked, oriented and "projected,"
undergone and heeded. Every philosophy, for example Spinoza's
Ethica, can be interpreted as the conceptual translation of an underlying experience. This makes it possible to ask what kind of spirit is evident in such a translation and to what extent it expresses the experience
of the individual or collective life in which it is rooted. The answer to

these questions cannot be found outside a careful reconstruction of singular oeuvres in their own contexts, and the results depend on the varieties of faith, experience, and reconstructive skills of the interpreters. There will thus be ample occasion for debates.

To further our inquiry, we must investigate whether Christian faith provides us with the means that permit us to diagnose the neutral, Christian, un-Christian, or anti-Christian character of the various theories that form the actual scene of contemporary and former philosophy. This question must be answered if we want to know whether concrete solidarity with all kinds of non-Christian philosophers is compatible with membership in the Christian community. The situation from which this question arises is in many respects similar to that in which the intellectuals of early Christianity found themselves. They too were confronted with a variety of non-Christian philosophers stemming from spirits other than that of Jesus Christ.

Integration

When Origen, for example, studied in Alexandria, or when Basil and the two Gregories studied in Athens, or when Saint Augustine was reading the Platonists, they saw themselves tempted and challenged by philosophies whose character they admired, although they recognized their pagan character. Something had to be changed in those philosophies in order to integrate them into their own thought and that of their Christian communities. Such changes could not be superficial because paganism, and, more concretely, Hellenistic philosophy, was a way of life, committed to specific practices and assumptions fed by a specific faith. The philosophies of the pagans could not be cut off from the experience in which they were at home. Integration into a radically different Christian frame demanded more originality than assimilation or competition according to accepted rules and uses; it demanded a *radical* transformation. Another spirit had to take possession of the elements gathered by the non-Christian inspiration in works that were offered as the highlights of civilization. Instead of rejecting the pagan philosophers wholesale, the early thinkers of early Christianity demonstrated the originality of their spirit by changing parts of those philosophies into seeds *(logoi spermatikoi)* and elements *(stoicheia)* of new ensembles showing a radically different inspiration. Not assimilation, but the combination of critical confrontation and inspired transformation generated a new *philosophia*, whose Christian character could not be denied. The refusal to betray the source of their Christian existence made the Christian philosophers creative in the constructive destruction of non-Christian philosophies. Insofar as they were successful, their appropriation of pagan thoughts makes it impossible to separate in their work some elements that would be called "philosophical" in the modern sense of the word from other, theological and typically Christian elements. The Christianization of thinking is neither a marginal business, nor a "super-added" level on top of an autarkic human nature. Grace transforms all the elements of life and thought. And this statement is not an abstract and speculative thesis without empirical basis; the Christian experience of life as a whole and in detail is radically different from that of an unredeemed existence. I do not want to exclude that certain works of the fathers or the medieval *magistri* contain unassimilated or badly integrated, and in this sense pagan elements, but the task was and is clear and sound. Christians cannot leave the secular elements of the actual culture untouched by their faith; neither can they refrain from participating in that culture by withdrawing into a ghetto. If their faith is alive, it inevitably transforms the elements of the existing culture, including its philosophy, into a body of its own. The assumption of culture is an ongoing incarnation, and the Christianization of philosophy is an important part of it.

Modern Philosophy

Students of our time are confronted with problems similar to those of the early fathers of the Church. What is the spirit of modern and postmodern philosophy? Did their great figures express a Christian inspiration in philosophy? In discussing the works of Descartes, Spinoza, Kant, and Hegel, I for my part would defend the thesis that their philosophies, including their appeal to Christian faith, in fact have betrayed it, but it is more important to show that the basic faith on which the whole enterprise of modern philosophy rests is not compatible with the faith of a Christian.

To be brief, I propose to characterize the source or principle of modern philosophy—that is, the philosophy that still dominates our institutions and manners—as a faith that combines the following convictions:

1. Reason, as interpreted in the modern logic and methodology of rationality, is the supreme and sovereign judge of reflective speech or writing.

2. Reason needs experience.

3. The experience that counts in the search for truth is a kind of experience that is or can be had by all people who have the normal use of the human senses, especially the eyes. Paradigmatic for this kind of experience are indubitable sensations and scientific observation.

One basic element of the concrete quest for truth is emphatically silenced in these principles: the element I have called *faith* or trust. Modern philosophy ignores the decisive role of its own faith in reason, in science, and in certain criteria for evidence and trustworthy experience. It also denies the relevance of good taste, virtue, religion, prayer, and dialogue for thinking and discovering the truth. Very different from the medieval and patristic *doctores*, but also from Plato and other Greek lovers of *sophia*, modern philosophy does not show much interest in the religious, moral, and aesthetic spirituality from which a well- or badly-oriented, an enthusiastic, moody, lazy, overheated, deathly boring, or hopeful thinking emerges. As is evident for everybody who is concerned about emotional economy, such a neglect has dramatic consequences for the course of a human life. If the practice of philosophy is a way of life, it cannot ignore the sources from which it in fact draws its energy, its desires and hopes and interests, its perseverance in the search and so on. Philosophical "research"—the word is revealing—has cut itself off from spirituality and faith, thus repressing what makes it so enjoyable and might make it an integral part of happiness. Deathly boredom and disgust are the inevitable results.

Experience

That philosophy cannot be autarkic is already clear from its dependence on *experience*, but it has tried to narrow the domain of experience to such a small and almost rational (that is, logically conquerable) part of its material that it still can harbor illusions of rational mastery. Fortunately, the phenomenological movement has shown us, for more than a hundred years, that human experience encompasses a much wider field of trustworthy and interesting experiences, but some schools continue to believe that we should restrict ourselves to indubitable impressions. They prefer not to consider the conditions of those more interesting experiences without which it is impossible to talk about genuine beauty, moral virtues, authenticity, love, phenomenality, and being. Their "democratic" ideal—often confused with universal validity—condemns them to neglecting or repressing all differences in receptivity, taste, open-mindedness, refinement, and civilization; the result is the utter trivialization of the matter on which they discourse.

The phenomenological revaluation of the entire range of authentic experiences reconnects us with a 2,000-year-old tradition that was disrupted by the methodical restrictions of the modern sciences. These made such an impression on the leading philosophers that they left all questions of existential wisdom to the experience of less scholarly persons. The historical split between philosophers who tried to be as scientific as the geometers and physicists of their time, and those who continued to search for wisdom outside the world of philosophy, has caused a long tragedy: for 400 years wisdom withdrew from thought because thinking withdrew from spirituality.

Autonomy of Reason?

The attempt at rational *autonomy* has been a disaster for our culture. Its failure is now recognized almost everywhere: we are not able to prove anything substantial without fundamental assumptions and experiences that we accept as plausible or credible, even though they cannot be fully justified. We are supported by a host of beliefs, yet we do not agree on the "logic" of these beliefs. The domain where "autonomous" reason has celebrated some triumphs is the domain of purely formal disciplines, especially modern logic. Since all of these disciplines presuppose but do not prove anything about the reality and the meaning of our existence in the world, they are abstract and hypothetical. As soon as we talk about a given subject, endless doubts about every possible description or analysis come up, doubts that can only be overcome by sticking to some belief. This situation easily leads to skepticism or agnosticism, and philosophy is tempted to see itself as a game or a particularly desperate way of "living dangerously." Skepticism is a child of rationalism, however. It stems from expectations that were too high and therefore *must* be disappointed.

The discovery that the dream of autonomous reason cannot be realized can also be the initiation to a further discovery: we should neither despair of reason and rationality, nor flee into the subjectivism of arbitrary preferences and beliefs; instead, we should find out where and how exactly reason's marvelous possibilities fit into the economy of human life. This discovery presupposes the recognition that philosophy, in the modern sense of the word, is not a sovereignly independent tribunal, but an element amidst other elements needed for the discovery of important truth. Philosophizing is only one, and not the supreme, activity among the activities and possibilities through which humans can approach meaning and insight. For Christians, participation in the tradition of modern and postmodern philosophy with their own authorities and canonical texts is only possible in two ways. Either we share with non-Christians the discussions of an ongoing history in which the participants methodically ignore all references to Christian faith *and* to any other kind of faith (from the preceding consideration, it is clear that I see this as an abstract, hypothetical, and provisional way of thinking); or we participate in the ongoing discussions, using at each occasion the appropriate rational and empirical skills, but without refraining from reflection on the meaning and the structure of our commitment to the Christian faith.

Philosophia

I would like to conclude this chapter with a summary sketch of the Christian *philosophia* that, by a creative retrieval of the premodern tradition, should find its place among the respectable and respected ways of doing philosophy. To prevent misunderstandings, I want to state clearly that I am pleading neither for any form of "neo-ism," nor for any other kind of conservative or reactionary return to epochs of the past. Repetition and archaeological nostalgia are signs of death; historical reconstructions, necessary and illuminating as they are, cannot by themselves solve the question of how we can achieve tasks similar to, but not identical with, those of Origen, Augustine, Anselm, Bonaventure, and Nicolas of Cusa.

In order to be radically reflective, the philosophy of Christians must develop as an integral part of a discipline that integrates theology and philosophy into one whole: a "philo-theo-logy" that accepts to be challenged by non-Christian philosophers. Such a challenge obliges advocates of this unified theory to be as competent as their non-Christian rivals who are committed to a godless, agnostic, relativistic, skeptical, or dogmatically anti-Christian faith. In philosophizing, Christians will necessarily be aware of the unbreakable connections that weave the philosophical elements of their reflection into the web

of their theological universe, while theologians will carefully scrutinize the philosophical elements of their own opinions, interpretations,
and theories. Since the evolution of the modern sciences confronts us
with an overwhelming mass of information, nobody is able to imitate
the encyclopedic knowledge of geniuses like Origen, Thomas, or
Cusanus; as mastery in both philosophy and theology demands a dou-
ble expertise, it is inevitable that many scholars will focus on partial
approaches to certain topics. However, it is necessary that the partiali-
ty of our investigations be practiced as an integral moment of the collective contemplation to which the Christian community is devoted. In
talking of a "collective" contemplation, I do not want to suggest that
we should prepare one overall system in which all individual attempts
at understanding Christian faith would fit nicely as parts of one whole.
The collectivity of thinking has structures and rules other than the systematic coherence of a dogmatic monologue. As a community of faith,
Christian life permits *and demands* a plurality of intellectual unfold-
ings that cannot be leveled to the unity of one theory or methodology.
But here we touch upon the problem of a nonrelativistic pluralism,
which demands a separate analysis.

Solidarity with other Christians within one historical community
cannot be separated from solidarity with all non-Christians, even if
their thought is oriented by another faith. On this worldwide level, the
communication can remain philosophical, but philosophy itself will
have to be more explicit than before about the radical differences
between the positions from which individuals and particular communities receive, perceive, experience, observe, understand, and methodically approach the historical world of human existence. Christians
should no longer be nervous or ashamed about their theocentric,
Christocentric and pneumatic inspiration. Their intellectual activity
should not feign to be separated from its theological, Christological
and pneumatological setting; on the contrary, the conversation with
individuals and communities who draw their inspiration from other
commitments demands that Christians manifest the breadth of mind
and the radicality of questioning to which the best of their traditions
have enabled them. If grace is the source and purpose of creation, it
can only fortify and illuminate our possibilities of understanding.
Perhaps *philosophia* will even lead us again to some sort of *theōsis* or
divinization through contemplation.

2

Why Plato Now?

IN THE *Seventh Letter*, Plato tells us that, as a young man, he had political ambitions and that the situation of Athens seemed to favor them. A revolution had just put an end to the democracy; the aristocracy of the Thirty had gained absolute power and some of Plato's relatives, who participated in the new government, invited him to join their political efforts. Plato had high hopes: the new regime would transform the formerly unjust *polis* into a community based on justice and internal peace. However, his hopes were cruelly dashed when the rulers committed crimes that were as scandalous as those of the former government. By way of example Plato mentions that the Thirty tried to make Socrates, the wisest and most upright of all men, an accomplice to their injustice by ordering him to arrest an innocent citizen whom they had condemned to death because of his democratic sympathies.

A few years later, when the supporters of democracy overthrew the aristocracy, things became even worse. Their new style of injustice was immortalized when they condemned Socrates to death for political crimes he did not commit.

Plato's third dramatic experience with politics and politicians occurred during his three visits to Dionysius, the absolute monarch of Syracuse in Sicily. Following the Athenian aristocracy and democracy, it was now the tyranny with which he was confronted. Dion, uncle of Dionysius, had urged the latter to invite Plato to be his adviser on the theory and practice of political justice. It is a myth that Plato would have tried to realize the ideas of his *Politeia* (better known as *The Republic*) in a new constitution of Syracuse (the *Seventh Letter* gives us a very different account of Plato's activities and inactivities in Sicily) but it is true that Dion wanted Plato to initiate Dionysius to the practice of philosophy and the virtues of justice. However, the latter was too full of himself and too much in love with his power to listen to Plato's lessons. Caught between two parties, Plato became the victim of blackmail and the arbitrary exercise of absolute power, while his friend Dion was exiled and later murdered.

Plato's report on these crucial experiences presents the phenomenon of politics as variations on a general pattern of injustice, which is the result of two factors: a bad constitution and unjust politicians. Reflection on his experiences led him to the insight that a just form of politics is extremely difficult or perhaps even impossible. All existing cities are badly governed, while their unjust laws and mores are practically incurable, and it is very difficult to assemble enough just friends and collaborators to form good leadership. There is only one hope: true philosophy.

> Only philosophy allows us to see all that justice demands in public and private affairs. The ills of the human race will never end until either the race of those who correctly and authentically philosophize come to power, or the governors of the cities, by some divine fate, begin to philosophize (*Seventh Letter*, 326ab).[1]

The contrast between the corruption of politics as usual and the purity of true philosophy is a central theme in many of Plato's writings, such as the *Apology*, the *Crito*, the *Gorgias*, and the *Protagoras*. Its development culminates in the systematic opposition of tyranny and philosophy that structures his monumental work on the *politeia* (that is, the cultural, political, and ethical constitution) of "the beautiful" but unreal "city" (the *kallipolis*). The thesis just quoted from the *Seventh Letter* is formulated in the exact middle of the *Politeia* (473d-e), thus emphasizing that the philosopher who is also engaged in politics—or the political ruler who is also engaged in philosophy—is the center around which all the parts of the drama revolve. The opposing figure of the tyrant on the other hand, appears at the two ends of the dialogue: in the beginning, where, in the "Hades" of Kephalos's house, the unjust politician is defended as the happiest of all people, and at the end, where he is described as the most miserable and is condemned as the most wretched inhabitant of the real Hades, together with other parricides and matricides.

In Books One and Two of the *Politeia*, the tyrant is defended three times: first by the sophist Thrasymachus, who—as the mythical Cerberus—wildly and violently praises him; second by Glaucon, a student in philosophy with good rhetorical skills and political ambitions; and third by Adymantos, who strengthens Glaucon's defense by quot-

---

1. Quotations of Plato follow the standard convention, which includes the name of the dialogue (plus the book number for *Republic*) and the page number and section letter of the 1578 Stephanus edition of his work.

ing abundantly from Homer and the classical tradition of literature and "music." Together, these advocates of tyranny exemplify the entire mythic, literary, moral, rhetorical, and intellectual culture that is the political backdrop of Athens. If Plato wants to attack this kind of politics, he must also indict the established *doxa*, the ethos, the art, and the entire culture from which it emerges. The diagnosis must then focus on politics as the powerful translation into practice of an overall mentality. If it can be shown that this mentality is expressed in various political systems, these systems do not differ essentially.

It is indeed Plato's conviction that the expression of the tyrannical mentality in a monarchical system does not differ essentially, but only in degree, from its oligarchic or democratic expressions. In contrast to a just king (*basileus*), the tyrant embodies the essential injustice that also inspires the average oligarchy (or "aristocracy") and democracy: all existing cities are corrupt and the average politicians are as corrupt as their culture is. This view is clarified in *Politeia* VIII-IX, where all the other existing constitutions, from timocracy to democracy, are understood as approximations of the tyranny, which is the worst of all. Although they are less unjust insofar as their corruption has not yet entirely destroyed the elements of an ideal *polis*, all of them are on the way to total injustice, unless some fundamental change of culture can turn them around.

Such a turn or conversion is not possible, however, unless at least two conditions are met. First, the citizens must discover the fundamental error in their culture; and second, they must acquire another moral, religious, literary, and intellectual culture that will urge them to rule with justice. The necessity and the conditions of such a conversion are explained in *Politeia* III-VII: not only does it demand the development of new institutions, but first and foremost it demands another way of relating to the world, other citizens, the community, one's own body, mind, desires, fear and hope, love and hate. Another way of life is needed, whose authenticity is shown by intellectual truth, poetical and musical beauty, moral justice, and religious purity. Theory is not enough for such a re-education. Before an adolescent can become a philosopher, he or she must acquire a truly "musical" kind of corporeal and spiritual health. The affective and emotional life in particular, including the many conflicting desires that move human beings, must be harmonized by a "sentimental education" that produces good taste and willingness to realize what is "good and beautiful."

In light of the two conditions for a true conversion, Plato thus has two tasks: to give a diagnosis of the ruling culture (including the education that prevails in it), and to outline a better, truly philosophical culture that will generate a better kind of politics.

DIAGNOSIS

Pleasure

What then is the principle of the corruption that makes the city and its politicians tyrannical? Plato's answer is that it lies in the absolutization of pleasure. What he means by "pleasure" is constantly exemplified in the pleasures of eating, drinking, and sex, but also, though less frequently, by pointing to wealth, power, and fame. Though Socrates sometimes states (for instance, in the *Phaedo*) that the evil principle lies in the *sōma* ("body") or the *epithumiai* (desires) as such, these expressions must be understood as metonymic for the absolute preference for "low" (*somatic* or "corporeal") pleasures over "higher" (psychic, intellectual, spiritual) ends. When he states that such a preference encompasses the desire for money, power, and fame, he most often represents these goods as the means for obtaining the gastronomic and sexual gratifications that are paradigmatic for all pleasures insofar as they seduce us to prefer private satisfaction over all that is good and just. It is not difficult to show, however, that power, wealth, and fame also by themselves (and not merely as means) tempt us to inflate our own private selves at the cost of doing injustice to others and ourselves. For power over other people and the possession of large portions of the earth make the owner large and most important: the earth is there for him and the others must look up to him. With money one can buy not only everything one desires, but also subservience and votes and fame, or even some sort of love.

Desire, satisfaction, and pleasure are not evil in themselves, but they become evil when they are preferred over the good of obligatory actions or when their pleasurability is hailed as the absolute goal of human life. This can be seen if we realize that pleasure is a feeling that, in a strict sense, cannot be shared. The desire to obtain (my) pleasure therefore competes with desires and duties that are directed toward your good or pleasure. As mine (not yours), pleasure has a tendency to enclose me in myself, thus making my own well-being more important than yours, even more important than your survival or entrance into this world, which is already mine. Thus, the absolute preference for (my) pleasure generates competition, war, hatred, robbery, murder, abortion, and all other kinds of injustice. In any case, it will prevent or destroy a peaceful community. For once hedonists are engaged in competition, their only choice is either to become a coward or a slave in order to survive, or to enslave the enemy in order to enjoy one's own might. Slavery or despotism are therefore the outcomes of hedonism.

There is, however, a second way from hedonism to injustice. This lies in the havoc pleasures can play with one's own life. By submitting to one's desires for enjoyment, wealth, power, and entertainment rather than to the good things that have to be done and loved, one becomes enslaved, imprisoned, and addicted. If pleasure-seeking is the first principle of life, it will resist all just actions or thoughts that are painful. Suffering is then a sufficient motivation for not doing or loving what has to be loved or done.

To adequately appreciate Plato's condemnation of hedonism, one must see that he is not primarily targeting singular acts or choices, but rather the overall attitude of a life obsessed with pleasure. Though pleasures are normal and natural—and as such nothing bad—the kind of life that allows itself to be motivated totally and exclusively by lust and greed and the thirst for power and fame is despicable and miserable. The opposition of the pleasurable and the good is an opposition of two different kinds of life.

All of these statements are illustrated in Plato's description of the tyranny to which the tyrant subjects himself (*Politeia* IX). By obeying the desires of his belly, the tyrant has transformed himself into a monster. The constitution that rules his own behavior is tyrannical itself: he is enslaved by the reversal of the right proportions between his *erōs* and the other orientations of his "nature" *(physis)*.

Authenticity and Semblance

A second step in Plato's diagnosis of the contemporary culture is taken when the absolutization of pleasure is associated with a more theoretical, and at first sight less ethical, perspective on the human world. Pleasure is associated with immediate sensation *(aisthēsis)* and appearance, semblance, superficiality, imitation, and inauthenticity. Again, there is nothing wrong with sensible impressions and perceptions. Seeing, hearing, feeling, tasting, and smelling are marvelous possibilities of human existence, without which no communication or knowledge whatsoever would be possible; they are indispensable for all theory and praxis. If they are opposed to or preferred over more lofty or profound ways of discovering what and how things are, however, they become evil because they then block these indispensable ways toward knowledge of the truly true. The truth of the cosmos does not lie on the surface of reality; it demands reflection, discussion, scrutiny, thinking, insight, intuition. Superficial people are content with sensations and impressions. They repeat available opinions and theories without investigating the phenomena themselves and swear by the images that appear on the television screens of their cave. Seeing, hearing, smelling, touching, and tasting fascinate them as means for entertainment and communication with other cave dwellers, but not primarily as integrated elements of a search for truth. Their lives are led by everyman's opinions and by the impression they try to make on their fellow citizens. The *doxa* and the ethos of "the many" rule their attitude. This makes them incapable of seeking the quintessence, the why and the origin of the phenomena with which they are confronted. Living on the surface of things, they are neither amazed at the splendor nor shaken by the terror displayed in the universe. They lack authenticity because shadows, appearances, and images separate them from the secret truth of things.

The Culture of Semblance and Pleasure

A culture that fosters the attachment to superficiality and indulgence is not authentic, because it does not take the reality as it (truly, genuinely, originarily, and essentially) *is*. Within the limits of this chapter we cannot enter into the details of Plato's critique of all the layers and levels of the culture that dominated the city of his time, but we must be aware of the solidarity between that culture and the political dimension if we want to understand his critique of the latter. Unjust politics and politicians are inspired by a mythology according to which the gods and heroes themselves behave in arbitrary, treacherous, and tyrannical ways. They are exemplified in the tragedies, especially those of Euripides, and hailed by the poets. They are made famous by the speechwriters, the marketers, and the media in general; and most citizens support them because they share their mentality, as is shown when they gain power in the form of a democracy. The most dangerous supporters of the politicians are those professors and intellectuals who, like Thrasymachus, Gorgias, and Protagoras, argue as if they possess the truth and therefore look like *sophoi*–but in fact neither possess nor seek nor love true wisdom; they are the pseudo-philosophers who give the tyrants an appearance of rational justification, while betraying the true interest of the people, its leaders, and themselves.

Philosophy

True philosophers cannot embrace this culture, because it despises justice and truth or is so indifferent to these ideals that it is not even bothered by the question of whether one should be or become truthful and just. A tyrannical *polis* despises authentic philosophers, preferring instead the ready-made sophistry of pseudo-intellectuals over the long-winded discussions about genuine reality by the likes of Socrates and his interlocutors. As Glaucon saw very well, this conflict can only lead to the death of the philosopher.

> the just man who has such a disposition will be whipped; he'll be racked, he'll be bound, he'll have both his eyes burned out; and, at the end, when he has undergone every sort of evil, he'll be crucified. . . . (*Politeia*, 361e-362a).

PLATO'S IDEAL

Does Plato offer us a theory of political justice that will heal the sicknesses of the ongoing practice?

The *Politeia* has been interpreted as the blueprint of an ideal constitution, but this interpretation is refuted by Socrates' remarks about the impossibility of realizing such a constitution in any of the existing cities. Moreover, even as an experiment in theoretical construction, the *politeia* that is slowly built up in Books III-VII abounds in gaps and inconsistencies. The comedy of the first two waves in particular expresses how unrealistic Socrates' proposals are, and there are many further indications of this.

What then is the purpose of this dialogue, whose explicit topic seems to consist in the basic institutions and mores of a good-and-beautiful city? At the end of Book IX, after it has become clear that no actual city can be perfectly good in structure and behavior, Socrates points out that the question of a just constitution and life primarily concerns the "city" that exists in each individual's soul. To rule one's own life according to the ideal paradigm that has been developed by Socrates in cooperation with Glaucon and Adymantos, that is the real purpose of their search for justice "in private and public" (592ab). True, Socrates does not deny that the moral, political, cultural, and educational proposals of the *Politeia* contain important advice for politicians; but first of all, they advocate a fundamental change in personal attitude: a turning away from the hedonistic and tyrannical kind of life to a more authentic and truly philosophical life. As is true of many other dialogues, the *Politeia* first and foremost is an exhortation to become philosophical in the broad sense that combines careful contemplation and courageous practice. Public life will never become just if it is not rooted in philosophical inspiration; but this inspiration cannot develop if it is not embodied in the lifestyle and the motivation of individual citizens. As long as the existing cities are dominated by a mixture of justice and injustice, truth and lies, authenticity and imitation, philosophically minded individuals will represent a marginalized minority. But once a person has grasped the difference between a true and a false or superficial existence, there is no way back: one has to be loyal to the demands of justice that have emerged from the demystification of politics as usual. How does Plato formulate these demands? Or, in other words, what are the principles of a truthful and just life?

Desire and Desires

The fundamental principle of a good life lies in its orientation toward the good, for this is what grants meaning, worth, and truth to all beings. The desire for the good, which is also a desire for the beautiful, must replace the addiction to pleasure as the supreme criterion. For it is only in the light of the good that all things can show what they (really or truly) are and what they are worth. Only this illumination reveals how we should perceive and receive and respond to them. Truth and authenticity depend on their being desired for the sake of the good because the good alone makes them genuine and meaningful. This orientation should not be impeded or obscured by pleasures that detract from it. No phenomenon should become an obstacle to its being appreciated for the sake of the authentic goodness it receives from the good itself. To do justice to phenomena, we must keep them in this light and orientation, without transforming them into absolute ends.

To discover the genuine truth and worth of the phenomena, we cannot abandon ourselves to immediate sensations and superficial impressions; neither can we accept widespread but unwarranted opinions or theories. Phenomena must be contemplated, deciphered, and understood as revelations of what they truly (or essentially) are. Plato's desire for truth is a passion for authentic being or "essence" *(ousia)*. It does not despise the senses, matter, or corporeality, but rather enjoys and respects them as embodiment of the hidden truth that is searched by reflection *(dianoia)* and discussion *(dialegesthai)* and "seen" by insight *(noein)*. The contrast between the desire for justice and wisdom, on the one hand, and the desire for sensual and other pleasures, on the other, is no more of an essential contradiction than that between the noetic truth (or "the ideas") and sensible appearances. The good is not hostile to pleasure but it condemns the addiction to pleasure-at-any-cost. Striving for truth and justice is imbued with its own kind of pleasure (which we would rather call by other names, such as "joy" or "delight"), but even when those pleasures are sought by a philosopher, the reason is not that they provide egocentric satisfaction: they testify to the presence of the good and anchor it in our emotions. Instead of condemning affections of the senses, pleasures, appearances, and opinions, these should be integrated into a harmonious and thoughtful life that does justice to all phenomena according to the true proportions that bind their various essences and dignities together. A sense for authentic reality, good taste, and—if necessary—patience are needed to acquire a well-proportioned or "good-and-beautiful" life. A "soul" that realizes this way of life is ruled by the good according to the demands of truth.

THE PHILOSOPHER IN THE CITY

If the tyrant and the philosopher are distinguished by a fundamentally different mentality and style of life, their mutual hostility is understandable. Under the guise of a fight between the political strategies of absolute power, on one side, and the vulnerable quest for wisdom, on the other, two radically contradictory manners of existing conflict in a drama that endures throughout history. The heart of the problem does not lie in the opposition of different strategies on the level of political institutions or decisions, but rather in the question of which kind of life does justice to the essence of being human in communion with others in a common world and history.

If, on the other hand, the public life of actual cities is, at best, a mixture of more or less just and unjust institutions and decrees, the real question for a philosopher is not how a perfectly good city should behave, but rather, how one can and should be part of a community that is dominated by a corrupt culture.

The purest philosophers will adhere to Socrates' principle that it is better to suffer injustice than to commit it (*Gorgias*, 466aff, 527b), even at the cost of their own life. However, philosophers would not love the good if they isolated themselves completely from the public interests of their city. In his explanation of the cave allegory, Socrates emphasizes that it would be unjust for someone who owes his education to the city not to descend back into the cave in order to assist one's unenlightened compatriots in the government of the community (519b-521b). A refrain that runs throughout the entire *Politeia* reminds us time and again that the search for virtue and truth has "a private and a public aspect" *(idiai kai dēmosiai)*. In a way, the philosophers are responsible for the most radical revolution that their city can and must undergo: the revolution of its culture. They are the catalyst for the emergence of another style of life. The political relevance of philosophers lies in their lived testimony to the spirit of justice and truth. Winning the fight against the violence of power, money, and the media is not their main concern. Loyalty to the search for a new inspiration is more important than success or survival.

Plato does not offer detailed advice on the public behavior of philosophers who are entrusted with power in a corrupt society; but it is obvious that philosophical education, despite its cathartic quality, does not guarantee complete immunity against corruption in situations where the usual wheeling and dealing sets the standard. How can genuine philosophers refrain from selling their souls when trying to transform their surroundings? They too are infected by collective sickness; where do they find the *pharmakon* that heals the soul?

As an antidote to the tyrannical power of the prevailing culture, philosophers appeal to eloquence, literature, arts and sciences, mythology and religion, hoping to convince their fellow citizens that purification demands philosophy. Such appeals imply a considerable degree of responsibility: are they able to create the conditions for a radically different culture? Veracity, contemplation, and the practice of courage and justice are more desirable than pleasure and wealth. Fortunate individuals can fall in love with them. But how can their love become popular? It *can* be recognized by all humans as natural and normal, authentic, "essential," and good; but philosophy is needed to *show* just how good such a kind of *erōs* is. Herein lies an answer to the question: "Why Plato now?"

3

Platonic and Christian Hope

For Kevin Corrigan

EVEN A SUPERFICIAL READING of the Gospels will suffice to convince the reader that incarnation is the alpha and—as resurrection of the flesh—the omega of Christian faith. And with the body, involvement in the human world and its history is part of God's self-revelation in his Word through the Spirit. The Christian community, whose faith is corporeal, communicative, communitarian, and sacramental, participates in this involvement. None of its activities is possible in the ether of incorporeal ghosts or spirits. All prophecies and fulfillments are facts of language; the entire liturgy is visible, tactile, and resounding; rituals have the smell of candles, incense, and sweat; the central union with God has the taste of bread and wine. Even in the itinerary of mystical experiences the body and the world are always present—often painfully—while the main outreach of Christians is addressed to neighbors whose hunger cannot be consoled by immaterial thoughts and wishes alone.

The Christian mode of transcendence, inspiration, and spirituality cannot be separated from corporeality and earthly spatio-temporality. The source of Christian hope is not a God in the heaven above or the depths beneath the earth of human suffering and delight, but rather the sacramental omnipresence of a Savior who loves his creation. "Incarnation" or "ongoing incarnation" is a good name for this amazing mystery.

But why, then, has there been so much concentration on immortality of the soul in the theology and philosophy of Christians? Is this topic a *Fremdkörper* in the Christian gnosis? Has it been imported by the "Greeks" and remained a foreign element, as many scholars—all too easily—have said? Where do the gnostic tendencies that have tempted Western Christianity come from? And why has the Christian faith been presented so often as a spiritualism, for which body and flesh were, if not bad and contemptible, accidental, more or less superfluous, dangerous, and low-class realities compared to the spirit, which was thought to be the true and noble core of human existence?

I cannot remember the exact wording of the catechism I had to learn by heart when I was six years old, but I am pretty sure that one of the first answers affirmed that a human being was composed of soul and body, that the soul was immortal, and therefore the most important thing was to take care of the soul and to keep it pure. Later, I discovered that these answers were quotes from Plato's *Phaedo*, which for a while made him a precursor of Christianity in my mind. Even in the new catechism, referred to as "a sure norm for teaching the faith," the immortality of the soul is clearly distinguished from the nature of the body and presented as a doctrine of "the Church."[1] I do not wish to flatly deny the possibility of such a distinction, though it should be preceded by a careful clarification of the different concepts of a living body, a corpse or dead "body," a psyche, soul, heart, or spirit. But I do think that an explanation of the Christian faith, even if it takes the twelve articles of the *Credo* as its lead, should focus on "resurrection of the flesh" and not immediately harmonize this faith with a Platonizing interpretation of human existence. In his attempt to win the Athenians for Christ, Saint Paul was less reconciliatory than many later theologians. If he had introduced Christ's survival with a speech about his immortal soul and—like the catechism—cautiously added that not only will our souls survive, but also, in some mysterious way, our bodies, the listeners might have been more receptive. However, his message about *anastasis* met with laughter, because his audience, not unfamiliar with Pythagorean and Platonic convictions about immortality, refused to consider the possibility of a re-emergence of the entire person (cf. Acts 17:31–32).

In order to discover to what extent Plato was the source of a theology that treats the resurrection of the flesh as an appendix or supplement to the immortality of the soul, we must begin by freeing Plato's texts from the misunderstandings through which Christian and non-Christian idealists, positivists, and logicians have obscured their meaning. This cannot be fully accomplished in one chapter, but allow me to

---

1. Cf. *Catechism of the Catholic Church* (New York: Paulist Press, 1994), nn. 363, 366, 997, 1005.

summarize here my rereading of Plato's *Phaedo*,[2] after which I will return to the Christian message of death and hope.

HOPE IN THE *PHAEDO*

In the *Phaedo*, Socrates converses with his friends for the last time about the meaning of life and death, knowledge and being, virtue and vice. Since he is to die that day, the thought of death occupies the minds of all who are present. However, Socrates is not the only one who is condemned to death—all humans are. The injustice of his judges and the aspect of rejection are no longer the issue; they must now meditate on mortality as such.

At the beginning of the dialogue, death is already present in various anticipations. While his friends weep, Socrates is more peaceful than ever, even joyous. The contrast between joy and sadness expresses a different attitude toward death, and therewith a different attachment to life. Xanthippe, the women, and the lamenting friends represent the "normal" attitude, while Socrates alone embodies the true philosopher.

The question of death is not a question that can be delayed until the last day of our lives; it is urgent from the moment we become conscious of our mortality. Death is always present, most clearly in the pleasures and pains of our bodies, but equally in the weariness of our thought, the needs and weaknesses of our will, and our dependence on anxiety and depression. Life is at every moment desirous of living on without end, yet threatened and condemned to death.

How can we accept this condemnation? Is utter sadness not the normal and appropriate response to our mortality? Is any kind of hope possible? Or must we simply limit our desires and accept the finitude of our condition?

A response to the inexorability of death is a response to the primary question of human life: what is the meaning (the desirability, the beauty, the sense, the light, the truth, the goodness) of a short, always all too short, life? If we experience this brevity as something painful, our

---

2. For my understanding of Plato's work and some of its (mis)interpretations, see Adriaan T. Peperzak, *Platonic Transformations: With and After Hegel, Heidegger, and Levinas* (Lanham, Md.: Rowman and Littlefield, 1997).

desire shows its ever reaching beyond. Is this genuine? Can we conquer our transcendence by a sort of radical modesty? If not, is radical
bitterness or cynicism then inevitable? Would it be better not to have
been born than to be born as a mortal being?

Socrates' answers to these questions appeal to an archaic tradition of
hope.[3] According to Orphic and Pythagorean *logoi*, the *psychē* sur-
vives its separation from the body *(sōma)* in death, and if the *psychē* is
pure, it will enjoy a divine existence, while the body rots away. The
body is a tomb[4] for the soul as long as the soul is glued[5] and nailed[6] to
it and imprisoned[7] within it. To become pure, one must undergo a
purification *(katharsis)*,[8] which encompasses *askēsis*, a virtuous way
of life, and the acquisition of *sophia*. An impure life will be punished
by a subsequent embodiment of the *psychē* in accordance with its character: a wolfish or a serpentine life leads to one's transformation into a
wolf or a snake.

The genre of these *logoi* is mythical. The Orphic *mythoi* proclaim
hope and preach the purification of life. In promising an afterlife that
confirms the quality of the life that has been led, they answer the question of how one should live. Their eschatology explains the *true meaning of life*, as seen by the *sophos*.

Socrates justifies his appeal to this religious message by referring
to our need for consolation by a special sort of *"mousikē"* (60d–61a):
the music of enchantment and persuasion through prophetic oracles,
religious poetry, and divination.[9] The child in each of us who is
afraid of death must be appeased by a trustworthy hope. Socrates
himself is not a "musician" *(mousikos)*, however; though he composed a hymn to Apollo and versified some stories of Aesopus, he
does not have the authority of a Diotima, a Pindarus, or the Pythia.
But Apollo has given him, too, a mission: Socrates' philosophy is his
music (60c–61c).

3. *Phaedo,* 63c, 66b–c, 68a, 70a, 98b, 114c.
4. Cf. *Gorgias,* 493a; *Cratylus,* 400c; *Phaedrus,* 250c.
5. *Phaedo,* 82e.
6. *Phaedo,* 83d.
7. *Phaedo,* 62b and 82e; cf. *Cratylus,* 400c.
8. *Phaedo,* 65e-69c, 79d-83d, 108b-110c, 114b-c.
9. *Phaedo,* 84e-85b, cf. 76b.

The combination of his appeal to a prephilosophical *mythos* together with the practice of a dialectical *logos* characterizes Socrates' meditation on death and life and hope as a hermeneutical theory. In retrieving a religious message by way of analytical thought, Socrates does what all theology has done since the beginning of Western philosophy: he attempts to understand that message and to discover to what extent it contains insights that can be universally recognized as well founded on the basis of common experiences and thought (85cd). What are the results of this experiment with a prophetic truth?

In order to uncover the meaning of the terms *psychē* and *sōma*, as opposed in the Orphic tradition, Socrates contrasts the life of "*hoi polloi*" and the philosophical life from an *ethical* perspective (*not* primarily from the perspective of psychology or anthropology). The first *bios* is constantly characterized as one obsessed with eating, drinking, and sex—vital activities that are sought for the pleasures they procure. Such a life is driven by hedonic desires and ruled by a calculus of pleasures and pains. The philosophical life, on the contrary, is oriented toward *phronēsis* and *aretē*. A wise person despises the pleasures that obsess the mind and heart of the many and does not complain about the pains ensuing from unsatisfied needs because it desires something very different: wisdom and virtue. These are also experienced as pleasurable, though Plato's Socrates seldom uses the words *hēdonē* (or *lupē*) and *epithumia* in this connection. Even in English we would rather speak of joy than of pleasure when referring to the intellectual and moral desiderata that dominate the activities of a philosopher. Can the reason for this hedonic difference be found in a distinction between corporeal and psychic (or spiritual) satisfactions?

In the *Phaedo*, Plato indeed opposes the two lifestyles as concentration on the "body" *(sōma)* and on the soul *(psychē)*. But this is strange, at least for the following reasons:

1. Virtuous behavior and thought, especially in the communicative forms of conversation *(dialegesthai)* and writing, are no less corporeal than eating and coupling.

2. The difference between gastronomy and philosophy is not experienced as corporeal versus merely psychic or spiritual, but rather as "lower" and "higher" and as less central and more intimate. Total concentration on the three vital functions seems to lower the person to the level of animals, while the quest for *phronēsis* clearly lifts one above

that level. This is not a reason to view typical human activities as immaterial and angelic, however. Furthermore, no human being is able to eat or drink or copulate in an animalistic way; human activity is typically human, be it in a noble or a beastly mode.

3. The difference between the ethical qualities of the two kinds of life does not lie in one being corporeal, while the other is psychic, but rather in the *attachment* and the *preference* through which a person is bound to one or another style of human life. By deciding that eating, drinking and sex should be my main fulfillment, and by declaring that the meaning of life coincides with the pleasures acquired through those activities, I make myself despicable, while devotion to philosophy unfolds the noblest possibilities of the human mind. The ethical difference between the two lives is thus founded on the different attitudes toward the desires that seek to orient and rule the entire person, body and soul included. But this means that the difference lies in the *preference*, that is, in the *will*, of the persons involved. Where is this will located? Certainly not in an *inanimate* body or corpse. In the soul? But then the soul itself would be accused of being "somatic" by its own desire and will. The contrast between lifestyles is thus revealed to be part of a discourse on *conversion*, rather than pertaining to a discourse on the composite elements of a human being.

4. Wonder grows about Plato's presentation of the *ethical* contrast between the two lifestyles as a contrast between *sōma* and *psychē* when, in the course of his drama, he extends the circle of the pleasure-seeking many to not only those who are concerned with all sorts of bodily cares, clothes, footwear, and jewelry (64d-e), but also those who make war (66c) and those whose highest good lies in wealth, honor (68de, 82c), power, injustice, and tyranny (81c-82c), and even to robbers and murderers (82a). The *Phaedo* does not explain how the vices of all these people are connected to the preference for the vital functions of the lower life. Must we understand that will to power, ambition, and all other vices are motivated by the pleasures of a well-kept body? But if the desire for honor and power and violence is somatic, why then not the virtues of courage and moderation?

5. In Socrates' translation of the Orphic promise into more philosophical language, he assures his friends that through death the true philosopher will find an even better company of gods and friends with whom he can continue, in a perfected way, the dialogical and virtuous

praxis to which he had accustomed himself prior to death (63b). The primary difference between life before and after death seems to lie in the fact that the soul in Hades is no longer hindered or hampered by the body. Death liberates the soul from its corporeal limitations (66a, 67cd, etc.). But how can a disembodied soul continue the conversation?

The weight, the restrictions, the obscurities, and the confusions imposed on us by embodiment are indeed phenomenally given. Confined to "this body," individually situated in a unique space and time, subject to physical and historical impossibilities and physiological exhaustion, involved in many needs and social necessities, and marked by cultural patterns and customs, we often experience our corporeality as a burden, a "glue," an obstacle, a confinement, and a "cage" (82e). Does this mean that I, who experience this, am incorporeal, a *psychē* that can distance itself from embodiment and worldliness? No, the desire that is expressed in that experience is oriented toward a perfectly docile, transparent, expressive, open, and far-reaching corporeality, one that does not become sick or tired or heavy or deficient in truth and harmony. Would such a body still require food and sex? What would be the orientation of this body?

Plato's answer is included in his eulogy of philosophy. To be oriented toward wisdom and virtue renders all other desires irrelevant. A philosopher must continue to eat and drink, but he does not do it for pleasure; he reduces such activities to the necessary minimum. Since they remain necessary until death, we can imagine that perhaps dying opens up the possibility of a philosophical life free from all nonphilosophical necessity. Liberated from eating, drinking, and sexual reproduction, we would be free to think endlessly. Instead of our involvements in earthly structures and affairs influencing our thought and action, we would understand and behave in ideal ways.

Must we be bodiless for such a freedom? Since the human body perishes in death, the only possible realization of such a dream seems to lie in the survival of a noncorporeal element that would survive the transformation of our animated body into a corpse. The full realization of the philosophical ideal must then presuppose the immortality of that element called the soul.

Plato's Socrates tests and confirms this postulate by showing a link between the constitution of human individuals and the ontological constitution of the universe. The dimension of sensibility *(aisthēsis)* and lower desires (*epithumiai*), to which most people remain confined, provides access to the variegated multiplicity of phenomena in continual change and exchange. The economy of sensible affections, emotions, pleasures, and pains is transcended, however, by *erōs* and *nous*, oriented as they are toward truth, beauty, and goodness. The secret truth of the sensible world is suggested in metaphorical language, when Socrates employs quasi-sensible and spatial metaphors to point to the "ideas" or essences as different from the sensibilia seen and touched in any superficial approach. By drawing an ontological distinction between the *ousia* of "*true being*" and the visible, audible, or tactile appearance of all beings, he *ipso facto* draws an anthropological distinction between the senses and thought. While in the *Phaedo*, he experiments with the hypothesis that the difference between these two dimensions can be understood as the difference between *sōma* and *psychē*, this hypothesis is abandoned in other dialogues. In the *Republic*, for example, the lower desires or inclinations *(epithumiai)* belong to the *psychē* itself, together with the *nous* and the source of all aggression *(thumos)*, which the *epithumiai* must obey.

The main motivation for Plato's distinction between the constellation of being *(ousia)*, truth *(alēthes)*, thought *(nous)*, and Desire *(erōs)*, on the one hand, and that of appearance, *aisthēsis*, lower desires or inclinations *(epithumiai)* and their pleasures, on the other, is anagogical: conversion to philosophy demands a turn from imprisonment within the horizons of a merely sensible universe to love of the truth and concentration on the truly desirable. The conversion cannot be a denial of the former's *reality*, but only a change in *attachment* and fundamental *attitude*. That both the sensible and the ideal aspects or dimensions belong together is the law and truth of human existence in the world, the truth of the unity of being and appearance (the *aisthetic* or phenomenal). If true being is the ultimate and primordial desideratum of *nous* and *erōs*, one could imagine a situation in which that truth would be contemplated without its half-revealing, half-obscuring appearance—unless it is clear and certain that the ideal essence of the universe can *not* be separated from its concretization in the corporeality of its sensible phenomenality. The *Phaedo* is a half-mythical, half-philosophical experiment with the postulate that the meaning of life ultimately and radically lies in the contemplation of essential truth and in the pure behavior that goes with it. Socrates' tentative interpretation of death as a separation that frees the purified soul from its un- and antiphilosophical "body" follows from his call to conversion: turn your true self from all attachment to corporeal and worldly involvement to the exclusive contemplation of the truth alone. Socrates' eschatology extends this conception of philosophy. His retrieval of the Orphic prophecies has inaugurated a long tradition of contemplative idealism or idealizing contemplation.[10]

CHRISTIAN HOPE

The reflection and dialogue among Christians about the meaning of their own lives and the lives of others is also preceded by the assurance of hope. How does this hope differ from the one that gave Plato so much to think about? What must a theological retrieval in the Christian context say about the promise of God who neither lies nor retracts?

Christians believe in "the resurrection of the flesh," as the Apostolic Creed formulates it. This expression not only refers to the enfleshment or incarnation of God's Son, but also extends his resurrection to all humans as potential sons and daughters of the Father. Since incarnation implies involvement in the affairs of world and history, resurrection, likewise, encompasses these dimensions of human existence. Faith in resurrection is therefore clearly different from any theory or belief that separates a mortal body from a surviving soul or ghost. "A spirit [pneuma] does not have flesh and bones, as you see I have" (Luke 24:39). All theologies according to which salvation first unites the soul with God before the soul "at the end of times" is rejoined by the body as a more or less superfluous addition, are attempts to combine a Greek theory with the promise witnessed by the sources of Christianity. But how is the realization of the Christian promise possible? What are the anthropological conditions of its possibility? The answers of faith are "God will provide" and "Love does not abandon, but saves." But even this formulation is already too thetical and theoretical. Faith itself does not talk *about* God and his plans or possibilities; it is too intensely turned

---

10. See Pierre Courcelle's second and third volumes of his *Connais-toi Toi-même de Socrate à Saint Bernard* (Paris: Etudes Augustiniennes, 1975) for the enormous influence of this retrieval on Western philosophy and theology.

toward God to indulge in reflection about its intimacy. When it reflects, in the form of meditation or theology, it wants to maintain the links that bind its thought to the attitude of confidence and adoration by which it has already overcome its doubts concerning the Promise.

A doctrine about God would be possible only if God possessed a horizon, a space or time or universe within which he could appear, similar to the gods of the pagans, or as a highest being that surpasses all others. However, faith and prayer testify to God's creating *all* horizons and possible contexts and yet revealing himself through a man, Jesus, the Christ, who—to a certain extent—is contextually present in one body, one world, and one history. All reflection must therefore refer to prayer and focus on the corporeal figure of Jesus, in whom God accepts to be somewhat thematizable.

How resurrection from the dead is possible, we cannot know; but it offers us a perspective when we turn to mortal life in order to decipher the meaning of death and salvation. We can know what salvation and resurrection mean if we know what in human lives is essential, loved by God, and heeded by the Spirit. If God loves humans, that which is most essential to them will be saved, assumed, united with God, divinized. If God is revealed in Jesus Christ, we must discover the central meaning or "essence" of Jesus' life and death; only then will we know to what sort of existence we are called and what, through death, will be saved if we respond appropriately to that call. The answer to our questions about God's promise refers us, therefore, to our embodied, involved, worldly, historical, and mortal life, insofar as this is assumed by the Son in his equally worldly existence.

CONVERSION

To become sons and daughters "in the Son," and thus to share the Spirit, a conversion *(metanoia, epistrephein)* is needed; but this conversion is very different from the Platonic *katharsis*. Jesus does not seem preoccupied by the pleasures and pains of eating, drinking, and sex. In contrast with John the Baptist, the Son of Man "ate and drank" without preaching ascetic practices or laws of purification. The New Testament speaks very little about pleasure *(hēdonē)* and pain *(lupē)*, but is full of joy *(chara, chairein)* and peace *(eirēnē)*. Even the narratives of the

Passion do not focus on the pains involved, but rather on the rejection, the humiliation, and the martyrdom of the prophet and Lord
who is the exemplary, but misunderstood, Son and Man. Jesus' death,
too, is the symbol of a life different than the average one, but the contrast here is not between the pleasures of a trivial kind of vitality and
the elite noblesse of high culture and philosophy. To follow Jesus
does not lead one away from *das Man*, but purifies one from Sin, that
is, from the loveless, arrogant, and idolatrous concerns that imprison
individuals within themselves. The turn of heart demanded by Christ
is the acceptance of Love as the unique and overall secret of heaven
and earth. Since the very existence of the Son is the result and proof
of God's absolute and complete self-giving, the Spirit in which the
Father generates the Son repeats this gesture in the complete self-giving of Jesus' Passion, for which the Christians say thanks when they
receive it in the eating of his body and the drinking of his blood. The
gratitude expressed in this *eucharistia* is translated into practice
when their involvement in body, world, and history shows itself
inspired by the same Spirit through a self-giving equally complete
insofar as their deaths reveal in retrospect how their entire lives have
been lived in love.

Turning away from the idols—that is, the divinized powers of
Money, Fame, Knowledge, Pleasure, or Autarchy—presupposes the
acceptance of an infinite desire that is met by the love revealed in
Jesus Christ and the saints. Conversion to Christ is therefore unconditional receptivity, acceptance, and recognition of the most incredible,
yet most desirable, gesture of a God who accepts human involvement
in everyone's world and history. Instead of the pleasures and pains of
idolatry, confidence, joy, and peace become possible because of the
absolute and total self-giving that enables desiring humans to live
without finite gods. Though not engaged in sin, the saints are no less
involved in the affairs of bodies in the world and their everyday activities, albeit in a different manner. Purification has now received a new
meaning: growth in the practice of the truth that *"tout est grâce,"*
including existence, world, and history itself. Not only forgiveness,
protection, guidance, and fulfillment, but creation itself are received
as gifts of the Spirit, that is, as expressions of God's internal communication. But how can a purified person remain involved in an unconverted milieu?

The joy of faith is not without pain. Inspiration translates into suffering and compassion because the world is a mixture of love and hatred. Christ's Passion shows that the inspired life yields rejection. Happy are those whose death is not due to exhaustion alone, but is rather the effect of a refusal to join the idolatrous liturgies. The passion and compassion of the saints is still experienced as annihilation and abandonment, but the total destruction of mind and breath and blood and body is lived, though perhaps not experienced, as the hard condition of pure and entire love, and therewith as union with God, who cannot reject those whom he loves. *How* God saves human bodies, we do not understand, but *that* he does is a question of trust, not theory. Is it so surprising that we cannot know how we "will be," if we cannot comprehend how God is? If we, as created by and destined for Love, are inspired by the Spirit of God, our lives must be hardly less mysterious and sublime than God's own respiration. Gratitude and hope then constitute the appropriate responses to the breath that precedes all existence, desire, and questioning. Meditation, contemplation, and theology come later—always too late to capture the horizon of all truths: God himself, who, as threefold self-communication, encompasses the human universe without being encompassed by it.

The admission of human lives into that communication, unfolding as love in gratitude and hope, is neither immaterial nor theoretical in a "Platonic" sense. "To love the Lord, your God with all your heart, with all your soul, with all your mind, and with all your strength" (Mark 12:30 and parallels) neither separates the soul from the body, nor exhorts the listener to develop a theory of love, but rather encourages one to join and practice the mode of God's own communication. The first commandment turns the entirety of the hearers' existence toward God as Lord of all possibilities, without leaving any of their attention free for speculation *about* what happens in this "face-to-face." If reflection emerges from the heart, it can only be practiced in a lateral or marginal re-turning to the position of prayer, for which God is never an object or topic or theme, because, as adored, he is without horizon or context—the unpreceded beginning and the end of all ends, *the nonplaceable origin of all contexts and horizons.*

"Philosophia" in Plato's sense or theology as hermeneutic retrieval of religious discourses about God cannot capture the truth of faith—not because faith contains a wider doctrine than that demonstrated by philosophical or scientific theory, but because faith relates differently to God than does thought. The Spirit of prayer inspires another attitude than contemplation. As hermeneutical theory, theology develops in the margins of adoration, gratitude, hope, and devotion. It is a lateral elucidation of those elements in prayer that can be translated into descriptive, imaginative, and conceptual language. Isolated from the praying position, however, theology degrades faith to a rather incredible doctrine or theory that must compete with other theories. It might then even go so far as to consider itself a basis for faith. Did not something similar happen when theology presented the idea of an immortal soul as the provable core of belief in the resurrection from the dead?

That the promise of salvation does not divide human beings into souls and bodies is obvious when we realize that the second commandment coincides with the first, and that none of these commands can be obeyed without obedience to both. The reality of love is proven by turning toward neighbors with a love as absolute and total as the one that constitutes an appropriate answer to God's own love for humans.

The Spirit of passion and compassion for humans is the same as the Spirit of prayer, and this is the same as the Spirit of God as revealed in Jesus Christ's passionate and compassionate giving. Examples of this love range from feeding the hungry, clothing the naked, visiting the prisoners, and healing the sick, to forgiving offenses and injustices, and taking on others' debts and sins. Eating, drinking, and sex are not spurned and no preference is shown for high culture over ordinary life. Care for the material beauty of flowers and the survival of birds is declared paradigmatic of the Spirit in which God and the saints act and speak. Eating, drinking, clothing, healing, and marrying do not belong to heaven, but neither do art, philosophy, theology, the sacraments, or the Church; yet the Gospels insist that Christ is not a ghost, because he has a heart and hands and feet, in which he carries the wounds of his passionate involvement in the world.

When we are amazed to hear that we fed and visited Jesus Christ himself, we learn that his resurrected body is identical with that of the least important of the hungry, the thirsty, and the naked (Matt. 25:31–45). A new humanity has apparently already begun. Paul insists that not only men and women, but the entire creation, is pregnant with a new creation (Rom. 8:21–22).

Reflection, theology, and contemplation take an idolatrous turn when they try to guarantee survival as the first and foremost aspect of faith in salvation. They might serve faith and gratitude and hope, however, by listening to the call that frees the mind of its concerns about security. Autonomy is arrogance when it is not humbled by the overwhelming directness of the Spirit's inspiration. The most appropriate reaction is not comprehension, but responding from the heart: correspondence.[11]

11. See chapter 5 of Adriaan T. Peperzak, *Elements of Ethics* (Stanford, Calif.: Stanford University Press, 2003).

4

Fulfillment

UNLESS THE CLAIM that one speaks in the name of Christian faith is confined to explications of ecclesiastical dogma, it is likely to be confused with the personal opinion of an individual marked by particular experiences and circumstances. However, even the official doctrine of a Church does not escape the law of historical concretization, according to which all dogma particularizes what it tries to establish by restricting its validity to determined epochs and milieus. Indeed, Christianity cannot be other than a mixture composed of "the purity of the Gospel," elements that belong to a culture, particular perspectives that hold sway at a given time over groups of individuals, and strictly individual versions of Christian life and thought. Moreover, because all education not only particularizes but also contaminates and distorts the purity of the Gospel, Christian life, as it is practiced and theorized, is always to some extent a caricature of what it should be. Inasmuch as it is evangelical, it involves consciousness of the gap between the purity demanded and the distortion that prevents it from being what it ought to be. This consciousness is *desire;* it constantly seeks a purifying "reform" through which a life more faithful to the authentic core of the Gospel can be born. The most profound meaning of Christian experience lies in this search for the Gospel in and through authentic concretizations. The mystic is devoted to this search, living each stage as an adventure in which he risks spiritual life and death. Ecclesiastical authorities—Councils, synods, popes, bishops, consistories, and so on—play an important role in this search, since the communion of Christians can exist only if it expresses itself through the authority of assembly and unity. On the other hand, the declarations of doctrinal authorities are dangerous to the Christian community when they claim to have a monopoly on the truth of the Gospel. The very multiplicity of Churches in flagrant contradiction with the union made possible and demanded by the Gospel shows what disastrous consequences result from replacing the Gospel with the official structure and authority of a

single Church. Ecclesiastical authorities both voice *and* resist the
Gospel by dogmatizing certain theologies. In guiding Christians
toward the truths of faith, they have often hindered, if not prevented,
the unfolding of living research into a more authentic understanding of
faithful truth.

Theologians have tried to sketch the contours of faith with the help
of scientific and philosophical theories that they inherited from non-
Christian thinkers. Some of their adaptations enjoyed great success
with the authorities; but much theological work has also been suspect-
ed of misrepresenting the truth by handing it over to extraevangelical
powers. Ordinary believers, on the other hand, have had a more earthly and humble experience of Christian life than most theologians and
official guides. Some of them, including saints and mystics, possessed
an existential knowledge that was more profound than the reflexive
theories of theology. Even though some mystics employed a decadent
theology to express their knowledge, they drew closer to the core of the
Gospel than some of the most qualified theologians who lacked the
same experience.

If the purest truth is neither guaranteed by doctrinal authorities, nor
by theologians, ordinary believers, or mystics, and if *none* of these
voices ever represent more than a particular concretization of faith,
then everyone who seeks the truth of faith—that is, everyone who
hopes to be or to become Christian—must, in the end, look for it at his
own risk and peril. "The purity of the Gospel" is not a given starting
point, but the horizon and goal of a search based on the hope of belonging to the great community of all who seek the ultimately necessary.
Without abandoning the communion of the search and the hope that
unites all believers, but at the same time without entrusting it completely to its official representatives alone, true believers must take up
for themselves the search for truth, while firmly holding fast to the
community of Spirit, to which they belong through their faith and religious practice. This search is not necessarily articulated reflexively or
theoretically; motivated by the desire of a reasonable being, it is an
integral part of *all* authentic faith.

The preceding lines presuppose that faith cannot be exhausted by a
series of theses or "articles of faith." It is not learned or taught by way
of a *dogma* or *theory*, although it is always tied to *doxic* and theoretical elements. The question of orthodoxy or heterodoxy comes into play

at a level secondary to lived truth. However, this level is not without importance, because the theology to which we commit ourselves reveals the quality of faith that we have. To counter the radical separation of faith and theology, we must defend their necessary and historical unity, while maintaining their distinction. Against any undue subjectivism in our interpretation, we should emphasize that we are taking part in the search of a historical community from a particular and individual perspective. In order to avoid the arrogance of thinking that we can possess the whole and only truth, we must see ourselves as participating in the communion of those who—in various traditions of Judaism, Christianity, Islam, Buddhism, and other religions—practice the search for radical meaning.

Our reflection takes place within a broken and divided community. Our ecumenism lies in the hope that we can agree on some basic conditions for a pluralistic but nonrelativistic communion of seekers who combine a profound, albeit initial, affinity with sincere respect for their differences.

THE QUESTION

Any attempted formulation of "the essence of Christianity" is permeated by elements that arise from non-Christian traditions. Among these, Judaism and Hellenism are uncontroversially most relevant. In this chapter, I will not try to define the core of Christian faith, but instead focus on the conviction that Christianity is the "fulfillment" (*plērōma*) of these traditions. That the word "fulfillment" is not univocal becomes clear when we meditate on the relationships that link the Christian to the Jew on the one hand, and to the Greek on the other. Although Christians believe that the Jew and the Greek have "become one in Christ," Christianity "fulfills" Judaism in a way different than it "fulfills" Hellenism. If we take "Greece" as the symbol of all the pagans or non-Jews, the constellation Judaism-Hellenism-Christianity summarizes all of history up to the *eschata* and the recapitulation (*anakephalaiōsis*) of the entire creation in Christ. In the time between their birth and the *eschaton*, Christians should meditate on the truth of this constellation, and their actions should display their capacity to integrate both Greek virtue and Jewish obedience into a Christian way of loving God and neighbor. In this way, Christian history has to fulfill what is proclaimed in the Gospel as essentially already realized. Theologies analyze the completion of the initial fulfillment and try to show the extent to which it faithfully reveals what has been revealed in Jesus Christ. The full revelation of the given revelation will uncover the sense in which the true Christian is a true son or daughter of Abraham and the extent to which the true Jew is the brother or sister of the true Christian. It will also show to what extent certain Christians are still Greeks, and to what extent the best of Greeks could be called Christian. The relation between Greek wisdom and Christian faith is very different from the relation between Christian faith and the Jewish religion, however. For the Christian, Abraham is a father, whereas Plato and Aristotle are only potential friends.

CHRISTIANITY AND JUDAISM

The relation between Judaism and Christianity is described in the New Testament as a *fulfillment* of the Law and its prophets. Jesus is the new Moses who brings the Law to its greatest perfection, the son of David who is at the same time different and greater than the most exemplary king, the Messiah, the Servant of Yahweh, the Son of Man. According to the message of the Gospel, the perfect Christian is a true son of Abraham, whereas the Jew who opposes its message betrays his kinship with the father of all the faithful. Although Jesus himself and all of his disciples were Jews, Christian writings often reserve the name "Jews" for those who have not accepted the Christian interpretation of Israel's destiny and its Bible. This usage expresses the first instance of an historical scission that was perhaps inevitable: the Jews and pagans who became Christians had to accept the impossibility of continuing their religious existence in the communion of faith and hope from which they emerged and within which they perhaps would have liked to remain. We do not ask the question of whether there is moral culpability in these events, but we must note that Jews who became Christians and the majority of Jewish authorities who rejected the Christian version of Judaism acknowledged that religious communion was no longer possible among them. In their polemic against certain priests and specialists of the Law, the Gospels bear traces of a disappointment that sometimes seems to turn into generalized scandal mongering. This was probably not entirely justified by the facts or by the ideals of pre-Christian faith. Whereas Christians claimed to be the true descendants of Abraham, Moses, and the prophets, non-Christian Jews were apparently convinced that the Christian interpretation betrayed the common heritage. For the Jews, Christian heterodoxy was a scandal, whereas for the Christians, rejection of Christ in the name of the Jewish tradition was blindness to the most profound meaning of this same tradition.

If the Christian is right, a reflection on faith must be able to explain how its claim to live the true fulfillment of the promises made by Abraham accords with its break from the Jewish interpretation of the same promises. For 2,000 years, the Jews have continued to deepen and develop their faith in a way that is different, although perhaps not *radically* so, from the Christian interpretation. This problem is complicated by the fact that after the two branches of the Hebrew tradition separated, a multiplicity of interpretations arose within Judaism as well as Christianity. Furthermore, within the biblical heritage there was already a great diversity of traditions, interpretations, and reinterpretations that could not be easily reduced to a coherent and harmonious position.

The first element of a Christian theology that addresses the difference between the Jewish and Christian interpretations of the message of Israel consists in an analysis of the concept of *fulfillment*, such as Christian faith understands it when focused on the *plērōma* of what it often calls the "Old Testament."

God is faithful. But after the persecution of the Jewish people by Egypt, Assyria, Babylon, the Ptolemys, Rome, the Christians of the Middle Ages, and the national states of the modern epoch, the promises and prophecies made to Abraham, Moses, and David do not seem to have been fulfilled. The proclamations of abundance on peaceful ground, restoration after exile, a worldwide kingdom, and so on remained utopian images unable to console the suffering people. How can we read Psalm 89 or Pseudo-Isaiah's "Book of Consolation" without being grieved by the distance between the happiness foreseen and the disappointing reality of unfulfillment? Any explanation that attributes this distance to exaggerated hope is unsatisfactory, because the content of prophetic promises (restoration—in a sublime form—of the Davidic kingdom, of the temple, of a united and happy people) has not even been realized approximately. The disappointment of expectations founded on divine promises urges us to consider another possibility: in order not to lose all faith, we can continue to believe in this God, without demanding that promises be kept in the way suggested by the apparent meaning of their wording. But how can we conceive of a fulfillment that does not correspond to the terms of the promises made? How could a prophecy be fulfilled in a way that is at least partially contrary to the obvious meaning of its words?

Before beginning my analysis, I would like to remark on the concept of prophecy. To purge from it all elements of magic or parapsychology, we can translate prophecy in terms of the continuity and discontinuity of history, insofar as history constitutes a time during which the human race approaches salvation. From this strictly religious perspective, prophesies express the conviction that they cannot be in vain, even when it seems clear that they are not fulfilled. The firm hope that salvation will be realized "one day" is necessarily projected in imagined paradises that correspond to the dominant desires of a certain present.

Reflection on the meaning and truth of biblical prophecies can begin with the thesis that *no fulfillment of a promise can exactly coincide with the representation of the future that is suggested by that promise.* When someone promises to do something in the distant future, we can be sure that the circumstances in which that promise will be fulfilled will be quite different from those in which it was made. No one can entirely foresee the transformations undergone between the here and now of the asserted promise and the time of its fulfillment. What is true of a promise that requires a long time for fulfillment is equally true, though to a lesser degree, for other promises that require only a short wait for their fulfillment. Belief in promises, then, involves abandoning ourselves to participation in a risky history. The future in which we must fulfill a promise is never known absolutely, but is more or less guessed at. The mistake of futurological projections, which were once quite popular, was to neglect the historical contingencies that fundamentally alter the framework in which the consequences of our current actions, ideas, and preferences take place. Any historical result of human action carries the mark of factors beyond our power. The fulfillment of a promise is not the simple execution of a desire, but the combined product of personal effort and historical intrigue that we have no choice but to accept. In all fulfillment, there is thus something unexpected in relation to the fulfillment that was imagined when the promise was made.

Inasmuch as certain prophecies proclaim a redemptive future, believers consider them to be promises made in the name of God, and they expect that such promises will be kept. However, their conviction also includes awareness that the exact form in which the promise will be kept cannot be known in advance.

On the one hand, every credible prophecy results in some kind of fulfillment, even if this is only the consolation it brings to one who places hope in it. Descendants of Abraham became a great people; the exiles were able to return; a temple was rebuilt; joy triumphed over misery and suffering. On the other hand, historical realizations were quite disappointing compared to the grandiose descriptions of prophetic messages. Was God too weak to accomplish what he promised, or did he lack loyalty? Or, perhaps, should we recognize a hidden plan in this apparent nonfulfillment? Although we are confused, we are at the same time urged to reinterpret the facts.

The perspective from which the prophets proffered their threats and consolations is that of human *salvation*. They presented God as the savior. Salvation cannot come from ourselves; under certain conditions, it comes to us from God. There is no other way of understanding what "salvation" means than to imagine in the here and now what, in the future, could be a situation of well-being, justice, reconciliation, and peace. How salvation is described depends on the epoch, the culture, and the particular circumstances marking the experience and imagination of the person providing the description. It cannot escape the situational and personal particularities to which it is bound. A representation of the proclaimed future *cannot* entirely coincide with the actual future. Those who experience the fulfillment in that future will be surprised by elements that were at least partially unforeseen. The prophesied future will therefore have a highly imaginary character. There is a difference not only between the fulfillment proclaimed by the prophet and the fulfillment awaited by those who later accept his message, but also between the imaginary world toward which the latter's wait is oriented and the historical realization of the message. Since the realization does not quite correspond to the expectation, it *must* be disappointing—at least to some extent—but it can also be surprising, enjoyable and overwhelming. If despite our disappointment we do not lose faith, then we must break with the obvious and traditional way of hearing the prophetic message in order to discover within it a more profound meaning hidden behind the appearances of the imaginary reality through which salvation was expected. Rejection of the "normal" way of interpreting religious promises obliges one to reinterpret them in a way that unseats normality. What appears to be nonfulfillment is revealed as an unexpected way of encountering the God of human salvation. For the believer, the series of historical disappointments *must* have the meaning of a redemptive process.

Fulfillment of a promise is not an exact replication of the initial utopia, and fidelity is not the repetition of real or represented events of the past. Moreover, the structure of fidelity with regard to a promised future corresponds to that of fidelity in relation to a commemorated past. Memory does not literally represent all the details of a factual past, but renews its core meaning in forms that belong to a new and different present. Because the future of a promise has its own possibilities of fulfillment, the promise of salvation can and must be realized in an unexpected way. Far from a repetitive literalism, fidelity demands that we recreate the hidden meaning of what we imagined when the promise was initially made. The actual future of a promise comes into being when the fulfillment previously imagined is transformed into a new representation and realization that fits into new circumstances. This process does not necessarily betray the meaningful core that made the old representation an authentic promise of salvation. In fact, we must grant that at least some surprising transformation is necessary for an historical fulfillment.

The only way in which to judge fidelity in religious matters is to determine if subsequent events, despite their disappointing aspects, take us closer to true salvation than does literal fulfillment. The prophets do not guarantee that the framework in which they pronounce their message in the future will be repeated or restored according to the rules of their own time. On the contrary, because they speak in the name of the Infinite, they encourage an endless, ever more radical reinterpretation of imaginary futures. We progressively discover then that these are assurances of ultimate deliverance.

All this is as true for modern utopias as it is for biblical images of a new world. The longing for liberation of humiliated nations, for a society without oppression, for a peaceful and just world expresses a messianic hope. But the most justified utopias in the end simply orient all our efforts toward the true life, which at the same time is seen as a task for us and desired as grace. According to the Christian message, the ultimate meaning, of which all utopias express only aspects, consists in the union of humans with God himself—a union already realized and still promised by "the Son of God." Even if this union can be realized only approximately, it clarifies the meaning of all prophecies.

From the perspective of the Christian *plērōma*, former prophecies appear as stages in a process that continually postpones fulfillment. Through the negation of "normal" fulfillments, the quest for salvation—oriented by utopias, yet ceaselessly disappointed by their nonrealization—discovers a hidden pedagogy directed at a more radical meaning. This education through disappointment can be compared to the purification of an individual in search of God as described by Saint John of the Cross. In renouncing perfectly legitimate pleasures, a welloriented individual is forced to discover deeper joys. Any union other than the union of grace is provisionally excluded in order that we become freer for "the uniquely necessary." Not only do the many renunciations open up the possibility of an unprecedented response, they also deepen the desire that motivates movement. A new response can then be accepted or expected without being previously known. The painful disappointment of desire opens up a depth beneath our questions, thus generating a more authentic desire than we would dare to have were its potential fulfillment not revealed to us. If salvation is the union of human beings with God, we can understand why no prophetic representation can respond to our most profound desire. All historical concretization, whether imaginary or real, remains symbolic in relation to the destination for which we exist, pointing beyond itself to the Unique that does not coincide with anything in particular. As representation, all prophecy is irremediably inadequate to what it tries to express. The meaning of its promise can be understood only after the fact and by virtue of unavoidable disappointments. Even a liberation theology that would identify heaven with the realization of universal fraternity in God falls into idolatry unless it insists on God alone as the ultimate source of all peace. The difficult learning process that prophecies impose prevents us from resting in the pure and simple hope of a more human world. This in no way denies that working toward a better world is an extremely urgent task. But the desert and the night that must be crossed on the journey to God are not empty and deep enough if we make *our* ideals of justice and peace the ultimate criteria of history.

While the Gospel fulfills and reveals the hidden meaning of the prophecies, the evangelical revelation is itself also an enigma whose hidden meaning must still be discovered and realized. The central "thesis" of the union of God and man points once again toward a future of discovery and realization of its truth. Not only the prophets of Israel but also Jesus and his witnesses engage us in a progressive revelation (or *"apokalypsis"*) of their revelation, thus providing us with a long education of hope. In giving himself as a response, God gives seekers a new heart; in leaving their desires unfulfilled, the revelation of the revelation already given lets God be known as "the sought" *(ho zētoumenos)*: one who still is and always will be sought. The fulfillment of the fulfillment is not clear knowledge, but an exodus oriented by a dark cloud that burns from within.

* * *

The fulfillment of a prophecy resembles neither a scientific prediction, nor a Hegelian *Aufhebung*. The latter has the structure of a synthesis that adds something new to its conflicting terms, concepts, or figures—it brings them to a higher level by uniting them despite their apparent contradictions—but the leap that this transition presupposes is completely determined by the terms involved and by the tension that binds them together in their difference.

Futurological extrapolation from a current situation would be possible if we had precise and complete knowledge of the essential data of the present society, the structure and rhythm of ongoing developments, and the historical contingencies that will change the present situation. A less positivistic prognosis that takes advantage of dialectical logic cannot compensate for the lack of such knowledge by globally understanding the internal dynamism of the terms at play. The fulfillment of a prophecy is not a result that can be determined in advance, like an oak tree that is somehow contained in its seed. A prophetic promise places the listener before many alternatives obliging her to follow the orientation and inspiration of the promise. The power of God is manifest in fulfilling the promise despite and by means of those historical contingencies and events that are hostile to it. This power does not eliminate human responsibility, however. Hegel's divine *Logos* dominates subjective choices according to a plan whose logic is superior to the realm of the arbitrary. Since this domination is rationally determined, it can be predicted by anyone who is "truly rational." Biblical Providence takes initiatives that cannot be foreseen by reason; they cannot even be reconstructed afterwards as necessary steps in a rational deduction. Certainly the fulfillment of a prophecy enables us to decipher its hidden meaning by a retrospective reading more enlightened than was possible at the time of its proclamation. Such a *post factum* reading does not have the character of a deduction, however; it rather celebrates the fulfillment as a consummation that, though foretold, remains surprising. Fulfillment differs from a dialectical outcome by being an event that, even retrospectively, cannot be taken for granted; even after its realization it remains unprecedented and free: a given in the strongest sense of the word—a grace.

A more suitable analogy than that of a seed evolving into a plant is found in the *birth* of a human being. The new phenomenon is surprising due to its absolute alterity. However, those who have engendered it also have an experience of the already-known and even of a certain identity that ties this little being to their own lives. No one can predict the style of life of a newborn, although the fact that another similar, but unpredictable and independent life is going to develop is certain and expected. The birth of a human being is thus closer to a repetition of the same than is the fulfillment of a prophetic promise of salvation, given that the latter goes beyond all finite completion.

Fidelity to a promise is neither the repetition of a past throughout a history of changing conditions, nor the dialectical development of a seed containing the totality of its unfolding. All forms of fidelity involve the faithful person in a process of adaptation to changing circumstances of history and individual lives. Consequently, a modification of the promised future is unavoidable, but exactly how one must adjust to the circumstances is not discovered by way of a rational *Aufhebung*. The promise can be kept if a generation or a person remains oriented toward the God of salvation, guided by a deeper desire than that for mastering or comprehending. The logic of the religious promise is the logic of desire, seeking, and receptivity with respect to what gives itself as grace. To retain the core of a commitment, it might be necessary to destroy the form and fashion in which it was concretized at another time. Literalism is perhaps as great a danger to fidelity as is its demise. Individuals and epochs must prepare an authentic and surprising future by means of well-oriented choices. They should transform the present into the memorable past of a future faithful to the sources of inspiration that determine their past and present. Nonliteralist fidelity entails working toward a more livable future than the futurological projection of today's customs.

Beginning with the question of how Judaism and Christianity are bound together through their relationship to biblical prophecies, the preceding reflection engaged in an analysis of the structure that characterizes the relation between a promise and its fulfillment. By way of a tentative conclusion, I propose the following theses: The varieties of Judaism and the various traditions of Christianity are divergent ways of continuing and fulfilling the foundational events of the Jewish people. For Christians, Jesus Christ is the key to the understanding of the promises made to Abraham and his descendants, but all of history is still insufficient for discovering what we "know" when committing ourselves to this faith. For Jews, the fulfillments of the same promises remain hidden in other ways: When and how will the Messiah come? Do we dare speak of a union between man and God without falling into idolatry? Jews and Christians approach God through an ethical perspective that is largely parallel: the encounter with the living God takes place in the "humanism of the other human." In the figure of John the Baptist, the good scribe of Mark 12:28–43, and Gamaliel, Christianity recognizes the possibility of other continuations of its own "Old Testament." Twentieth-century Christians have discovered that they still have much to learn from their Jewish brothers and sisters. While pursuing another path, the latter have continued to interpret the signs of God, aided by their greater affinity to ancient Israel and its Hebraic bible.

CHRISTIANITY AND "GREECE"

Following the plan outlined above, we should now address the question of whether and, if so, to what extent "Greece" can be considered a promise of which Christianity is a fulfillment. However, "Greece" refers to a multiplicity of Greek epochs, some of which (such as the Athens of Pericles) have been idealized in different ways by the many renaissances of European history. Being unable to speak of all Greeces, I will here restrict my task to a very incomplete meditation on one expression of the Greek spirit: the relationship between the Platonic conception of salvation and Christian faith.

Plato's Ideal

The Platonic conception of the meaning of life can be gathered from the analogy of the cave, located at the beginning of the seventh book of the *Politeia*. It becomes even clearer if we combine this text with reflections and analogies that are found in the *Phaedo*, the *Phaedrus*, and the *Symposium*.

The cave symbolizes the "normal" state of people who eat, drink, make love, watch television, and chat. They do not live for truth; not even for a "true" life. Their thoughts are only shadows of the truth. In contrast, Plato presents the wisdom of one who, after many lessons and trials, has found the right attitude. Not only does this person see the world of phenomena from the perspective of their true essence, he has an idea about the source of the light necessary to discover their ultimate meaning. There would be neither light, nor reason, nor understanding without the Good, which is the ultimate source of all meaning and through which there is truth and being. A wise person is directed toward this source of light, the generous One beyond all finite meaning.

The distance between a so-called "normal" life and the superior life of those who befriend wisdom can be traversed by studying under the guidance of one who already knows the way. To begin with, the transition demands a critical reversal with respect to the habits and views of "normal" life, a deliverance from the bondage of superficiality through a fundamental reversal of one's theoretical, practical, and affective perspective. Such a reversal is not possible without a certain violence. Who would be able to turn away from the land of shadows where one is very much at home, by the sole means of one's own will? The nontruth of "normality" can be seen only in retrospect, though it might begin to shine in the form of uneasiness and self-doubt. An escape from the cave presupposes a master of truth who is already turned toward the light. How would the prisoner be ready for an ascent without someone pushing or convincing him to climb toward the blinding radiance of the hidden source? Plato's Socrates is this master, but his violence is gentle: he uses seduction. By asking questions in the form of innocent requests for definitions *(ti estinē)* he engages his listeners in a strategic discussion. Once they enter into his reasonable game, they are caught in the net of a certain logic. How, then, can they escape from his "onto-theo-logical" net leading to the ideas and beyond—to the "idea" of the Good?

If he did not awaken a similar desire within the student himself, Socrates' dialectical seduction would be pure violence; he would thus be unable to capture any smart student in his net. Humans must already be attracted to the "up-there" *(ekeise)* in order to feel drawn by the suggestions of the one who comes from there. *Erōs* is the intermediary force on which the educator must be able to depend. Like a type of *mania*, it moves irresistibly. Without *erōs*, Socrates himself would have nothing truthful to say. However, dialectical reasoning is not enough to clear the path that leads to the Good. Without inspiration, no one will submit to the fascination of the Good-and-Beautiful. The rhetoric of the initial seduction will be forgiven later, when the student has become a master who applies the same pedagogy.

Arrival "up-there" does not end all violence. Once you are used to the purity of the truth, you must return to the community of "normal" people. The descent from the enlightened Academy into the *polis* of earthly concerns is motivated by a kind of pity. This descent does not make the wise happier—on the contrary, they must sacrifice their happiness in order to help others gain a more truthful existence. The practice of wisdom includes political involvement, but free time for contemplation is granted to those who are still learning. *Theoria* remains the true salvation and the ultimate refuge.

Taken together, the upward and the downward paths constitute a back-and-forth between theoretical delight and political service. An analogous image is found in the *Symposium*, where Diotima teaches that the same *erōs* leads in two directions: toward Beauty itself, the revelation of which is the greatest delight imaginable, *and* toward other human beings in need of wisdom and truth. Here, too, birth serves as an analogy to evoke both the new and traditional character of wisdom acquired by an individual in search of ultimate meaning.

The ascent toward wisdom requires study and asceticism. Corporeal exercises, musical training, mental hygiene, formation of a noble disposition, as well as scientific and philosophical studies, prepare one for the sudden vision that reveals the ultimate meaning of the entire universe. Total liberation, however, presupposes breaking with the back-and-forth between low and high, and high and low. Death is not necessarily a complete liberation, for in most cases it is followed by multiple reincarnations, which each time impose a new existence similar to the last. Only the very pure and persistent philosopher will escape the vicious cycle of human life and death to rejoin the endless contemplation of the happy gods.

Plato interprets the higher region as the proper dimension of the soul and identifies the lower region with the corporeal realm. Although certain inconsistencies relativize this view (for example, according to *Phaedrus* 246d, gods have bodies), the aristocratic existence of the philosopher is described in terms of the *psychē*, whereas the body (*sōma*) is responsible for the banal existence of the multitude. Death is defined as the separation of body and soul, but how can this be true if what remains after death is not a body, but a corpse? It is also easy to show that philosophical existence is in no way less corporeal or more *animated* than the existence of those who exhaust themselves in eating, drinking, chatting, making love, and watching television. However, the Platonic conception of the "normal" and the superior life and the conversion separating these two kinds of human existence can be thematized without introducing the dualism of body and soul.

Metanoia

The reversal preached by the Gospel is not the beginning of a philosophical ascent toward the supra-ideal source of ideas, but an opening of the heart to the "kingdom of God." We can study it in the résumé of the evangelical message given by Mark 1:14: Jesus . . . proclaimed the Good News: "The time has come and the Kingdom of God is at hand; repent and believe the Good News."

The condition for the conversion demanded here is that the awaited time, that of salvation and foretold by the prophets, has finally arrived. Although religious messengers have often appealed to a radical change of heart, the *metanoia* demanded by the herald of the Gospel is different in that it responds to the definitive fulfillment of old promises: God has begun to reign; from now on, the human race can live the life of God himself. One cannot enter the kingdom, however, without turning one's heart from pseudo- and antidivine powers and attaching oneself to the only true God, the Father whose sun shines on good and evil people alike.

The state one must escape in order to enter into the dimension foretold by the Gospel—the state of humans who have not yet noticed the approach of God—is not the banal existence that Plato contrasts with philosophical existence. According to the Gospel, the meaning of unconverted existence is dependent upon the meaning of the new life made possible by the reversal, but the promised life cannot be described as a higher kind of theory. The Gospel attempts to rouse people from a situation described in terms of sleep, sickness, death, or slavery under the evil powers that, without compassion, terrorize the human race. Insofar as we submit to these masters, we are sinners; sickness, suffering, and death itself are thus experienced as symptoms of Evil. The evangelical message, however, proclaims that God has begun to break down this power by substituting his own dominance. The world is still seized by great crises, but the outcome is no longer in doubt; true life has begun its conquest.

The domination of sin is not the banality of material existence, but the idolatry continually denounced by the prophets of Israel. The root of all sin does not lie in a trivial hedonism, but in the closing of the heart to God. Not to open oneself to God's approach, to prefer something else to God's offer of deliverance, not to accept all existence as entirely given, not to expect from God alone the ultimate meaning of all life, but rather to rid oneself of all guilt by mere self-justification— all of this is resistance to the Unique, and therefore adoration of the Opposite. Idolatry encloses us within the domain of private property, well protected against the intrusion of the uninvited Stranger. Even *theoria*, if it is practiced as the supreme mode of life, impedes the heart in welcoming the approach of God.

The Christian conversion away from idolatry is named faith or trust *(pistis)*. Through the Greco-European tradition we have been seduced to understand the meaning of *pistis* within a framework of theoretical knowledge. We thus distinguish between certain knowledge (philosophical, scientific, or empirical), and various degrees of uncertain or unproven knowledge. The latter range from very probable knowledge, which should only be doubted in exceptional cases, to frivolous opinions, easy to supplant with other, equally doubtful, opinions. If we let ourselves be imprisoned within this framework, we are forced to set faith in the category of "uncertain" or "insufficiently established" knowledge, as for example, when we say, "I don't know, but I believe that. . . ." We define it then as a belief, a form of opinion or conviction without proof, while distinguishing it from scientifically or philosophically justified knowledge. Thus Kant defines faith as a "taking-for-true," which combines a fundamental lack of insight with subjective certainty about its content. However, biblical faith escapes the categorization of knowledge that we inherited from the Greeks and their modern successors. It is neither a theoretical certainty concerning "articles of faith," nor a provisional *doxa* that could be transformed into a conceptually justified theory. It is therefore impossible to oppose this faith directly to theoretical conceptions, as if faith itself contained a vision of the world that would render all philosophical or scientific visions superfluous. Faith is neither a weak form of solid and certain knowledge, nor an apologetically defended dogma. Proofs for the existence of God or the soul's immortality, such as philosophy has tried to establish, belong to a different dimension than that of faith.

The dimension of faith is one of confidence in God, grateful acceptance, and attendance to the realization of grace in history. As entry into the dimension of God's allegiance to the human race, faith participates in pity, which, according to Luke (6:27–38), is the specific perfection of God. The reversal demanded by the Gospel is achieved by the practice of this pity. Although we have never seen the Lord, we have met him by giving water to one who thirsts (Matt. 25:35). We participate in God's eschatological coming not through intuition of the Beautiful or the Good in itself, but through pity and fraternity (Matt. 24–25). We do not reach God through contemplation of the dazzling divine, but in active compassion.

Like the reversal that delivers one from the Platonic cave, evangelical conversion presupposes a form of violence. This does not lie in any separation of the spirit from the body, or in seduction of young fellows to the elite existence of philosophers. The Gospel promises a rebirth in the image of a merciful God, but the path from an estranged life to that of union with God is not reserved for an elite who have the money, the time, and the courage to engage in extensive education; it is rather the shortest path possible: that which passes through love. Whereas Platonic *erōs*, according to the *Symposium* (206), disappears as soon as it possesses what it lacks, Christian *agapē* does not diminish, but rather increases as it approaches the loved one. Its aim is not possession, but giving. The aim of the latter love is not different from love itself; it is its radicalization. One who loves does not cease loving; love deepens the "need" to love. We have never loved enough, because love itself is the infinite. Its goal is not an eternal possession of the Same (cf. *Symposium* 206a), but a desire (growing as it is satisfied) to become more and more generous. Without merging with the other, love gladly shares in the other's existence, joys, and pains.

The contrast between *agapē* and *erōs* has a parallel in the difference between Christian admiration and the wonder that Plato and Aristotle see as the beginning of philosophy. According to Aristotle's *Metaphysics*,[1] amazement diminishes and eventually disappears when thought is able to understand what initially amazed it. For a believer, however, reflection can only heighten, not diminish, one's admiration for the given world. As gift or grace, not only does the world symbolize, but *is*, the proximity of God. Admiration and love increase as we approach the marvel of a mystery that deepens in revealing itself. Revelation intensifies the mysteriousness of the mystery. Mystics teach us that a specific mixture of joy and suffering indicates the indissoluble unity of God's proximity and his obscurity.

Faith and Theory

Although the Christian path does not necessarily aim at the acquisition of a superior theory, and though its essence cannot be captured by dogmatic theses, evangelical life does lead to a certain form of wisdom (cf. for instance, Matt. 11:25–27). God reveals himself without being seen to one who receives a poor person (Matt. 25). Jesus' word, "I am" (John 8:58), is not equivalent to a philosophical "I think"; rather it says, "I am here for you," as God had said to Moses (Exod. 4:14), "I carry, support, and hold you; I take care of you and grace you." Revelation reveals not only something more and better than a doctrine; it urges us to "*do*" and to live the truth.

Unlike the Platonic reversal, the Christian conversion does not involve an ascent toward the ideas, followed by a descent back into the obscurity of a corrupt community. The path that leads to God *coincides* with the path leading to our world. God is neither in heaven nor on earth; God's interest is identical to that of the human race, and there is

---

1. *Metaphysics,* A 2, 983a11–23.

no difference between true religion and authentic fidelity to the earth. By encountering the Other in a *particular* way, we find ourselves close to God and vice-versa: praying is a lie if we are not devoted to other humans. There is thus no opposition between love of "heaven" and dedication to the world—not even provisionally. Although contemplative life has its psychological and historical difficulties with respect to action, these cannot be justified by the opposition between God and the world or between religion and politics, and even less by the opposition of the spiritual to the corporeal. Within the interpretation given here, the Christian religion is as earthly as any agnosticism or atheism, even more so; the *metanoia* does not escape the historical world of corporeal, intersubjective, and socioeconomic communication, but embraces it. Although it rejects what Saint Paul calls "the flesh," this rejection differs radically from Plato's and Hellenism's suspicion about matter, which, through Manichean and other influences, has infiltrated historical Christianity. In fact, like "the world" of Saint John, "the flesh" does not express matter in opposition to the soul, but the misery of human existence insofar as this is abandoned to itself. In this sense, the most "spiritual" philosopher who is not hospitable to the poor is "carnal" and "worldly"; he does not have access to the dimension of the divine.

Praeparatio Evangelica?

Can we defend the thesis, shared in some respects by Justin and Clement of Alexandria, that Greek, and especially Platonic, thought, like the history of Israel, prepared Christian faith?

From the comparison sketched above, the answer seems to be negative. The orientation of Plato's *eros* differs too much from the evangelical orientation, although some affinity can be recognized in the movement toward the high, the pure, the beautiful, and the good. All these words ("high," "pure," "beautiful," and "good") are equivocal, however, and their Christian interpretation is not a straightforward unfolding of their Greek understanding, nor even a synthesis into which the Greek interpretation is preserved as an element. A certain integration of Greek philosophy does occur in Christian theology, but faith itself is no more a fulfillment of Greek culture than that of a Persian, Chinese, or Germanic culture, even if one believes that all cultures are essentially oriented by the same desire for the Absolute, despite differences in their concretizing of this desire.

The idea that Greek thought is a second preparation for the Gospel is ambiguous. It can mean that Christianity owes much to Greece (or to a *particular* Greece)—which cannot be denied—but it can also indicate an attempt at monopolizing all the good produced by "Greece." Were Justin and Clement, in their theory of the relationship between Greece and Christianity, not too Greek? The idea of complete integration rather fits the Hegelian conception of a philosophical system or the political practice of an absolute State, but how could it encompass the Christian ideal of a worldwide fraternity of many cultures? The tendency to unify all differences through the monologue of one orthodoxy might characterize Western civilization, but the Christian attitude seems at once more modest and more universal. Is it not too convinced of God's incomprehensibility to enclose His omnipresence in one theory?

Plato and Christ

To conclude this chapter, I would like to reflect on some aspects of the old question: To what extent has Christian theology either betrayed or enhanced the content of faith by its attempt to integrate the Platonic distinction between "soul" *(psychē)* and "body" *(sōma)*? I will restrict my meditation to Plato's *Phaedo*, and do not claim to give an exhaustive account of it.

The problem posed in the *Phaedo* is introduced by the question of whether it is not better to die rather than go on living. The response that it is better to be separated from corporeal existence, because the body is a prison for the soul, develops through a meditation on the composition of human being. Both the framework and the central issue of the entire dialogue lie in the following double—yet indivisible—question: What can we hope for, and what life should we live? (Or what should we do?) The *Phaedo* thus combines two different questions: an ethico-religious question concerning the quality of life (a question further developed by Aristotle in the *Nicomachean Ethics* when he asks in which *bios* the happy life resides),[2] and a second question concerning the constitution of human beings. The unity of ethics and metaphysics characteristic of Platonic thought is a virtue that distinguishes it from all philosophies in which the dualism of the good and being is due to a lack of depth. However, as we will see, Plato draws a false metaphysical

---

2. *Nicomachean Ethics* I, 5, 1095b14–1096a10.

conclusion from his ethical considerations: the separation of the soul
and the body is not a necessary consequence of his contrast between
two ways of living.

The principal question of the *Phaedo* urges the reader to discover
the best sort of human life. The clear response is illustrated in the life
of Socrates: the perfect philosopher is the best and the happiest of all
humans. From this response follows an entire pedagogy. By means of
physical, ethical, aesthetic, moral, and theoretical education, we
become experts in philosophy, which leads to the intuition of the Good
that grants beings their essence and truth. This goal is achieved through
the personal effort of an astute individual guided by a wise master. All
effort is in vain, however, if one does not have a "divine destiny" (*theia
moira*) that provides the necessary talents.

As we have seen, Plato opposes the outcome of this education to the
banal life of "the multitude," which he characterizes in terms of their
favorite activities: eating, drinking, and having sex. It should be noted,
however, that (a) Plato adds *chatting* and a series of vices unrelated to
eating and sex, to this list (66c), and (b) these activities do not by themselves distinguish common people from philosophers. The ethical difference is that the philosopher does not eat or drink more than is necessary.
The banal life is not distinguished by eating, and drinking, and so on, but
by its *concentration* on these activities and the extension and intensity of
the interest it devotes to them. If we have excessive esteem for the pleasures of food and sex, preferring them to more noble satisfactions, we can
be neither philosophers nor happy. There is then nothing left but to fill
the pauses between pleasures with work and chatter.

The conversion that liberates us from the banal life and introduces
us to the philosophical life can be compared to a kind of death. By con-
verting to the search for wisdom, a seeker "dies" to her previous life.
The asceticism following this reversal is then a kind of agony during
which the dying person meditates on the advantages of this death.

Plato passes from metaphorical death to real death when he introduces the thesis that by its dissolution of the human composite, death
is able to deliver the soul from a trivial existence shackled to vital
needs. Instead of sketching a phenomenology of different lifestyles
and their phenomenal (and thus corporeal) characteristics, he passes
quickly to a very different question: what remains of a human when
she dies? It is obvious that the orphic response that Plato adopts is

false. If death were the separation of the soul and the body, following death there would be not only a soul, but also a body. In fact, however, there is only a corpse, which is something entirely different than a body. In order to espouse the orphic thesis, one would have to say that the human being is composed of a soul and a dead thing—deader and more different from a body than an insect or plant, so much so that it is already changing into earth. The existence of any human body necessarily includes animation by the soul, but death changes the substance of a body into earth. If the soul is distinct from the body, it can exist in two different ways: (a) in union with the thing that, *through this union*, is a body, and not a corpse, or (b) independently of all ties to a material substance. In the second case, the function of animation would not be essential to the soul; the human being would fundamentally be nothing but an angel, and corporal existence would be an accident. History, language, and the world would simply be superfluous or worse—a punishment for the soul that has not yet become completely pure, that is, purely and simply angelic.

The Platonic attempt to explain the difference between the two ways of life by opposing two metaphysical entities is wrongheaded. The specific quality of a philosophical existence is no less empirical, visible, audible, and tangible than a completely trivial existence. While it is true that the superiority of a wise person can only be perceived if the observer possesses a certain openness in regard to phenomena that show themselves, nothing phenomenal suggests that such a person is less corporeal or material than others. The differences in lifestyles can be formulated by a description of their diverse appearances. The characteristics of a wise life are as much corporeal, animated, and spiritual as those of "the many." The manner in which ordinary people eat or make love is not more material than that of an accomplished philosopher. All human life is, in this sense, corporeal as well as "spiritual," but the specific way it is lived demonstrates a particular and individualized "spirit." The equivocity of the words "spirit" and "spiritual" is thus demonstrated by the distinction between the ethical and the metaphysical perspectives. Even "bestial," despite its reference to inhuman behavior, expresses a "spirit" that can only be human. A "spiritual" life is a *certain way* of being alive and corporeal; being a human body is a *specific way* of being animated by a spirit, because it is able to speak, love, enjoy, desire, adore, and so on.

The error that generated the dualism of soul and body originated because the activities of eating and procreation seem to tie us more firmly to the material world than theoretical discussions and training in the virtues. But even if there is some shade of truth in this, we do not become more human or more "spiritual" by leaving our body behind; suicide does not produce spirituality.

Without entering into a phenomenology of different lifestyles, I will end this chapter with two remarks and a conclusion:

1.   The resemblance between the eating and sex of animals and humans is entirely superficial and does not touch on the meaning of *human* nourishment and sexuality.

2.   The reversal to which Socrates invites his pupils tallies well with the Platonic eulogy of the philosopher's superior life, but it does not lend itself to a conception that sees liberation from the body as part of the philosophical way of life.

The shortcoming of base people does not consist in their corporeality or material activities, but in their *slavery*. Liberation is found when the addiction to the hedonic pleasures of eating, drinking, and sex is replaced by a more noble (because more intellectual) allegiance: the love of thought, which leads to perfect wisdom and has its own pleasures and joys. The ascent is neither murder nor suicide, but a specific love and discipline of life. Christian faith sees a dangerous slavery in any passionate love that adores *theoria* as if it were the absolute itself. Such contemplation, very different from mystical contemplation, is another idol to smash. This judgment does not imply any contempt for philosophy, virtue, eating, drinking, making love, or chatting, but it relativizes all of these activities, because none of them can claim to be the absolute or God.

Because Plato thinks that corporeality, or belonging to the sensible world, prevents the soul from enjoying perfect knowledge, terrestrial existence as such seems to him a burden and, if we cannot escape it, a cause for despair with regard to a divine sort of life. Reincarnation solves nothing, because it requires repetition of the same imprisoned existence. Only the very constant philosopher, after many lives, achieves a perfectly free existence by escaping the corporeal atmosphere once and for all.[3] It is thus clear that even for Plato it is not death as such that should

---

3. Cf. *Phaedrus* 247a ff.

delight us, but a certain kind of death: that which—like the death of Socrates—puts the final seal on a life dedicated to the search for truth.

The evangelical message does not recommend death as a way of delivering the true human from the earth. If many saints desired death, it was because they wanted to be with God. Dying is not desirable in itself; God does not like to kill; but perfect union with God is not possible without the completion of a life lived in desire. According to Plato, death is the ultimate form of a reversal through which the philosopher separates himself from the shadows and directs himself toward the source of light. For the Christian, it is the loss of autarchy. The acceptance of mortality is a response to the gracious gesture that creates mortals *ex nihilo* and saves them, despite their tendency toward an illusory autarchy. Nothing can protect me from final destruction except God. The ultimate meaning of my life cannot come from society or history, which, though longer, are as finite and mortal as I myself. The secret of the *metanoia* is to wait for God, while accepting the extreme poverty of human existence. Death is necessary, not as liberation, humiliating destiny, or punishment, but as the overcoming of the temptation to sovereignty. In dying, human existence is converted into receptivity of Grace.

These statements are not a direct denial of the metaphysical thesis that the soul is immortal. They respond to another question, namely, that of hope: What can we hope and from whom? Plato's hope pointed toward the region of astral gods and the Good as source of light. He focused on the immortality of the soul because this seemed a necessary condition for the fulfillment of that hope.

The resurrection of Jesus Christ indicates the contradiction that separates Greeks and Christians by symbolizing a more radical reversal. Either the soul can acquire happiness through its own actions, or else human beings, even the purest, cannot by their own power save themselves. Salvation is given as grace. Resurrection is not the opposite of incarnate or reincarnated human life, nor does it occur in an otherworldly heaven of angels and bodiless souls, but it is the ultimate fulfillment of the promises and prophecies. A prophecy is nothing parapsychological, but insists on the human, and therefore bodily, character of the ultimate meaning. Prophecies express a religious perspective on mortal life taken as a whole. They testify that the ultimate meaning presupposes God. As ultimately fulfilling, resurrection does not belong to history; the final meaning does not take place as an occurrence in time. The beyond of history is not an atemporal theory, but it comes to us in the form of inspiration and participation. The amazement caused by prophecies that seem unfulfilled, grows with the conviction, surprise after surprise and disappointment after disappointment, that such is the manner of God's coming.

Without disdain for the joys of the earth, yet distancing itself from all that is not God, Christian faith testifies to the gracious structure of existence as a gift. The *hōs mē* of Saint Paul (1 Cor. 7) expresses the inevitable rejection of all idolatry. Christian asceticism counterbalances the "carnal" tendency of idolization by a series of nonabsolute *No*'s. Denial *(Nada, nada, nada)* is only a moment or a phase (which may last a long time) within a history of gratitude that delights in everything. Because the gesture of donation is more important than the content of the gift, ascetic distance testifies to a love of Love.

The contrast sketched here between Plato's philosophical approach to death and the meaning of death according to the story of Christian salvation is only one element of theological eschatology. A deconstruction of European Platonism cannot stop at a naïve rejection of metaphysics in the name of hope. Leaving aside a more fundamental reflection, this chapter has served to sharpen some questions about life and death that no Christian who practices philosophy can avoid.

5

Anselm's *Proslogion* and Its Hegelian Interpretation

HEGEL ON ANSELM

Saint Anselm is the only philosopher of the Middle Ages whom Hegel discusses seriously in his lectures on the history of philosophy and his lectures on the philosophy of religion.[1] There are two main reasons for Hegel's interest: 1. In contrast to those of his colleagues in theology and philosophy who proclaim at every turn that the human mind cannot know God, let alone prove his existence, Hegel agrees with Anselm that genuine faith not merely permits but requires the believer to seek to understand what he believes. 2. According to Hegel, Anselm's proof of the existence of God, presented in the *Proslogion*, is an expression—clumsy though it might be—of the heart of all philosophy and all theology that deserves to be called an absolute science.

When Hegel dealt with the argument that Anselm makes in the *Proslogion* he probably had not read its entire text and so missed the emotional context within which, according to Anselm, thought must move in order to attain a certain understanding of God. In fact, all the quotations that Hegel offers to his students are taken from Tenneman's *History of Philosophy*.[2] That book makes no clear reference to the indissoluble union between the religious sentiment, expressed in chapters 1, 14, 16–18, 22, and 24–26, and the work of conceptual understanding presented in the context of prayer. Without a sense of that union, Hegel interprets the *Proslogion* as though it were a thematic

---

1. G. W. F. Hegel, *Vorlesungen über die Geschichte der Philosophie,* ed. Hermann Glockner, 19 (XV) (Stuttgart: Frommann, 1927), pp. 164–69, and *Vorlesungen über die Philosophie der Religion,* ed. Hermann Glockner 16 (XII) (Stuttgart: Frommann), pp. 214–18.

2. Wilhelm Gottlieb Tennemann, *Geschichte der Philosophie,* 11 vols. (Leipzig, 1798–1819), vol. 8^I, pp. 115–53.

discourse, comparable to the philosophical treatises of modern thinkers such as Spinoza, Leibniz, and Kant.

Not only in its form, but also in its content, Hegel's interpretation is dominated by the perspective of eighteenth-century philosophy. He does not give a precise analysis of the definition from which Anselm starts, namely *id quo maius cogitari nequit* (that than which nothing greater can be thought) or *IQM;* instead, he declares this formula to be equivalent to a number of different expressions: "the concept of the most perfect" and "the universe of reality" *(der Inbegriff der Realität* or *das Allgemeine der Realität)*—expressions that suggest the *omnitudo realitatis* (totality of reality) of Leibniz and Kant—and, on the other hand, "the thought of a highest" *(der Gedanke eines Höchsten)* and "the highest thought" *(der höchste Gedanke).*

But even if Hegel did not know the framework within which Anselm introduces his argument, there is nevertheless a surprising resemblance between their conceptions of what Hegel calls the "proofs of the existence of God." Hegel tells us, in his *Lectures on the Proofs of the Existence of God,* that any such proof is nothing but a way of conceptualizing "the elevation of the spirit towards God" *(ein denkendes Auffassen dessen, was die Erhebung des Geistes zu Gott ist).*[3] In trying to include what is true in the various proofs, Hegel starts from Christian faith, just as Anselm did, in order to comprehend its content. If the proof is to succeed, the comprehension that it reaches must include the necessity of its conclusion, and the hypothesis from which the argument starts must show itself to be a self-evident truth. According to Hegel, Anselm's great discovery is that the concept from which he deduces the necessary existence of God does not have any foundation outside of itself. Even if it is only taken as the notion of a hypothetical possibility, it imposes by its own force the necessity of what it hypothesizes. Belief in the existence of God— which, as an empirical fact, is prior in time to the deduction of that existence—is then no longer required for the knowledge that God exists as God. The proof shows itself to be a proof *a priori,* a deduction of the necessary implications of a pure concept. The task that remains is the deduction, from the concept of God, of a subjective and historical expression, which is the Christian faith. Such a deduction

---

3. Hegel, *Philosophie der Religion,* pp. 392 and 399.

will also show that the initial concept is at the heart of the emotional faith that is prior in time to its conceptualization.

In Hegel's judgment, Anselm's argument contains all that is necessary for a foundation of philosophy: the concept of the perfect, or of God, is nothing but the concept of the *Logos* (or of "the Logical"—*das Logische*—as Hegel often says), which includes within itself all being and all thought. The argument, rightly called "onto-logical," is merely a way of proving that the *Logos*, or God, is the absolute identity of thought and being, the first and the last, the foundation and the end of all that is and all that must be thought.

For Hegel, like Anselm, faith has an affective side. But Hegel goes much farther than Anselm, thinking as he does that the essence of faith lies in its emotional form and that its content is identical with the theological content one discovers in transforming emotional adherence into rational knowledge. Although the truth of reason does not depend on faith, faith is not superfluous: insofar as humans have knowledge, they must also express the truth in the emotional side of their lives. A complete philosophy would also have to undertake analyses of the representational, imaginary, and narrative dimensions of faith, but in order to be brief I limit myself to its emotional aspect.

Both Hegel and Anselm trust the power of reason to advance the understanding of what they believe. However, Anselm is convinced that there is an insurmountable gap between God as he reveals himself through a living faith and God as he is known by rational thought. He certainly believes that reason can shed light on faith through a conceptual clarification of "the elevation of his soul in faith toward God," but he would never use reason to oppose the faith of the religious and historical community in which he is at home.

Hegel likewise is convinced that faith and reason cannot contradict each other, but he subordinates the former to the latter. He professes a "faith in reason" *(Glaube an die Vernunft)*, and tells his students that this is the only certainty they have to bring to his courses.[4] From Anselm's perspective, we might say that Hegel bets on two different sorts of faith: a faith in God and a faith in the Reason of Logic. According to Hegel, however, these amount to only one faith. God is the *Logos* and Reason,

---

4. See Hegel's inaugural address at the University of Berlin on October 22, 1818, in *Berliner Schriften* 1818–1831 (Hamburg, Meiner: 1956), pp. 8–9.

understood rightly, is God. Faith is only a provisional way of being attached to the truth of the *Logos*. Once Reason or *Logos* has permeated faith, the latter is understood as the emotional and imaginative prefiguration of its rational core. Reason is thus the supreme measure with which faith is measured; it judges all religions, including the absolute or Christian religion. "The elevation of the spirit to God" must obey logical necessities if it is to be fully worthy of God and humanity.

The concept that lies at the basis of Anselm's argument is understood by Hegel as the concept of the highest perfection and as the abstract concept of the absolute. In Hegel's terminology it is the concept of the Idea insofar as this is the original identity of thought and being. Hegel's praise for Anselm's argument is understandable: through an analysis of the abstract concept of perfection, the argument shows that the supreme thought, the thought of what is most universal, implies being. Thought and being are, then, two aspects of the One, which is also the totality. The thought of perfection is the Infinite. It encompasses not only the universe of finite beings and thoughts, but also the pseudo-infinite that most theologians contrast with it. Despite certain blunders, a monk of the Middle Ages—which Hegel considered very obscure—here surpassed Kant in affirming with all lucidity the central truth of Hegel's absolute idealism: as identity of thought and being, the *Logos* is the Infinite and the Perfect. According to Hegel, the Idea of all ideas, the Essence of all that is, is not surpassable by any thing or any thought. It exists as the beginning and the end, as the meaning of all that is and is thought.

Hegel sees, however, two weaknesses in Anselm's effort:

1. An adequate proof of his thesis would have to start either from thought and show that it includes being, or from being and show that it necessarily implies thought. The difference between the two paths is the difference between the *a priori* and the *a posteriori* proofs of God's existence. In either case, the proof would have to begin with the most objective and necessary sense of thought or being and not with a particular instance, whether subjective or otherwise contingent. Anselm starts out from the subjective consciousness of a certain individual who ponders the notion of perfection. He does not begin with the *Logos* as it displays itself in a Logic that is universal and necessary.

2. Anselm limits himself to a phenomenological perspective, but Hegel in his *Encyclopedia* shows clearly that such a perspective is not

sufficient to prove that the secret of the universe consists in the self-realization of the absolute as the spiritual identity of subjectivity and objectivity. Only ontology, a logic that encompasses all that is, can prove the thesis Anselm sketches out in the *Proslogion*.

ANSELM

Having seen how Hegel transforms Anselm's *argumentum unicum* into a foreshadowing of post- and anti-Kantian idealism, let us now consider the text of Anselm himself.

Any interpretation of the "single argument" must begin with a correct grasp of the framework in which it exists, its text and context; to begin with, I will consider the title. *Proslogion* means "allocution," or "address," as Anselm remarks in his preface. He contrasts this *alloquium* with the *soliloquium*, or soliloquy, of his earlier written *Monologion*. The *Proslogion* is thus neither the meditation of someone "who would seek what he does not know by a reasoning in the silence of his interior," nor is it a theological or philosophical treatise. Rather, it is a speech addressed to someone. In fact, the *Proslogion* is addressed to many people, in the first place, and like all writing, to its readers. Anselm also speaks, in many passages, to his soul *(anima mea)*, to his heart *(cor meum)*, and to the "little man" *(homuncio)* that he is. The principal addressee, however, is continually present as someone who hears and intervenes without making a sound. It is God—*Deus meus*, my God, or *Dominus meus*, my Lord, or simply *tu*, you. The frequent repetition of *meus* in *Deus meus* and *Dominus meus* shows that the relation between Anselm and "his" God is more intimate than the relation between a philosophical mind and a theme it tries to comprehend. The relation between the writer of the *Proslogion* and the heart he exhorts or reproaches seems to create a distance between the text and Anselm himself, but he undermines this impression by directing himself primarily to God and by constantly identifying himself with his soul or the *homuncio* to whom he speaks. The little book, oriented as it is from the beginning toward God, is a prayer that Anselm's heart directs toward "his God." All of the analyses that compose the text are presented as parts of one long prayer, a prayer that tolerates no distractions.

This prayer is a direct and utterly natural expression of faith. It is not subjective—if this word means "arbitrary." On the contrary, in describing the content of his faith, Anselm appeals to what he has received from the historical community that calls itself the "Body of Christ." Hence the use of the plural in *"credimus"* (we believe) in chapter 2. This community had, in its thousand years, borrowed from the languages of many cultures in order to translate and interpret the heritage of its faith, a faith that was not particular to any of those cultures, and yet was capable of redeeming them all. One of those languages was the language of Hellenistic ontology, as translated into Latin, which Anselm read in the writings of his abbey's library. He uses that language when, after the invocation at the beginning of chapter 2, he reformulates the rock of Christian faith: "Grant that we might understand, as much as you think it beneficial, that *(quia)* you are, as we believe it, and that you are what *(quod)* we believe. Now, we believe that you are something *(aliquid)* greater than which one can think nothing."

If we take the understanding *(intellectus)* that Anselm seeks to be a synonym for "wisdom," the prayer seems to carry on a biblical tradition that is expressed, for example, in the wisdom literature and in many of the psalms. However, Anselm changes the "You" *(credimus te esse)* into a "something" *(aliquid)* that one can "think" *(cogitare)*. Is this not a *metabasis eis allo genos*, a change of kind? Hasn't Anselm here left the biblical tradition in order to abandon himself to a pagan philosophy? Are we confronted once again by the insurmountable difference between the God of Abraham and the God of the philosophers?

Anselm's intent is to show that the God of faith is the one and only Lord, and that all the value of our life and intellect depends on this single God. He uses a reason that has been educated by pagan and Christian thinkers in order to "somewhat understand" (*aliquatenus intelligere*, chap. 1) that God is what he is, but he always maintains his radical and intimate connection with the emotional fountain that springs from desire and hope, and is the fruit of religious maturity.

Although Anselm would firmly deny that any contradiction could rise between the God of faith and the God of philosophy, he often warns us not to overestimate the power of the intellect. Yet he never deprecates the gift of reason that characterizes man as an image of God.

Although the beginning of chapter 2 might suggest that faith is primarily a doctrinal belief in true propositions, this is not the case. Like the *pistis* of which Paul speaks, Anselm's faith *(fides)* is, from the start, utter abandonment and complete confidence. By God's grace, faith engages the believer in the practice of love on the basis of gratitude and joy in hope. In faith, a life is seized by an orientation that has become a habit and a disposition of soul and heart and body. "God" is thus the name of the Unique who orients, supports, and consoles even before granting a clear awareness of what he is bringing about in the soul.

At the same time, a living faith inevitably unfolds itself in all the essential dimensions of the human being engaged by it, and so also in the intellect that lets itself be moved by its inclination toward more light. Having received their faith in the community that heeds its tradition, authentic believers are engaged in an effort to comprehend the lives they live. If they have learned certain methods of reflection, they will use these to acquire a certain wisdom. Christian faith has never required that all believers be intelligent, or that all of them should dedicate themselves to philosophical or theological studies. Just like the blind and the deaf, those who are not intelligent are equally called to essential wisdom. But when an authentic believer is also an authentic philosopher, it is impossible that his or her philosophy remains isolated from the deepest inspiration of their lives.

The orientation of a life that seeks God is thus the moving force of the philosophical investigation Anselm proposes to us. This investigation is not an autonomous enterprise, because belief and love accompany it and support it. It is therefore natural that the investigation opens with a prayer in which "my whole heart" *(totum cor meum)* asks God to help, to teach, to illuminate, and to renew the man who looks up from his miserable state of ignorance, in order to see whether, in hope, his God will grant what he desires. Anselm's project is in no way apologetic: *neque enim quaero intelligere ut credam* (for I do not seek to understand in order to believe); he hopes only to acquire or receive a certain understanding: *credo ut intelligam* (I believe in order to understand).

In concentrating on a philosophical task within a prayer, Anselm links two fundamental attitudes. The more radical of the two is that of the faith in which he finds himself naked before the face of his God, whereas the other reflects upon God by reaching out through a thought in which God appears as a theme or an object. Can these attitudes be combined? Anselm's wager is the hypothesis that the philosophical intent, according to which God is manifest as a theme or thought, can be integrated into the intent of prayer. If such an integration succeeds, a believer who is also a philosopher will have expressed his faith by speaking to God about God himself, offering to him the perspective, the presuppositions, and the means of philosophy. Philosophy will then have lost its autonomy, but its insights are saved by becoming elements of a prayer that prolongs its quest. While seeming to reduce God to a theme, Anselm's allocution continually calls him "You," "my Lord," and "my God." He offers God what he thinks of him, submitting whatever he thinks he knows to God's judgment. Anselm's understanding is thus determined by desire and expectation; even when his understanding is thematic, his thought is drawn, guided, and illuminated by the "You" that hears it. The investigation is an exercise in speaking, and, insofar as grace has preceded his faith, this speaking is first and foremost a way of responding to the one who is his Light and Life. The wisdom he seeks is discovered to be a gift in the giving of which he himself played a part. The God in whom he believes allows him to think that very God.

A living faith in God is not only a good point of departure, but also the criterion that allows us to judge whether the investigation effectively reaches its end. That faith guides reason is, for example, clearly evident in chapter 14. Having proven that God exists as omnipotence, life, truth, justice, mercy, goodness, and eternity themselves, Anselm must note to his regret that this God, as (re)presented in the fullest of concepts, does not coincide with the God of religious experience and piety who appeared prior to all philosophy. The gap between the truth of God revealed in faith and the truth of God thought by reason is the gap between the wisdom of an emotional attunement to God as "*Tu, Deus meus*," and the lucid concept of God's rational contours. Faith is not prevented by any lack of speculative brilliance from guiding and evaluating the results of philosophy, whose inner logic obeys only itself. Can philosophy, without faith, discover the right perspective and the orientation that leads to the living God? Can it find the right direction if it does not have an idea of the sought for end?

The movement toward a more illuminated faith is a process by which an abstract concept becomes concrete and "fulfills" itself little by little. Chapters 14 and 15 show that the doctrine that can be deduced from the starting point does not so completely fulfill the concept that the God of thought in it can be recognized as the true God of faith.

When Anselm asks, in chapter 14, whether his "soul" has found what it sought by means of the deduced concept—namely, to know God as it knows him by a faith that has not yet been transformed into ontological understanding—he notes that it has not: "that which is the highest of all beings, beyond which nothing better can be thought, which is life itself *(ipsa vita)*, light, wisdom, goodness, eternal blessedness, and eternity utterly happy, and who is all this everywhere and always," is not the God that the prephilosophical faith recognizes as its God, the God it prays to and depends upon as its "creator and recreator." This discovery plunges the disappointed soul into a crisis, which is as much emotional as intellectual.

The disappointed soul must learn to accept two things if it is to overcome the depression that threatens it: the ontological argument has made the soul see something of its God—"the soul sees you in a way" even if "it does not see you such as you are" *(sicuti es)*, but this "something," which becomes more visible through the course of twelve chapters, is still an abstract thought. The logic that has been uncovered has not yet reached the sense in which the soul feels that God is truth and goodness, eternity and blessedness.

The second movement of the *Proslogion* (chapters 16–26) is a new attempt to identify the God of philosophy with the God of faith. Though Anselm strongly affirms their thorough identity, he acknowledges in the last chapter that the utter lucidity that belongs to faith in reference to itself remains an ideal that will not be realized on earth. Anselm seeks the reason for the gap between the two ways in which God reveals himself in the wretched fate of men as the inheritors of a heritage of sin. The tradition of evil (starting with Adam and Cain) that cuts across the tradition of faith (starting with Abel) plunges us into a darkness of ignorance and deformity that we are unable to depart from entirely. This is to say that we all, believers and unbelievers, carry the opposite of wisdom at the heart of our existence. We are all fools, *insipientes.* We all tell ourselves in one way or another: *Non est Deus*, "there is no God."

What prevents the fool from becoming wise? Anselm asks himself this question at the end of chapter 3, immediately after he has set out the core of his single argument, thus sandwiching that argument between two quotations of the fool who says in his heart that there is no God. The fool hears with his ears and grasps with his consciousness the thought of something "than which nothing greater can be conceived," but he does not realize what this thought necessarily includes. The concept with which Anselm tries to formulate the core of what "we believe"—abstract and enigmatic as that concept is—does not stand, for the fool, as a thesis affirming that existence is contained in the essence signified by the words he heard. The fool grasps the (pseudo)definition of God, but he cannot pass from the reference it contains to the thing to which it refers.

Why not? What prevents him from making that transition? If Anselm is right in saying that the transition is logically impeccable, it would seem that the fool lacks intelligence or logical ability. But if that is where the obstacle lies, we would have to say that all atheists are bad at logic and that all those believers who do not see the logical necessity of the argument are just as "foolish and stupid" (*stultus et insipiens*, chapter 3) as the fool who says there is no God. While explaining why the fool, even while truly "thinking," says in his heart there is no God (chapter 4), Anselm makes a distinction between "thinking the word *(vox)* that signifies a thing *(res)*" and "comprehending what the thing is," but he does not say why the atheist is stupid and foolish enough to deny the connection between the two. Immediately after his "explanation," however, Anselm thanks God for having given to him what he sought: the understanding of the concept that he previously had possessed by faith alone. Thanks to divine illumination, a "little man," full of darkness, understands that the abstract concept *IQM (id quo maius cogitari non potest)* demands that one transform it into a phrase affirming the existence of what is thought or represented in the concept. Apparently, logic alone does not suffice in order to pass from the abstract concept to the evidence of a concrete thought. But why is the fool unable to pass from the nearly empty concept of God to its merely partial fulfillment? What experience or motivation does he lack?

If we can suppose that the fool represents not only the atheist we find outside of us, but is also someone living in our heart, then the answer to the question seems to be found in the first chapter of the *Proslogion*, where Anselm asks God to grant him the right orientation, the attitude that will allow him to progress from a blind faith to one that has been illuminated by the comprehension of its contents. Without God's assistance, man is bent over *(incurvatus)* so that he cannot look above. Anselm writes, "I am not able to look [anywhere] but down" (chapter 1); without the illumination that comes from the face of God, the eyes of man remain blind. That is why the writer asks: "Lift me up, until I am able to direct my gaze above."

What humans lack, what prevents them from using philosophical reflection to intensify and elucidate their faith in God, is a perspective that distinguishes between the high and the low, and looks upon the being of the world in the context of that difference. Instead of speaking of high and low, one might also speak of more and less, of smaller and larger, or of better and worse. The need for such a perspective is evident in the initial concept that Anselm uses to summarize the heart of faith in a universally valid way. The formula *IQM* has no meaning— what it is trying to say cannot be grasped—if one does not understand that the ultimate dimension of all beings is characterized by a gradation in greatness. Only then is it possible to compare beings with one another. Anselm's ontology presupposes both a comparison of different dimensions of the universe and an intuition of the directions that distinguish the more and the less.

The meaning of "greater" or "more" and "smaller" or "less" is not very clear, but it is in any case far removed from the emphasis on quantity characteristic of modern science. If we point at qualitative differences, like many commentators do, those expressions become somewhat clearer; at least *maius* and *minus* point then to something about value. A reading of all the relevant passages confirms that *maius*, as it is used in *IQM*, refers to what has more value. It is thus a synonym for *melius* (better). In fact, as early as chapter 3, Anselm passes without ado from the concept of *maius* in the formula *IQM* to that of *melius*. He writes: *Si enim aliqua mens possit cogitare aliquid melius* (for if some mind could think something better . . .) This latter concept will in fact dominate the rest of the *Proslogion*.

The perspective that dominates the whole argument presupposes that all beings form a ladder according to their greater or lesser "value," "goodness," or "greatness." God is not sought within this universe, because that would imprison him in a more encompassing horizon. It would then be possible to think of something greater or to identify God with the totality of all the kinds and degrees of being. The God who is sought is clearly separated by an absolute "not" from anything that can be thought to be great, greater, or greatest.

If the indicated manner of approaching the universe and God is a condition *sine qua non* for understanding of the abstract concept Anselm offers us, it is clear what the fool would need in order to follow his deduction. It is not that the nonbeliever lacks logic, but that he has no sense of what is high and what is low. His world does not point toward summits, because it is tilled with indifference. Neither the nonbeliever, nor his world has a radical orientation that directs his life, actions, and feelings toward the beyond that awakens our most radical desire.

Who would not be reminded of Plato here? For him, not only the *psyché* and the *polis*, but the whole *cosmos* appears as a wonder within a dimension greater and higher than the essence of ideas: the dimension that is dominated by the *agathon*. The *agathon* is neither a being nor an essence, nor an idea among the ideas, nor the greatest or highest idea. It is the Good Itself, beyond the whole gradation of beings, outside of the totality of gradual differences that can be compared. All of Plato's work is set in a "space" oriented by what is low and what is high. To understand it one must discover the meaning and the necessity of the references expressed by words like "*ekeise*" (up there) and "*epekeina*" (beyond). To understand it is to know—or at least to surmise—what the upward orientation that results from true conversion *(epistrophē)* demands.

Like the sophist and the tyrant, the fool cannot discover the true Good because he is not looking in the right direction. He does neither love the Good, nor recognize what is better than all other things, even when it is presented in a concrete experience. That is why *IQM* seems to be "without any (real) meaning" or to have a meaning that is alien to its concept (chapter 4). The fool does not follow the movement of the concept but he denies what it suggests, because his way of being in the world is not religious. Bent toward what is below, he cannot see the light that comes from above.

Are we not being unjust when we accuse an atheist of indifference and insensibility to the differences between the better and the worse? It goes without saying that the atheist of whom Anselm is speaking cannot be defined as someone who pronounces the words "there is no God." But even if in restricting atheism to those who say in their hearts that God is an illusion or a pseudonym for some finite reality, it would be unjust to claim that they lack the required taste or culture to distinguish the degrees in value of a long ladder of beings. What they deny is not that there is a multitude of degrees in being, quantity, or quality, but that there exists a single "thing" beyond all things that can be thought to be extremely great and good. They admit the possibility of something better, but not of the Good itself. Anselm wrestles with their quite civilized relativism when he identifies what exceeds any possible maximum of being and goodness as that which exists independently as the absolutely Good on which all the degrees of goodness and being, including all possible *maxima*, depend. He presupposes not only a ladder from what is lowest to what is highest or a chain without definite endpoints, but also an attraction exerted by "something" that escapes all gradation, the non-graded that is beyond what is endless or "infinite" in a finite way, the Good beyond all that is. The philosophical enterprise presents itself as an attempt to conceptualize the orientation that the heart of the believer experiences in faith. This attempt cannot succeed if the "orient" of this orientation is not present both in the perspective and the movement that guides and transforms his thought. The logical task must be sustained by an inkling of the wisdom that might result. Otherwise, the initial foolishness will block the possibility that a logical transition is experienced as the transformation of an abstract concept *(IQM)* into its affirmative concretization. Logic alone is not enough; an orientation and a prelogical movement—that is, a good desire and an emotional attunement—are necessary.

The *Proslogion* is one ongoing deployment of an emotional certainty that becomes conscious of itself by means of an (onto)logical strategy. That is why its second half, beginning after the disappointment expressed in chapter 14, is dedicated to a deepening of the discovery in two respects: (a) the prayer becomes more insistent, giving free rein to the fundamental emotions that testify to the proximity of a God who seems far away because even someone bathed in his light cannot see him; and (b) the discovery that the light of God is "too much for me" *(nimia mihi)* and "inaccessible" (chapter 16), develops into an amendment of the initial formula. Anselm writes, "Thus, Lord, not only are you that than which one can think nothing greater, but you are something greater than can be thought" (chapter 15). Even so, this correction does not abolish the initial formula, because the new "definition" can be justified rationally by it. If God were not great enough to exceed all that can be presented or represented in human thought, the latter would still be able to think such a thing, and God would not be *IQM* (chapter 16).

Thought can thus think something beyond all that enters into it. It can think beyond what it thinks, beyond all beings and all ideas, beyond the being of beings itself, beyond the universe.

We must conclude that the true sense of the abstract concept of God with which the investigation begins is not yet evident in chapters 2 and 3. Nor is it present in chapters 4–13, where God is understood as truth and goodness, eternal and omnipresent, the source of all that is true and good, and so on. A truer grasp requires the opening of one's soul to a reality that surpasses all that can be thought.

Is it possible to experience this reality? As the end of the *Proslogion* shows, there is a joy *(gaudium)* that reveals that one can. However, the path that Anselm pursues is not the path of a purely emotional experience but that of an (onto)logical investigation sustained and guided by such an experience. That is why, after a long prayer that constitutes a new departure, Anselm goes on to deepen the provisional outcome of his investigation by making a new appeal to the concept of that "than which nothing better can be thought" (chapter 18). "The second sailing" which occupies chapters 18b-26 does not bring much new knowledge, however. Instead, it reinforces, unifies, and simplifies aspects deduced in the course of the first part of the *Proslogion*, by emphasizing that God is not the highest, the best, and superior, the most lasting and the most extended being, but rather that he exists "outside of all time" (chapter 19) and "before" and "beyond" everything (chapter 20). The "presence" of God (chapters 20, 22) is a presence that is utterly unique and not temporal in any sense. It is thus no longer a presence, a here and now, opposed to the past and the future. The eternal presence of God differs as much from the present, which is opposed to the future and past within temporality, as transcendence differs from the totality of beings. "You alone, Lord, are what you are, and you are who you are" (chapter 22). The "Greek" question as to the being of God seems here to coincide with the question of God's presence as it was revealed to Moses and was translated in Anselm's bible as *Ego sum qui sum*: I am who I am. At the same time, the expression "you are who you are" seems to allude to the word by which Jesus ventured to identify his omnipresence in history as *egō eimi*, or "I am."

The deepening of the argument that occurs in chapters 15–26, culminates in a very simple formula whose radiance the three last chapters celebrate: "God is the good Itself," (chapter 23). In order to know what divine goodness means, one must not only know all that has been said about God's existence, properties, and unique essence, but also that God is a tri-unity of truth and love. Or, to summarize it in an (onto)logical manner, without excluding all allusions to the New Testament: God is the Good that is simple and uniquely necessary, the one and total perfect good, the only one that is good. Or, to say it with Anselm and Plato, God is the Good.

ANSELM AGAINST HEGEL

The reaction that Anselm would have had to the Hegelian interpretation of "the ontological argument" can now be summarized as follows.

The faith that seeks understanding neither wants to nor can abolish itself as the foundation of existential and noetic meaning. It thinks of itself as more than an expression of speculative truth because to reduce it to such an expression would remove its character as a face-to-face encounter with God. In its faithful encounter, the soul speaks to God about all that it has grasped of God's presence and absence, knowing all the while that it has grasped only very little compared to the invisible light by which it is surrounded.

God is not the Identity of being and thought that encompasses all things, but the Unique One, which, of course, contains the fullness of being and goodness in a way that separates it from the universe of beings. The ascent towards the absoluteness of God is the heart of human being and its dynamic *logos*, and thus the source of all other truths. But faith is not an idea: it leads and judges the entire history of the intellect, because it precedes and exceeds reason through an adherence that is older and more prophetic than philosophical rationality. This adherence, manifest in love and hope, is as different from (onto)logical comprehension as God is different from the ideas of speculative thought.

TWO REMARKS

In the course of the preceding analyses, Plato and Neoplatonism have been present in the background. In fact, the *Proslogion* shows more affinity with Platonic inquiries than they do with the Hegelian system. In particular, the "idea of the *agathon*," which occupies the center of the *Republic*, seems close to the *bonum* that dominates the *Proslogion*. Like Plato's Good, the God of the *Proslogion* is before, outside of, and beyond (*epekeina, ante,* and *ultra*) the universe of beings. Anselm's God rules, as the absolute end, not only the desire that initiates the entire process of the investigation, but also the whole universe, which is his gift. By multiplying the structural parallels between Plato and the *Proslogion*, one might explain why several fathers of the Church believed that Plato had read Moses, whom God had sent to the Greeks in order to prepare them for his most authentic self-revelation.

However, a complete comparison of the investigations undertaken by Plato and Anselm requires that their words be understood within the horizons of their different lives and cultures. Thus Anselm's Good is not the sun of Plato's ethical, aesthetic, and religious universe. In Plato's cosmos, where wonders both mortal and divine show up in the luminous space that separates and unites heaven and earth, the Good shows itself in the beauty of essences, the excellence of communities, the virtues of human individuals, the nobility of art, and the natural justice of a good education. *Kalokagathia* does not leave enough room for the Good to manifest itself as a person who can listen and forgive. The meaning of "giving" is tied to an anonymous source of light, which neither hears nor speaks, while ethics is dominated by admiration for their beauty. *Aretē* ("virtue") is the glory of human beings in the various forms of well-proportioned harmony. The Good is identical with Beauty. Neither a thing nor a person, the Good-and-Beautiful is the anonymous Beyond without a face. The destiny of all beings is to fulfill each of them as the wonder that, at its core, it always already is. It must shine forth in order to let their idea, which is also their ideal, come to the fore in the splendor of a phenomenal universe.

For Anselm, the Good is admired in a different way. When he says to God: "You are nothing other than the unique supreme good . . ." (chapter 22) or "This good, it is you, God the Father . . ." (chapter 23), he is attempting to make the name "good" coincide with the revealed names of God. In calling God "good," he expresses, first of all, biblical reminiscences, and only secondarily, while transforming their meaning, the concepts of *agathon* and *bonum* he had received from the tradition of noble pagans. This is obvious, for example, in chapters 8–11, where the first stage of his "onto-theo-logical" discovery reaches its culmination: God's mercy that seems so difficult to reconcile with his justice is surely not inherited from Plato, whose aesthetic ethic does not abhor Greek cruelties toward infants, handicapped, and criminals.

At the same time, it is remarkable that, in his prayer, Anselm does not address himself to God by calling God *bonum* or *summum bonum*. His preferred vocative is "Lord" *(Domine)*, but he also, though less often, calls God *altissime Domine, bone Domine* (chapter 4), *Domine Deus, Deus meus et Dominus meus*. Only once does he address God through the words *immensa bonitas* (chapter 9), but in all cases it is the word *tu* (you) or *es* (you are . . .) that accompanies these names, and what Anselm desires above all is to see his God face to face. God, the creator who has "formed" and reformed the universe, to whom all being and all knowledge is indebted for what it is, evidently does not allow himself to be reduced to a theme or topic or idea about which we can talk. Even the most beautiful words, like "good," cannot name him unless they are integrated in an address from face to face: God is the incomparable "you" *(tu)*. Saying "you" affirms God in an act of allocution; it prevents us from reducing God to a theme or the content of a dogmatic thesis. In using the second person singular pronoun, Anselm distinguishes himself not only from Plato, but also from his own argument. The thesis that God is the Good, and even Goodness itself *(bonitas ipsa)*, belongs to the genre of a thematic discourse. Everything must be done to harmonize such a statement with the full richness of the biblical heritage and the spiritual experience of Christianity, but the truth of speaking to God will always surpass the truth of a philosophical reflection that treats it in the third person, reducing God to an object, despite the thinker's desire to express the transcendence of the One who does not fit into any system. The language of (onto)logical discourse can result only in a provisional name, a pseudonym rather or a pro-pronoun of God.

The second remark I would like to make concerns the ambiguity, no doubt inevitable, of the onto-logical language. It is evident in the *Republic*, where Plato is careful to separate the Good itself from the whole collection of beings, even while, in the very same context, he treats the Good as an "idea," calling it "the idea of the Good," and presenting the knowledge of the Good as an ideal knowledge.[5] The Good cannot be what is beyond *(epekeina)* all being—and thus beyond all

---

5. Plato, *Republic* 509b and 517c.

the ideas—it cannot be transcendent or infinite and at the same time be an idea. It cannot even be the idea of the summit. As Plotinus saw very well, the One is absolutely separate from the totality of beings or ideas. Although Anselm likewise knows very well that God is neither a being nor the being of the totality of beings, he also juxtaposes an insistence on the fact that God is outside of *(extra)*, before *(ante)*, and beyond *(ultra)* the universe, with expressions that call God the highest good *(summum bonum)*, which seems to mean that God is the end of a ladder of values. Against such an interpretation we might insist, for example, on his formulas "the truth itself," "the good itself," or "the essence itself." However, we also might acknowledge that even the initial concept of the *Proslogion* is open to two different interpretations. *IQM* can be understood as an indication of what does not in any way belong to the ladder of gradations, but it can also be read as that which is the greatest of all finite beings. Anselm would probably reject the second interpretation by arguing that one can think something greater than the entirety of all finite beings, but the atheist could answer—and not just the atheist—that he commits a *petitio principii*, because it is not immediately evident whether an idea of the infinite is possible at all.

But this is to begin a new reading, a re-reading of the *Proslogion* from the point of view of its logic. What I have tried to show is, however, that a reading that restricts itself to the logic of the argument is a second reading, because it requires first of all that we understand how the "onto-logical argument" is experienced and lived by the author. In other words, we must not forget the intimate connections that tie the (onto)logical argument to the religious experience that is its dynamic and prophetic support.

Confiding in his religious experience, Anselm did not think it necessary to explain at length that *"id quo maius non cogitari potest"* is neither an *id*, nor the greatest or the summit of all beings, nor universal being. God is the horizon that rules all other horizons. For a thinker who tries to think God, that horizon reveals itself as the You to whom all being and the experience of thought belong.

6

Ascent: Plotinian Motifs
in Bonaventure's
Itinerary of the Mind to God

For Louis Dupré

MARKED BY THE SHIFT from modernity to postmodernity, our epoch shares the ambiguities of both. The hubris of an emancipation that burdened humanity with a superhuman responsibility for the well-being of the entire world; greedy concentration on human, all-too-human needs; generous proclamations of universal human rights and deficient attempts at concretizing them; a humanistic moralism in conjunction with the greatest mass murders of history; a highly ambivalent relationship to religion and faith; a combination of blatant ignorance and repressions with fine scholarship about our past; an exaggerated veneration of science and technology; ruthless exploitation and romantic divinization of nature; the musealization of works and entire cultures, with the ensuing relativisms, skepticisms, and cynicisms; a nostalgia for simple forms of life, close to animals and flowers in an unspoiled nature . . . ; these and other features of modernity have marked our ways of living our lives and thinking our thoughts. At the same time we participate in this epoch's agony and in a longing for otherness. The death of modernity has filled us with postmodern anxiety: a desert seems to have replaced the spiritual wealth of the modern and premodern Occident. Nostalgia is tempting. How could we give up our attachment to that wealth? Our memory, filled with the highlights of our Greek and Roman, Christian and humanistic civilization, does not want to be repressed by total immersion in postmodern—or even posttheological, postphilosophical, postoccidental—museality. Since education has made us feel at home in 3,000 years of Western civilization, we cannot but resist the skepticism that seems to follow naturally from a dying culture. Rather than being objects for destruction or decon-struction, the achievements of our past awaken awe and gratitude, inviting us to comparable attempts at realizing meaning. We participate hermeneutically in the unrepeatable but inspiring lives and works of our history and celebrate their ways of coping with human existence. Despite our separation, we celebrate exemplary figures in a hopeful kind of *memoria*. Perhaps we may even link such celebrations to a sacramental memory in which *the* Meaning comes to light and life.

* * *

The following pages sketch how Saint Bonaventure received and transformed some Neoplatonic motifs in writing his *Itinerary of the Mind to God*.[1] More specifically they compare Plotinus' conception of the ascent to the One with Bonaventure's description of approach-ing God through speculation. Although Bonaventure never studied any work of Plato or Plotinus itself, he was obviously inspired not only by the *liber Scripturae*, as old as Revelation, and the *liber nat-urae*, as old as Creation, but also by the books that transmitted a (Neo)Platonic, Stoic, and Aristotelian heritage to him, thus giving him a chance to transform pagan wisdom into an element of his Christian contemplation. Perhaps his way of "receiving" and "reduc-ing" a past more than a thousand years old gives us a better example of remembering than any variety of destruction.

PLOTINUS' TRAVEL GUIDE TO GOD

In order to see how philosophy, according to Plotinus, functions in discovering the meaning of human life, I turn to the well-known and central treatise VI, 9 [9], titled "On the Good and the One." One can read this treatise as a more or less well-organized travel guide for the soul in its search for what it most desires. Although *erōs* appears rather late (in section 9), the allusions to Diotima's discourse on its

---

1. I use here the edition, with an introduction, translation, and commentary, of Saint Bonaventure's *Itinerarium Mentis in Deum* edited by Philotheus Boehner (St. Bonaventure, N.Y.: The Franciscan Institute, 1956).

nature and workings in Plato's *Banquet* (201d-212c) are spread out over the entire treatise. The soul *(psychē)* is driven by a necessity (9, 27: *ex anagkēs*) to seek her origin and father; the deepest desire, which constitutes or co-constitutes the *psychē*, is directed to the first and ultimate (the *archē* and *telos*) of the universe *(ta panta)*. The beloved is none of all the things or persons of the world; it cannot be found in any being, not even in the totality of beings. It is neither all beings together nor their being as such *(to on hēi on)*. The Intellect *(Nous)* itself cannot still the soul's desire because, as a totality of thinking thoughts, it encompasses the entire cosmos of being and is thus multiple. *Erōs* flees plurality and points to an extremely simple unity, the unity of the One "before" and beyond all beings and ideas, a unity to which the soul responds by trying to become as simple and one as it was when it was born from that unique and simple One. The soul's journey is a progressive self-transformation; at the same time it is the discovery of the soul's true nature. The encounter with the One demands and grants it the greatest possible simplicity. It reveals what the soul has always been, although this fact has become obscured by its falling down into the dispersion of worldly existence. United with a body, entangled in material change and history, obsessed by all kinds of wants and sorrows, the soul is estranged from its original state. The journey is a return; therefore it requires a conversion from dispersion and a systematic exercise of unification.

The stages of the return to the One can be distinguished according to the hierarchy of the universe: from material things to the *psychē* itself, from the *psychē* to the *Nous*, and from this to the One. The levels of progressive simplification through which the soul proceeds show a progressive spiritualization. The greatest obstacle lies in being tied to the material world through corporeality. Askesis, virtues, meditation, abnegation, and purification are necessary for becoming what one originarily and most authentically is. As separation from corporeality, death is welcome, on the condition that the soul has prepared itself by practices that express its most intimate desire.

Chief among these practices is the practice of philosophy. A. J. Festugière, Pierre Hadot, A. Hilary Armstrong, and other scholars have shown that philosophy in the Hellenistic epoch is not identical with the modern project of scientific and autonomous rationality. It is much more religious and ethical, intimately connected as it is with the

existential search for meaning and ultimate wisdom. It cannot be dis-
sociated from a specific way of life, the particular orientation and tone
of a *bios*, including the basic attitudes and *tropoi* of the thinking that
is part of such a life. These insights have important consequences for
our concept of philosophy and its history. The relations of philosophy
with science, moral practice, religion, beliefs, and faith have to be
revised, and postmodern as well as medieval criticisms of theoretism
will appear to have ancient precedents. Yet we must concede that the
philosophical spirituality proposed by Plato and his followers heavily
emphasized, and probably overemphasized, the role of *theoria*, and
that this emphasis, which in modern times developed into an extreme
scientification, has marked the history of our culture.

Plotinus' treatise VI, 9 [9] shows that thinking as theoretical practice is an indispensable guiding principle in the human search for
meaning, but he also insists that theory is not enough. First, no theoretical endeavor would be possible were it not driven by *erōs*. Second,
and more important, theory does not reach far enough to get in touch
with the desired end. One cannot approach the One without passing
through the discursivity of *epistēmē* and ideality, but since the *kosmos
noētos* is a totality composed of many ideas, knowledge of it is unable
to realize the simplicity of a union with the absolutely one. The exclu-
sion of all plurality from the Origin itself is responsible for the fact that
theory alone cannot satisfy our deepest desire.

To settle in the noetic realm of ideas and arguments does liberate us
from the dissemination that typifies the world of *aisthēsis* and *aisthē-
ta*, but with regard to the One, which can only be "seen" or "touched"
through an immediate contact, thinking—or, more generally, "speaking and writing"—can do no more than awaken the mind from its
immersion in *logoi* and point out the conditions of the ultimate union.
Instruction *(didaxis)* and reflection *(dianoeisthai)* prepare the soul, but
to go the whole way in order to experience the vision is a farther-reach-
ing task *(ergon)* of the person who is longing for it (VI, 9, 4).

The threefold way from *aisthēsis* to *noēsis* and from *noēsis* to contact with the One can be represented as an ascent. To describe this
ascent, Plotinus borrows many metaphors from Plato's *Republic*,
Banquet, and *Phaedrus*. However, another mode of spatializing—and
one that perhaps is closer to the truth—describes the search as a turning inward. The One beyond being is present *(paresti)* within the soul,

at the center of its center. It has always been there, even if most people neither know nor notice it. To approach the One is to free the core of your soul from all its additions and complications. You must divest yourself of the many things, thoughts, and elements that surround and obscure the One. To become *eudaimōn* is to become simple in union with the One, which is also the Good. Plotinus' guidance urges his readers to open their souls to the presence of God who has never left them, although their turning away from him to earthly things caused them to forget their origin and destiny.

The urge for unity suppresses every attachment to multiplicity and demands an affective distance from corporeal and material realities insofar as these tend to seduce us to a scattered way of life. Intersubjective and social relationships, friendship and love do not play a direct role in the discovery of our destiny except as conditions for the authentic practice of thinking on the way to insight. God can be found within our soul, but to get in touch with him, one must practice detachment with regard to the entire universe of beings, including the manifold of ideas, souls, and communities. The ascension is therefore a solitary task (4, 23: *monos anabebēkēs*). The recommended life does not find enjoyment in the things here below *(bios anēdonos tōn tēide);* it is a flight of the single *psychē* alone to the One alone (*phygē monou pros monon* 11, 50–51, cf. 9, 52–54). The meaning of human existence lies in its becoming angelic: a soul at home in the spiritual cosmos of being and thought, but reaching out beyond this dimension, since even spirit is still too diverse and complex.

The most beautiful and fecund aspect of Plotinus' spirituality' lies in his conviction that neither morality nor philosophy in the purely theoretical sense of this word fully responds to the desire that drives us. Emphasizing that the words "seeing" *(thea)* and "intuition" *(noein)* fail to describe the soul's union with the One, since they still presuppose some duality, he does not fall into the theoretism that has been a strong temptation for the entire history of Western civilization. However, his interpretation of transcendence as a super- and supranoetic return to the undivided Principle through detachment from all multiplicity has exacted a high price for which we still are in debt. Plotinus' spiritualistic turning away from matter, which—as dispersion—is the cause of evil (I, 8, 14), seems to preclude finding the One in devotion to singular and corporeal beings. Love for the One who—despite its admirable generosity—is uninterested in the totality of beings and thoughts (which, for their part, are totally dependent on it) demands distance from everything else. The One is present everywhere: in all thoughts and souls, including the cosmic soul that encompasses all individual souls and things. The order and beauty of the visible universe, which Plotinus defends against the Gnostics, testify to the generosity of their unique Source; yet the experience of its presence in them cannot coincide with service or grateful enjoyment of human or other beings. Though nothing that exists is bad (except the dispersion of a materialistic existence), all ideas, bodies, souls, and spirits point to the only One that can be loved without restriction. The search for union with this Beloved leads through its resemblances, but to what extent does the Good send us back to involvement in the corporeal, sensual, and historical world of human life? Once the union with the Good has made the soul a god, politics seem below one's dignity, although it is possible that intimacy with the Good expresses itself by telling others about it and giving them indications about the way to reach it (VI, 9, 7). True communion between humans ultimately depends on each one's own approaching the unique Source. Instead of concentration on the material conditions of a just society, it is the attempt to become wholly spiritual that gathers us into a community (cf. I, 4, 3–4).

It is obvious that death will have a very different meaning according to whether it is seen as a flight from the world or as a total destruction for which in the end no other meaning can be found than that of an extreme opportunity for selfless love. Salvation through spiritualization is radically different from a redemption that transforms the entire human constitution by turning a deviated heart back to God's outgoing love.[2]

BONAVENTURE'S GUIDANCE FOR THE ENCOUNTER WITH GOD

Many Platonic and Plotinian elements can be found in chapter 5 of Bonaventure's *Itinerary*, although it contains only two explicit quotes from Greek philosophy (n.4 and n.6) as well as an allusion to the

---

2. I want to thank Kevin Corrigan and Eric Perl for their observations on an earlier version of this text. If my picture still fails to do justice to Plotinus' attitude toward the corporeal and social universe, the responsibility is entirely my own.

Neoplatonic *Liber de Causis* (*propositio* 17 in n.7). The quotes are not from Plato or Plotinus but from Aristotle's *Metaphysics* (II, 1, 993b9–11) and his *Topica* (V, 5, 134b24–25), but the subject of chapter 5 is very similar to that of the Plotinian treatise VI, 9. However, whereas Plotinus identifies the One *(to hen)* with the Good *(to agathon)* and clearly separates it from Being, which belongs to the *Nous*, Bonaventure presents the unicity *(unum)* of God as an aspect of God's being *(esse)*, contrasting this to God's goodness *(bonitas)*, which in chapter 6 will be shown to be another name for God.

Chapters 5 and 6 taken together describe the penultimate station of the mind's ascent to God. They must be situated in relation to the preceding four chapters and the final, seventh chapter, which describes the rest that comes after the traveling. Chapter 1 stipulates the conditions of the journey. It shows how typically Christian the whole journey and its stages are but also how much in conceptual analysis and terminology their description owes to (Neo)Platonic predecessors.

Following the Greek tradition as expressed, for instance, in Aristotle's *Ethics* and in the Stoic treatises on well-being, the first chapter begins by stating that the goal of the journey lies in *beatitudo*. This word translates the Greek *eudaimonia*, but, as we will see, it also evokes the paradise of *Genesis* 2 and a *peace* that surpasses all human powers of acquisition. (The coincidence of these meanings in Bonaventure's text already indicates how much the Greek *eudaimonia* and the Roman *beatitudo* have been transformed in their encounter with the biblical *eirēnē, pax*.) Plotinus, too, pointed out that union with the One cannot be conquered by the soul's own forces; after having settled in the *Nous* and looking up from there, one must wait until the union overwhelms one's ethical and theoretical possibilities, but the character of the One, of the soul, and of their relation, as Plotinus depicts them, is different from their parallels in Bonaventure's travel guide.

Bonaventure defines *beatitudo* as "nothing other than the enjoyment of the utmost good" (*nihil aliud est quam summi boni fruitio*, n.1), a formal definition that seems to fit many ethics. However, since the utmost good is "above us" *(supra nos)*, its enjoyment can be reached only through an ascent. The mind must therefore transcend the possibilities of its own being. This transcendence is neither a corporeal movement nor a liberation from corporeality. It is a "cordial"

(cordialis) ascent: a task for the human heart, not for reason or intellect or behavior alone. As the phenomenological core of the human
compositum, the heart is the center that mobilizes human interests and
provides them with passion for what really matters.

Since human beings are not able to surpass themselves by their own
forces, they must look up to God's grace. According to Plotinus, no
soul can even begin its ascent unless it is driven by *erōs*, which, like
all good things, comes from the Good itself; through its union with the
soul, the Good shows that it always already has been present. The
union is nothing other than the full unfolding of an original but hidden
and often inhibited unity. The natural, necessary, and anonymous character of this presence differs from Bonaventure's more dramatic conception of God's gracious dealings with the contingencies of human
history, but it is not so easy to determine this difference without doing
injustice to Plotinus.

The normal response to grace is an attitude of looking up, which
Bonaventure calls *oratio*. By stating that "prayer" is the basic condition for approaching God, he declares that thinking, in order to point
in God's direction, must emerge from a pretheoretical turn of the heart
that can be characterized by the words "humble" and "devout" *(petunt
ex corde humiliter et devote*, n.1). "Prayer is the mother and origin of
all upward-action" *(oratio* [. . .] *est mater et origo sursum-actionis*,
n.1), including philosophy and theology. Theory is thus rooted in the
dimension of the heart, or—as I would like to translate—theory is born
from and nurtured by spirituality. The necessity of *oratio* for the
authenticity of all God-talk does not imply that philosophers or theologians cannot do their work successfully without saying a host of
prayers. Without excluding these, "prayer" means first of all a specific mindset or turn of mind *(a tropos)* through which humans respond
in an appropriate way to the infinity of the One who is interested in
finite beings that thereby are also interested in Him.

The relations and proportions involved in this mutual interest must
be clarified according to two perspectives, which traditionally have
been contrasted as *nature* and (sacred) *history*. According to the first
perspective, the situation of the human mind can be determined with
the help of the parallelism between *macrocosmos* and *microcosmos*
(n.4) that was introduced into philosophy by Plato's *Timaeus* and
became very popular in the course of the twelfth century.

Creation

Typical modes of feeling, knowledge, and practice relate the human mind to the three main dimensions of the universe: the dimension of things outside us *(extra nos)*, the dimension of our own interiority *(intra nos)*, and the dimension of what surpasses us *(supra nos)*. Corporeality enables us to know and handle the world through the senses; having a will and intellect opens us up to the everlasting dimension of the spirit; transcendence to the suprarational enables us to enjoy God himself in a relation of affection that surpasses all kinds of discursivity and behavior.

Bonaventure's originality lies in the doubling of each of these levels through the application of a distinction between a seeing *per speculum* (through the mirror) and a seeing *in speculo* (in the mirror): each level of reality mirrors some other reality in two different ways. The schema itself can be understood as a development of Platonic and Neoplatonic speculations about *mimesis*, but it is profoundly transformed in a Christian context.

Finite realities, such as the human mind, a tree, or a mountain, can be taken as points of departure for the ascent insofar as each of them, in its own way, mirrors God as the creator—and therefore also shows God to be the "formal cause" *(causa formalis)* of all things. In concentrating on the tree (or the mountain or the mind), we can discover certain traits in it that suggest an essential reference to its first cause, and thus, by way of conclusion, direct the mind to God. Having found God *per speculum*, the mind can then enjoy its discovery by realizing that the reference of finite realities to God entails a certain presence of God *in* those realities, not only behind them or concealed under the surface of their being, but also *in* them and *as* their ultimate and primordial truth and "essence." God's infinite being then becomes visible, audible, touchable as displayed (be it in a finite, limited manner) in the mirror of finite entities *(in speculo)*.

Bonaventure's retrieval of Platonic *topoi* transposes into the language of speculative theology the Franciscan experience of a world that shows and bespeaks God. Corporeality is not an obstacle to meeting with the One. The phenomena invite us to decipher their phenomenality, or, as Bonaventure repeats again and again, they "preach" *(praedicare)*, "clearly indicate" *(manifeste indicare)*, "insinuate" *(insinuare)* and show *(ostendere)*, "evidently proclaim" *(evidenter proclamare)*, "declare" and "clarify" *(manifeste declarare)* God's presence in all beings and lead us by the hand *(evidentissime manuducere)* to him. All these expressions are found in chapter 1, which treats the "lowest" level of micro- and macrocosmos. A human mind that discovers the omnipresence of God's self-manifestation is awakened by the "shouts" of the phenomena.

Nothing in this universe is despicable, and the Good does not demand any separation or destruction. What we must flee from is not matter but instead a wrong manner of concentrating on and relating to God and the universe. If goodness lies in corresponding appropriately to all that exists, evil is a mode of turning away from it toward its negation, a manner of existence that distorts the proportions of the original creation. And here we meet with the typically Christian explanation of why the mind has so much difficulty in following the path that leads to God through appropriate behavior toward the universe.

History

Instead of being caused by materiality or multiplicity, the great and unique obstacle lies in the noncoincidence of human factuality with what we originally and "naturally"—through creation—are. Our basic orientation is deviated; human desire is inclined to betray itself by preferring finite satisfactions over the enjoyment of the *summum bonum*. To climb the "ladder" of the universe would be easy if we were pure and innocent, spontaneously looking up toward the complete and perfect good. However, our orientation has become bad through greed and arrogance, and a lifetime of bending one's tendencies straight is necessary for becoming genuinely what one was meant to be from the outset. It is the heart that generates and encompasses theory and practice, and the deviation of this heart, not the body or materiality, is the source of guilt. The negations and abnegations imposed by our search for the ultimate should not be shaped by contempt for corporeality, but rather by respect for the true proportions that rule the universe and promise *beatitudo* to those whose behavior and reflection take them into account.

The hierarchical model of the microcosmos develops certain Greek analyses of the human psyche, but Christian faith integrates it into a history of sin and redemption. The entire microcosmos, including its most spiritual levels, is curved and crooked *(curvatus)* because of its turning away from the real good and the light of truth. Since the root of this deformation lies in a self-willed or consensual deviation from God's presence, a return to the lost straightforwardness can only come from a more benevolent force than human reason and will. Grace is this force, but it is powerless if it is not welcomed by will and reason, imagination and the senses that attach us to the world. The first expression of this cooperation is purification. What Plato and Plotinus said about the role of "justice" *(dikaiosynē)* in the discovery of the truth is integrated into Bonaventure's theory of a union of grace and human effort. He, too, sees justice as the necessary condition for acquiring true knowledge, and he agrees with Plotinus in making a distinction between the highest form of science and the wisdom of a nondiscursive union with the One. But Bonaventure's conception of wisdom is one of an affectionate and communicative kind of embrace rather than that of a vision. This preference is intimately linked to his belief that justice and wisdom in their belonging together have been perfectly revealed and realized in the charitable way of life that was accomplished by Jesus the Christ. The encounter of the One who is the Good and the acceptance of grace cannot bypass the historical reality of a person who lived the ultimate truth of goodness by unreservedly giving himself for others (n.7).

The One (Chapter 5)

Chapters 5 and 6 outline the highest level of contemplation before entrance into the promised land of well-being and bliss. The mind looks here to that which is above us *(supra nos)*: the light that enlightens our mind, presupposed in all former discoveries as the condition of their possibilities. Appealing to Psalms 4:6–7 and a text of Saint Augustine,[3] Bonaventure states that this light is the eternal Truth itself insofar as it "forms our mind immediately." In this light we experience all things, but we could not enjoy it if it were not *"signatum"* (marked, sealed, signed) on our mind.

The light of the eternal truth has two aspects. The first aspect manifests God as *esse;* the other becomes manifest when we consider his

---

3. Boehner (p. 80) refers in a note to Augustine's *83 Quaestiones,* q.5,2,4. When Bonaventure quotes from the Bible, he uses the Latin translation of the Vulgata. This explains that sometimes it is difficult to find his quotes in modern translations of the Bible.

goodness. The divine names "being" *(esse)* and "good" *(bonum)* are thus disclosed as the ultimate discursive possibilities to recognize God. Bonaventure compares the contemplation of God's *esse* and the contemplation of his goodness *(bonum)* with the "two Cherubim of Glory that stand over the Ark, overshadowing the Mercy Seat" *(propitiatorium*, Exod. 25): the first mode of contemplation *(per nomen primarium esse)* concentrates on the *essentialia Dei*, the other *(in nomine quod est bonum)* considers what is proper to the three persons in God. As the contrast between *per* and *in* in the titles of chapters 5 and 6 suggests, these modes differ in degree of proximity to God. Although both cherubim seem equally holy, being *(ipsum esse)* is the radical principle through which all other aspects of God's essence *(essentialia)* are discovered, but *bonum* is the "*most* principal *(principalissimum)* foundation for the contemplation of the emanations," that is—as we will see—of the communicative structure of God.

The parallels and differences with Plotinus' *theoria* are obvious. There the One is discovered *through*, not *in*, the knowledge of being *(Nous, ousia, to on);* the ascent leads from the knowledge of being to the experience of the Good "beyond being," which shows its goodness by overflowing into emanations. Bonaventure does not separate being from the good but synthesizes both names by subordinating God's being *(esse)* to the goodness that is revealed in God's trinitarian structure and movement. He thus integrates a certain plurality into God, the plurality that is indispensable for love.

Because his treatment of being *(esse)* in chapter 5 seems to be a synthesis of Neoplatonic and Aristotelian ontotheology, whereas the disclosure of God's trinity obviously depends on Christian faith, one could expect that the first of the cherubim with whom Bonaventure compares the two highest kinds of contemplation would represent the summit of Greek philosophy, whereas the second cherub would then symbolize the Biblical tradition, in which there is little speculation and even less ontology, but a lot about God's communication and compassion. This is not the case, however. Almost all of chapter 5 is a rigorously philosophical analysis of the concept of being *(esse)* that shows how much Bonaventure has learned from Greek ontology. However, his summary of that ontology is framed by two quotes from the Bible and presented as a speculative summary of its faith in one, unique God. The first cherub represents the Old Testament, while the second stands for the New Testament. Bonaventure's presentation is thus not meant to be a synthesis of Greek wisdom and Judeo-Christian faith. Although his whole deduction of God's *essentialia* (chapter 5, nn.3–6) is purely philosophical and hardly supported by Biblical texts, Bonaventure offers his retrieval of Greek ontotheology as a speculative translation of God's self-revelation in Exod. 3:14. The truths contained in the expression *"Ego sum qui sum"* were revealed to Moses long before Parmenides inaugurated the ontological language that permits us to conceptualize them. "He, who is" *(Qui est)* is equated with being itself *(esse ipsum)* and this is shown to be the pure actuality of being, which is the first that is "thought," or rather the preconceptual *a priori* of all thought *(quod primo cadit in intellectu,* n.3), the first, unique, most simple, most perfect, eternal, infinite, creative, most present, immutable origin and end, the center which is also the circumference, and so on. Since all these "names" can be shown to include one another, God is the One in the most extreme and absolute sense of pure simplicity and one-ness. While the self-revelation of God to Moses as told in Exod. 3:14 opens the analysis of *esse,* the beginning of the *Shema Israel* closes its first, fundamental part (n.6). Bonaventure concludes his analysis with these words: "If 'God' is the name of the primary, eternal, most simple, most actual, most perfect *esse,* it is impossible to think that he is not or that he is not one." But then he immediately connects through the word "therefore" *(igitur)* a Latin translation of Deut. 6:4: *Audi igitur Israël, Deus tuus Deus unus est.* "Listen [therefore] Israel, your God is One God."

The Good (Chapter 6)

Although Bonaventure places his consideration of the Good beside *(juxta)* the "ontological" cherub of chapter 5, there is a difference of degree: being *(ipsum esse)* is the radical principle *(principium radicale)* for the contemplation of God, but the *good (ipsum bonum)* is the most fundamental principle *(principalissimum fundamentum).* Although "being" is the name through which all other predicates of God are known, it is somehow included in, and to that extent also subordinate to, the good, as Bonaventure points out in n.2. For stating the identity of the One and the Good, he could have appealed to the Neoplatonic tradition, but again he finds himself more inspired by the New Testament than by philosophy. Yet he builds a logical argument by showing the necessary connection between God's being and his goodness through an Anselmian formula. If God is the Good, he is the best, namely "that better than which nothing can be thought." "Since it is absolutely better to be than not to be," the Good (or the best) "cannot be thought not to be" (n.2). Being is therefore contained in the Good. And since being is absolutely one, God's goodness entails his one-ness.

The great admirer of Dionysius here clearly takes a distance from negative theology. Far from dismissing ontology as failing to name God, Bonaventure suggests that it can explain the Jewish and Christian faith in God's unity, and that it is an essential part of the contemplation of his goodness. By the same token Bonaventure bridges the abyss Plato and Plotinus maintained between the Good and the *kosmos noētos* of the *Nous*.

An even greater difference from Neoplatonic thinking shows up in Bonaventure's view on the emanations. The goodness of the One is not only the source *(pēgē)* and origin *(archē)* of the ideal, essential, psychical and material universe that flows from it, but it multiplies the One within itself. Appealing to the pseudo-pseudo-Dionysian dictum *"bonum est diffusivum sui,"* understood as a summing up of the Gospel's testimony about God's love, Bonaventure infers without much ado that the supreme good *(summum bonum)* must be diffusive and self-diffusive to the utmost degree. To be good is to be communicative and self-communicative. Its absolute mode (neither a degree nor a mode) is realized in God's communication of his own essence within the unity of this same essence. Goodness is love, and infinite love is the sharing of God's substance with another who thereby is generated in one and the same God. Since love between two persons is not complete without a third, God and his "Son" together "breathe" the Spirit as the third person within the same essence.

Surprisingly for modern minds, Bonaventure does not seem to consider the trinitarian structure of God a strange truth too difficult for philosophers to swallow. He presents it as a logical consequence of God's absolute goodness. It is clear, however, that his understanding of goodness, quite different from that of Plotinus, would not have been possible without faith in God's love, a love which he explains here as extreme self-communication. What Bonaventure finds really surprising, incomprehensible, and admirable is not so much God's unicity and God's trinity taken separately, but rather their simultaneity and mutual inclusiveness. He even warns the reader: See that "you do not deem yourself to comprehend the incomprehensible" (n.3). Instead of promoting insight into the triune nature of God he affirms it as an inevitable but incomprehensible certainty.

The combination of incomprehensibility and certainty forces the thinker into a change of attitude; the ontological approach yields to another kind of relation to God. Instead of seeing or comprehending, affections come into play. At the summit of the intellectual contemplation the traveler is urged to achieve a radical shift: admiration is now more appropriate than the most rigorous form of ontotheology. In the end, theory is shown not to be an overcoming of amazement, as the beginning of Aristotle's *Metaphysics* had suggested, but the preparation of a more sublime surprise and wonder. However, the theological concentration on God's being one *and* threefold in love is not the end stage of the journey to which the mind is invited. Once the traveler has identified with both cherubim by contemplating the union of God's essence and personal relationships, the mind must direct its eyes to the "Mercy Seat" (*propitiatorium*, Exod. 25:20) on top of the ark in order to admire the expression of God's own life in the "superadmirable *(supermirabilem)* union of God and man in the unity of Christ's person" (n.4). This is the center and synthesis in which God's self-communication expresses itself as the perfect union of the Creator and his creation: Christ is the human icon in which the Word of the Origin has become the open book where all essential truths can be found. Whoever has become able through the stages of the journey to read this book has found the perfect source of illumination. After this discovery no other progress can be made, except by an ongoing intensification of appropriate affections.

By emphasizing that admiration should take over when reason and intellect have exhausted their capacities for truth, chapter 6 prepares the reader to enter the end station of the road, which is somewhat similar to but also very different from the extasis that crowns Plotinus' posttheoretical union with the One. Discursivity has made room for a suprarational kind of mood characterized as *peace*. Only at the end of the road can the full meaning of this word be experienced. The mind enters into peace through an "excess"; the speculative attitude, maintained throughout the six stages of the road, undergoes a final conversion (n.2). Bonaventure's excess is not the Plotinian unification in which the mind loses its self-consciousness. "To be perfect, this transition must leave all intellectual operations behind, while the tip of affection *(apex affectus)* entirely is transformed into God" (n. 4). The supratheoretical disposition needed is composed of faith, hope, devotion, admiration, exultation, appreciation, praise, and jubilation. Bonaventure's phenomenology of emotions, virtues, spiritual senses, gifts of the spirit, and "*beatitudines*" should be brought in at this point to get a better idea of the mindset and the kind of life that are demanded as a response to the central mystery (the "*propitiatorium*") in which God is most adequately manifested. This mystery is the simultaneously divine and human fact of Jesus the Christ as crucified. The final meaning of human existence, introduced in chapter 1 under the name of *beatitudo*, is now revealed in a dying man, who is God. The *theōsis* of human mortals is realized in God's mortality. Encountering God is not an escape from corporeality, but the acceptance of death as a symbol and concretization of absolute generosity and self-communication. The journey of the mind to the *eudaimonia* of peace is a passage (a *pascha*) through the Red Sea under the guidance of the cross. Death is necessary, not in order to free the soul from its imprisonment in corporeality, but rather to pass over into the dominance of grace.

7

Bonaventure's Contribution to the Twentieth-Century Debate on Apophatic Theology

For Theo Zweerman

GOD HAS DIED, at least in science and philosophy. He is agonizing in religious study, perhaps even in some divinity schools. Atheism and a careful sequestration of God from current business are the two main forms in which academia deals with the long history of religion, which, notwithstanding academic reservations, goes on. For scholarship, faith, God, and religion have become curiosa. The theoretical intention has separated itself from religious commitments; it abhors edifying language and has forgotten or rejected the long history of its association with contemplation. *Curiositas* is the word Bonaventure would use to characterize the study of religion that ensues from such a situation. But what is the relevance of such curiosity? Does at least philosophy accept that the question of the ultimate and its inevitable connections with science, education, ethos, politics, art, literature, and philosophy itself cannot be ignored in a discipline that is proud of its reflexive and universalizing capacities? Where the question of the ultimate (the ultimate concern, the ultimate meaning) is still alive, the climate is dramatic: after God's death nihilism seems inevitable, but how can human beings live without rejecting it? Not everybody appreciates Nietzsche's dramatic accents; the majority of scholars in philosophy seem quite satisfied with their way of life, but those who have seen the depths and felt the radicality of great traditions of thought from Parmenides to Hegel and from Amos and Isaiah to Saint John of the Cross and Pascal, cannot be impressed by the boring mediocrities of philosophers that ignore the life and death of God.

Fortunately, there are still philosophers who are not afraid of making explicit the inevitable and necessary connections between their faith and thought. Some of them agree with Nietzsche, but they point out that his "God" is different from the God of Abraham, Isaac, and Moses, and from the Father of Jesus Christ. Was Nietzsche the messenger of the death of a Victorian God, the God of Kant, or the God of the slaves' resentment only? Similar questions should be asked with regard to pre- or non-Nietzschean atheists, such as some exponents of the Enlightenment, certain nineteenth- and twentieth-century scientists, and those contemporary philosophers who deny even the relevance of God. How do they understand the word "God"? What exactly do they deny when they declare God nonexistent? What is the meaning, the possible or impossible relevance of "God"?

According to certain philosophers and theologians, only "the God of metaphysics" has died, not the God of Abraham, Moses, and Jesus. Others do not accept that the history of philosophical theology can be summarized in the word "metaphysics," if this signifies the "onto-theo-logical" mode of thinking with which Heidegger identified it; they want to free and retrieve the nonmetaphysical insights of that history to show that there are better modes than the metaphysical one to approach God in theory. Still others think that the Heideggerian and post-Heideggerian use of "metaphysics" is a caricature of what metaphysics was in the high times of its history; they want to show that the works of premodern Christian thinkers contain important elements for a postmodern theory of our relations to God and of the names through which we can approach and somehow reach Him or Her.

In the context of these attempts at naming God in our secularized world, apophatic theology plays an important role because it permits us to criticize the deficiency of all the names and concepts that are used in talking about God, thus showing the essential limitations of our understanding, but at the same time permitting us to point—and in a sense to pass—beyond the borders of our knowledge. Negative expressions are closer to the truth than affirmations about God, because they indicate more clearly that God surpasses any intellectual grasp. The darkness into which one ascends through contemplation is more appropriate than clarity because the infinite splendor of the superessential Good can only blind finite intellects if they are not protected by a cloud of unknowing.

There might be a certain similarity between the gesture of those who killed "God" or announced His death and those who retrieve the work of Pseudo-Dionysius and other masters of apophatism. If the murdered God is "human, all too human," a denial of such an all-too-human being is necessary, but this denial does not solve the question of whether our existence in the world can be conceived of without essential connections to the living God who surpasses all names.

It would be unworthy of a (theological or philosophical) theologian to always want to agree with non- or anti-Christian heroes of thought, but many motivations of those who reject "God" can be shared by Christians, and this strengthens the suspicion that the god they hate must indeed be denied or at least surpassed by something better: the unique God, who in all respects, or *simpliciter*, can be called Good. But is even "good" a perfectly appropriate predicate or name? Again, we must correct the finiteness of our concept ("good") by denying that "God is good" is a fully true expression.

Going beyond all affirmations concerning God through negations does not mean that we forget, leave behind, erase or cross out the negated affirmations. Although "good" and "not-good" seem to contradict each other, both must be maintained: "good" must be kept together with "non-good" in a subordination that can be understood neither as species of a genus, nor as part of a whole. The negation does not fall back behind the affirmation, as if it tried to re-establish the indeterminacy that precedes all determinations; it urges the thinker to think beyond that which we know as "good": a determination that, although its contours escape us, surpasses it and therefore demands us to express its noncoincidence with any good. God cannot be identified as good, but he is beyond-good *(hyper-agathos)*. Dionysius even calls him super-divine, *"hypertheos."*[1]

The tension created by the simultaneity of affirmations and negations is expressed in the return of the affirmations on a higher level, indicated by the word "hyper." The transition from the level of the affirmative predicates to the level beyond, a transition urged by negation, would not be possible if affirmations and negations did not translate an orientation and a dynamism that urge and move the thinker who is looking for appropriate names. Only if thinking itself is an oriented

---

1. Dionysius, *On Mystical Theology* 1, 1 and *On the Divine Names,* for example 1, 5 and 2, 3.

movement can the negation of its affirmations force it to go farther, to
pass over to a stage that is closer to the Orient. *Theologia* could not
make any progress if it were not driven by an originary movement. The
source of this movement can be called Desire.

When thinking about God originates in desire, the investigation is
an ascent that does not let itself be stopped by the denials of its affirmative experiments. It rather understands these negations as a warning
not to take any affirmative result as definitive; all results are only
pointers to a higher level of approaching God. The desire of God precedes and anticipates the end of thinking. What the thinker in the end
must learn—and this is most painful and humiliating for someone who
has put his heart into *theoria*—is that theory does not reach far enough.
The highest stage of thought is the obscurity of a well-prepared,
thoughtfully entered ignorance: the learned *agnōsia* of a union that
cannot be expressed in language, a silent union in dark transcendence.[2]

BONAVENTURE AND APOPHATIC THEOLOGY

Can a study of Bonaventure's work enrich the actual discussion of negative theology? A certain expectation in this respect seems justified.
Jacques Guy Bougerol[3] called Bonaventure "without a doubt the most
Dionysian mind of the Middle Ages" and although Bonaventure did
not write extensive commentaries on any of Dionysius' works, he
quoted them at least 248 times, as Bougerol has shown. The influence
of Dionysius on Bonaventure was relativized by Marianne Schlosser in
her book *Cognitio et Amor*, and Bougerol himself recognizes that
Bonaventure at times thinks very differently, and, in any case, "entirely transforms Dionysius' system."[4] However, transformation does not
erase influence and is normal between great thinkers. For our question,

2. Dionysius, *On Mystical Theology*, 1, 3 and 2.

3. Jacques Guy Bougerol, *Saint Bonaventure: Études sur les sources de sa pensée*
(Northampton, England: Variorum Reprints, 1989), *avant-propos*.

4. Marianne Schlosser, *Cognitio et Amor. Zum kognitiven und voluntativen Grund
der Gotteserfahrung nach Bonaventura* (Paderborn: Schöningh, 1990), pp. 123–24
and 128–30; Bougerol, *Saint Bonaventure*, pp. 113–23. See also Zachary Hayes,
Disputed Questions on the Mystery of the Trinity (St. Bonaventure, N.Y.: The
Franciscan Institute, 1979), pp. 22–25.

the attempt to find out to what extent Bonaventure retrieved Dionysius' apophatism must be made. However, this chapter will not offer the result of such an attempt; I rather will insist on a few aspects of negativity in Bonaventure's conception of contemplation that seem to me relevant for a correct evaluation of the possibilities contained in apophatic theology. For a thorough investigation of Bonaventure's reception of Dionysius' work, I refer the reader to Bougerol's precious studies, "Saint Bonaventure et Pseudo-Denys l'Aréopagite" and "Saint Bonaventure et la hiérarchie dionysienne."[5] The role of negative theology in Bonaventure—without emphasis on his relation to Dionysius—has been laid out in Marianne Schlosser's excellent study, "Lux Inaccessibilis. Zur negativen Theologie bei Bonaventura."[6]

What I would like to offer is a sketch of the way in which Bonaventure points out how the human search for insight, if it is accomplished appropriately, terminates in the *docta ignorantia* of an obscure and silent, but very awake union with God. In doing this, I will draw heavily on Bonaventure's second conference on the *Hexaemeron* *(Hex.)*, but I will also use other works, such as his Commentary on the *Sententiae* and his *Itinerary of the Mind to God (Itin.)*.

Desire for Wisdom

Continuing the Platonic and Neoplatonic tradition, Bonaventure sees desire as constitutive for the nature of human beings. We are driven and in movement by a desire that we have not chosen. It is important to realize that this drive and this movement determine all our activities, including our thinking, contemplating, and speculating. A philosophical or theological vision is continually on the move from stage to stage, according to the quality of life of the thinker who unfolds such a vision. Thinking is not separable from the rest of a human life; the moral and religious—and we could add the aesthetical and psychological—level of a thinker conditions and codetermines what the thinking of this thinker projects and how it proceeds. Without an intense desire

---

5. Bougerol, *Saint Bonaventure,* pp. 33–123 and 131–67.
6. Marianne Schlosser, "Lux inaccessibilis. Zur negativen Theologie bei Bonaventura," *(Franziskanische Studien* 68, 1968), pp. 3–140.

(concupiscentia, vehemens desiderium) of wisdom *(sapientia)*, for example, we will never acquire true insight, not even discover the way that leads to it. Moral decency too, a pure heart, even holiness *(sanctitas)* are necessary conditions for being perceptive and receptive enough to discover the truth: the truth of a universe created, loved, saved, illuminated, and inhabited by God, that is, the truth of God as mirrored in the universe *(Hex.* 2, 2–6).

Contemporary phenomenology recognizes what all traditions of spirituality have known for millennia, namely that thinking needs specific affective and practical conditions in order to let things show and unfold, to do justice to humans and animals, and to be receptive to the manifestations of God's presence. Reason and intelligence must be oriented by a desire for genuineness and purity. This is the cathartic law of perception and thought, often forgotten, despised or suppressed under the domination of scientism in philosophy and religious studies.

A corollary to this law is that the search for insight cannot be achieved as a project for which, in a first stage, we could lay the foundation in order to build other levels on it in later stages. Most often, the first stage will not represent a completely authentic and noble mode of life, and therefore will be deficient in perception, sensitivity and willingness to accept truths that are painful or humiliating. The movement of thought can thus not take for granted that its first stage is trustworthy enough to found a system. If the question of the conditions and their purification is taken seriously, a thinker must start many times: each progress in honesty and sensitivity makes new fundamental insights possible.

Someone who has perfectly realized humanity's radical desire, is wise: a saint is *"deiformis"* and "wisdom [itself] enters immediately in him" *(Hex.* 2, 6). Yet, Bonaventure holds also that wisdom cannot be acquired without intellectual labor. The dialectical relation between insight *(intellectus)* and wisdom *(sapientia)* is one of the central problems of his oeuvre. He underlines that wisdom—as discovery of the ultimate understanding of existence—is a grace and given only to a pure heart; but analysis and reflection enrich a naive reception of that gift. Intellectuals can become wise only if they are as pure as the "simple" saints; these do not miss anything essential for their glory, but they avoid the temptations of intellectual arrogance and vain curiosity. Theologians, however, have a chance to love God not only with their heart, but also with a fully unfolded intellect.

Bonaventure distinguishes four "aspects" *(aspectus)* or "faces" *(facies)* of wisdom (*Hex.* 2, 8–34):

1. Its basis lies in a network of *a priori* principles that constitutes human consciousness. These principles owe their universal certainty and immutability to the radical orderliness *(ars aeterna)* of God, which is the source of light without which no human action can be performed. This light inhabits and unites all humans; it can be discovered through a reflection on the conditions of knowledge and practice. Faith, however, recognizes the presence of God's Word in it (*Itin.* 2, 9; cf. 5, 1).

2. Sacred Scripture mysteriously reveals the meaning of human existence to those who are humble enough to receive it as a grace and sensible enough to understand the symbols and signs through which the sacred mysteries are revealed. This revelation provokes faith, hope and love without abolishing the enigmatic character that belongs to a mortal life on earth. Human beings need allegorical, anagogical, and tropological explanations to show them what and how they must believe, expect and act. *Faith* unites the members of the ecclesiastical body with its head; the anagogical unfolding of *hope* prepares the soul for a way of existence that is ruled by active and contemplative *love.* Faith, hope, and love guide the soul on its ascent from existence in a closed universe to the enjoyment of an infinite space between God and human souls.

3. In light of the Scriptures, the universe becomes understandable: "the entire world is like one full mirror" in which God's own wisdom is mirrored. The "book of nature" *(liber naturae)* receives its explanation from the "book of Scripture" *(liber scripturae)*, but intellectual labor is necessary for their interpretation. The key for the explication of Scripture and the entire universe is Jesus Christ, since he is the center of all things. Any attempt to understand the whole of reality must start from this center because all wisdom is concentrated in Him. As the uncreated, incarnated and inspired Word of the Father, Christ encompasses the whole creation and manifests how everything is an expression of God's living presence (cf. *Hex.* 1, 11–37).

It is difficult to find passages in Bonaventure's work that speak of God's absence. The overwhelming presence of God's light and grace to which Bonaventure constantly refers corresponds to the affectionate openness that, according to his descriptions, characterizes a well-disposed subject. However, God is always hidden, enigmatically present in the form of humiliation, rejection, and suppression. The Word that precedes creation and rules the world through its inspiration invites the seekers for truth to participate in the drama of a persecuted guide. I will come back to this aspect of wisdom toward the end of this chapter.

4. The ultimate secret of God's wisdom cannot be understood, but neither are we condemned to total silence about it. Bonaventure calls this aspect of true wisdom "extremely difficult" (*dificillima, Hex.* 2, 28). It is "the depth of God" *(profunda Dei)* of which Saint Paul in the first letter to the Corinthians writes: "Among the perfect we speak about a wisdom that is not of this age [. . .], a wisdom that is hidden in mystery *(in mysterio abscondita)*, which no eye has seen and no ear has heard; it has not emerged in any human heart; but God has revealed it to us through His Spirit. For the Spirit investigates all things, even the depths of God" (1 Cor. 2:6–10). This quote introduces a transition from Paul to Dionysius. Bonaventure must have experienced this highest moment of wisdom, since he writes: "this [namely the experience of the beloved beyond all substances and knowledge] nobody knows who does not have an experience of it." Yet, he prefers to appeal to the authority of "the Apostle" himself, who "taught this wisdom to Dionysius and Timotheus and other perfect [Christians], while he hid it to others" (*Hex.* 2, 28).

The mysterious concealment of the highest wisdom, as indicated by Paul's expression "hidden in mystery" *(in mysterio abscondita)*, is explained in a commentary on the first chapter of Dionysius' *Mystical Theology.* Bonaventure calls it the text with which Dionysius brought his work to completion (*consummavit, Hex.* 2, 29). To prevent misunderstandings, he reminds the reader that this text cannot be understood and that the wisdom indicated in it cannot be discovered unless one has passed through all former stages of discovery. He quotes the second section of *Mystical Theology,* where Dionysius addresses himself to Timotheus, whom Bonaventure apparently sees as Paul's pupil and companion. Since Bonaventure, in *Hex.* 2, 29, cites only the first words of the text, which must have been familiar to his listeners, referring by an "etc." to the rest, I will give here a more complete text, as it is found in the *Itinerarium* cap. 7, n.5. The text is also quoted in *Hex.* 2, 32, again in an abridged form ending in "etc." Several details of the quote are different in the three versions, a fact that Bougerol explains through the use of different Latin translations; perhaps we could also see it as an indication that Bonaventure quotes from memory.

Here is a translation of the Latin version used by Bonaventure in his *Itinerarium*:

> However you, my friend,[7] concerning the mystical visions, be steadfast on your way;[8] leave the senses and the intellectual activities behind, as well as sensible and invisible things and all being and non-being; then you will be brought back as much as possible and without knowledge to the unity of him who is above all essence [or beingness] and science [or knowledge]. Indeed, by an immeasurable and absolute excess of your pure mind you will transcend yourself and all things toward the superessential beam of divine darkness, leaving all things behind and free from everything.

In his commentary, Bonaventure emphasizes the necessity of becoming detached and free from all grasping and "apprehensive" activities: the secret of God surpasses all beings and knowledge, including sensibility, imagination, evaluation and all intellectual operations. The summit of the ascent to which desire drives human beings, is a union in love beyond all understanding and representation. "Nobody has an idea of this, who does not experience it." And Bonaventure concludes rather laconically: "This shows that *beatitudo* does not entirely lie in our intellectual possibilities" (*Hex.* 2, 29). Thus, the tradition that started from Plato's *Republic* and was developed by the Neoplatonists is retrieved by Bonaventure as a theory about the character of God's secret and the nature of human perfection. The union *(henosis)*, which, according to Dionysius, surpasses the ontological dimension where thinking *(noein)* and being *(einai)* coincide, reveals itself in a nonintellectual experience: the experience of love.

Desire reaches farther than reason. It cannot grasp, but it can receive as a grace the desired and beloved, if it separates itself affectively from all beings insofar as these are not God. These beings include one's own self— "if this were possible." By adding "if," Bonaventure apparently wants to mitigate somewhat Dionysius' phrase about transcending one's own self. He could also have said that the detachment from one's self should target this only insofar as it does not yet fully participate in God's life.

---

7. *Hex.* 2, 32 has here: "dear Timotheus" *(amice Timothee)* and 2, 29 reads: "O Timotheus, my friend" *(O Timothee amice).* For the different translations of Pseudo-Dionysius into Latin and those used by Bonaventure, see Bougerol, *Saint Bonaventure,* pp. 39–40 and 59–64.

8. *Corroborato itinere. Hex.*, 2, 29 has: *forti actione et contritione* (with strong action and contrition), while *Hex.* 2, 32 reads: *forti contritione et actione.*

Affectivity, in the form of *caritas*, transcends intellect and science; it reaches the infinite and experiences the depth of God and humans simultaneously. Beyond the dialectic of affirmations and negations, trust, hope, gratitude, peace, pure enjoyment, and authentic love establish the self in the secret of the ultimate. "The soul enters into its own intimacy and thereby reaches its summit, for the most intimate and the highest are the same" (*Hex.* 2, 31). This union, which is "affective only" (*Hex.* 2, 30), is sought by all of the empirical and conceptual experiments in philosophy and theology. Through a supraintellectual intimacy, the Spirit reveals the truth—not to the brain, but to the heart. We might vary Pascal's well-known dictum in stating that the heart has experiences that reason does not know.

If the perfection of wisdom lies in an affective event beyond theory and discussion, the importance of the opposition between affirmative and negative propositions is relativized. Although Bonaventure, like Dionysius, Plotinus, and Plato, emphasizes that consummate wisdom presupposes a thorough preparation in which intellectual and moral elements play important roles, all of them point out that the fulfillment of desire toward which all human endeavors and cultures converge does not lie in knowledge but in the simplicity of an ignorance *(agnosia)* that is experienced as trust, hope, love. Those who walk the path of theory are oriented by an experience that somehow already is present in their departure. The desired union with God, who is "greater," "more than" and different from all realities theoretical speculation can fathom, codetermines the search, even if the searchers are not aware of it. The Spirit is present in their moods, their courage, and their enjoyment. Indifference or mere curiosity harms their attachment to the ultimate desideratum. What they must learn during the unfolding of their disciplines is detachment from all that is not God, but this does not mean that they should despise or lose the enjoyable wealth of creation, for this is not opposed to God, as if God were another, higher or highest being. The turn to God is a turn to universal love and participation. "All that is not God" is a name for those elements—or rather, for those nonelements and privations—that do not contain God's creative presence. To love God, who is "all in all things,"[9] is therefore the purest form of love

---

9. *Itinerarium* 5, 8; cf. 1 Cor. 15:28.

for all beings in the world and in history, for these have their being not only "from him and through him," but also "*in him.*"

The negation through which pure attachment to God becomes possible is a total, not merely theoretical, abnegation; it is the affective and effective abstraction *(aphairesis, remotio)* of perfect poverty with regard to the totality of Godless realities. The ultimate relationship presupposes death, as is clear from the statement in the *Song of Songs*: "love is strong as death" (Cant. 8, 6). But the mortification that is demanded by love opens the lover for an encounter with the infinity of the living God who lives in all creation.

*　*　*

In his conferences on the *Hexaemeron*, Bonaventure's style is often polemical: he scolds those philosophers who prefer Aristotle's interpretation of the human universe over the theological tradition. Although he had often shown how well he knew and how much he appreciated "the Philosopher" when Aristotle did not contradict the Christian faith, Bonaventure could be very harsh in speaking of the idea that philosophy would be able to operate independently from the dimension of faith; for example, when he calls the philosophers *magi Pharaonis* who sell their bad food in the darkness of Egypt (*Hex. 2, 7*) or talks about their preference for having sex with an ugly maid over marrying the king's daughter called *Sapientia* (*Hex. 2, 7*). This polemic might explain why the conferences of Bonaventure's last years seldom celebrate the greatness of human reason, but rather insist on its limitations. To prevent an all too sentimental reading of his texts, we can turn to less polemical works, such as his impressive *Commentary on Lombard's Sententiae*, the very detailed *Questiones Disputatae*, or the masterpiece which is his Summa: the *Itinerary of the Mind to God*. I will concentrate here on the last three chapters of the latter, in which Bonaventure offers a summary of his metaphysics, his theology, and his epistemology of religious experience, including its mystical aspects. These disciplines are unified by an image: the image of a contemplative traveler who, after having successfully sojourned in the temple court *(atrium)* and the holy *(sancta)*, has entered the holiest *(sancta sanctorum)*, where the wings of two cherubim overshadow the ark on which the "mercy-seat" is placed. These angels represent the two supreme degrees of speculative contemplation. They extend to the farthest boundaries of human understanding and can only be followed by a supraintellectual stage of contemplation.

THE WISDOM OF THE CROSS

Chapter five of the *Itinerarium* focuses on the most fundamental condition of knowledge as such: the light of the eternal truth *(aeterna veritas)*. It is thus concerned with the first face of wisdom as indicated in *Hex.* 2. A reflection on this *a priori* light shows the most fundamental reality under two names: "Being" *(esse)* and "Good" *(bonum)*. The second name is better, but being is included, not negated in goodness. Although Bonaventure mentions and quotes Dionysius several times in chapters 5–7, he does not follow his versions of Plato's "good beyond being." Although he accepts a certain subordination of being under goodness, he reconciles them as mutually inclusive. The name "Being" *(esse)* revealed God to Moses (Exod. 3:14) and summarizes the wisdom of Israel, while "Good" summarizes the New Testament (Matt. 28:19; Luke 18:19). Damascenus represents the theological tradition that is oriented by the first name, while Dionysius developed a theology of superessential goodness.[10] Bonaventure wants to honor both traditions and distributes them as complementary perspectives among the two cherubim.

In a splendid compendium of his onto-theo-logy, Bonaventure shows that being *(esse)* as such, that is, as pure, completely actual, eternal, simple, perfect and unique, can only be the divine beingness of God and that all its characteristics mutually imply one another. The blinding light of a thorough ontology reveals God's uniqueness as expressed in Deut. 6:4: "Hear Israel, your God is the one, unique God."

The other cherub, that is, the other supreme mode of speculation (cap. 6), discovers that the goodness of God implies God's trinity.

---

10. Philotheus Boehner, ed., *Itinerarium Mentis in Deum* (St. Bonaventure, N.Y.: The Franciscan Institute, 1956), p. 80, refers here (at *Itin.* 5, 2) to the first book of Damascenus' *De fide orthodoxa,* chapter 9, and to Dionysius, *On the Divine Names* 3, 1 and 4, 1.

Quoting the Dionysian "bonum dicitur diffusivum sui,"[11] Bonaventure shows how the principle of all principles *(principalissimum fundamentum)*, which is the good *(bonum)*, can be contemplated through its most radical, *un*created emanations. By way of preparation, and differently from Dionysius, he first makes sure that there will be no opposition between God's being, through which we discover his absolute unicity, and God's goodness. His argument for their unbreakable unity is Anselmian.[12] The Good, as purely or perfectly good *(optimum)*, is "that better than which nothing can be thought." Since it is clearly better to be than not to be, however, it is impossible to think that God is not *(Itin.* 6, 2).

Bonaventure's "deduction" of God's trinitarian constitution is given as a concretization of the principle that the good is self-diffusive. If to be good is to give from oneself, the perfect Good cannot but totally communicate its entire being to another, who then is identical with and, as receiver who thereby exists, also different from the origin. Bonaventure gives here (in chapter 6) only an incomplete sketch of the arguments that are unfolded in his *Disputed Questions on the Mystery of the Trinity.* For our purpose, I would like to underline that the concept of "good" that underlies Bonaventure's argument is a Christian transformation of the generosity that was characteristic for the Neoplatonic One. Emanation is now understood as creative and compassionate *agapē*: absolute donation of all that a person is to another person; sharing, in the most extreme way, one's being *(esse).* The "deduction" is, thus, based on the infinitization of Christian *agapē*.

To discover God as One Divinity in three loving and beloved Persons is a possibility of human reason but we cannot "comprehend" what we "apprehend" through it.[13] The greatest difficulty lies here in

---

11. According to Bougerol, *Saint Bonaventure,* pp. 81–104, this dictum is quoted 26 times in Bonaventure's work. The connection between God's goodness and the Trinity seems to be hinted at in *On the Divine Names* 2, 11, where the *diakrisis theia* (the divine difference) is explained as "the forthcoming emanations that fit the goodness of God's originariness" *(hai agathoprepeis tēs thearchias proodoi).*

12. Cf. *Proslogion* cap. 5: "Tu [Deus] es itaque [. . .] quidquid melius est esse quam non esse," and the title of the chapter: "Quod Deus sit quidquid melius est esse quam non esse."

13. Cf. Schlosser, *Lux inacessibilis,* pp. 18–27, on the certainty of our knowledge of God, who remains incomprehensible. The human intellect is able to know the entirety of God, but not in a comprehensible way *(totus, non totaliter).* See *I Sent.,* dist. 3, pars 1, qu. 1; *II Sent.,* dist. 3, pars 2, art. 2, qu. 2–3.

the combination of God's being One and God's being Three, that is, in the understanding of how being and goodness are intertwined. God can be known with great certainty, but we cannot acquire an insight into God's triune constitution. Knowledge and incomprehensibility are here one: we can know how un-understandable God is. However, this ignorant "knowledge" is not developed through apophatic discourse about its darkness; it is enacted in a transition from understanding to another, deeper and higher dimension of the human search: un-understanding speculation turns into *admiration*. Wonderment not only precedes philosophy, it also crowns its endeavors by introducing the investigating mind to an affective relationship with God (*Itin.* 6, 3).

This level of admiration is not the end of the spiritual journey, however; not even the end of its theoretical part. The *ascent* from the lowest level of creation to the sublime heights of the Creator's inner life, must be followed by a *descent* that confirms our belonging to the corporeal, earthly, corruptible and historical reality in which we live.[14] The perfect life does not consist of looking upward while leaving the messy history of humans to its own miserable destiny. "This is the eternal life: that they know you, the only true God *and* the one you sent: Jesus Christ" (John 17:3).

Continuing his interpretation of the cherubim in the *sancta sanctorum*, Bonaventure points out that their faces (that is, the faces or aspects of wisdom, as mentioned in *Hex.* 2) not only are turned to one another, but are also looking at the *propitiatorium*, the place of reconciliation, or the "mercy-seat" on the ark (6, 4). The wonder of all wonders is not the mystery of God's triune essence and internal love, but the "superadmirable" realization of God's human, that is, corporeal and mortal reality in Jesus Christ. Here we rejoin the beginning of Bonaventure's conferences on the *Hexaemeron*: as the central sacrament, Christ is the beginning and the end, alpha and omega, of contemplation. Perfect spirituality is the fully unfolded experience of its beginning in faith (6, 5).

Bonaventure addresses himself (in *Itin.* 6, 5) to the reader whom he has identified as the synthesis of the two cherubs: focusing on the "essentials" of God (cap. 5), you are admiring the paradoxes of God's

---

14. In *Republic* 519c-520a and 539e-540a Plato insists on the unity of the ascent *(anabainein)* and the descent *(katabainein)*, but the latter is hardly emphasized by Plotinus and Dionysius.

being first and last, eternal and totally present, simple and greatest, perfectly one and encompassing all modes of being. Yet, do not forget that to be a good cherub, you must concentrate on the drama in which the reconciliation between God and humans is realized. The ultimate secret is not found in the unique, perfect, immense, and eternal Present of the unique Divinity; it is hidden in the corporeal, humble and suffering history of that Presence. In the figure of the other cherub you are full of admiration for the mystery of God's trinity, but look at Christ's person, who makes this Trinity concrete in a human destiny (6, 6). Perfect enlightenment shows how the intention of the Creator and the internal life of God's self-communication are realized in the perfect image of God: a man who translates God's love in the elements of human history. The union of Creator and creation, known by faith, is experienced at the highest level of knowledge in an "experimental cognition," which, by surpassing comprehension, provokes admiration.

Having shown how intellectual perspicacity reaches its limits and turns into an affective response, Bonaventure finally dwells on the peace that crowns the journey to God. This peace is not the peace of heaven, but rather participation in a final passage or transition *(transitus)* to God in company with Christ *(Itin.* 7, 1). Once the stages of intellectual speculation have purified the mind, it is able to fully concentrate on the reconciliatory "sacrament that was hidden for ages" *(a saeculis absconditum*, Eph. 3:9): a man who is God, hanging on a cross. There the secret of God is spread out in all the dimensions of space and time, thus showing "the breadth and the length and the height and the depth" of a love "that surpasses knowledge."[15] The only appropriate way of responding to the self-manifestation of God in the midst of human history is an affective one that encompasses all the moments of mind, intellect, and heart. Bonaventure enumerates the following moments of this final conversion: trust, hope, love, devotion, admiration, exultation, appreciation, praise, and jubilation *(Itin.* 7, 2). Instead of maintaining a speculative distance, these affections unify the soul with the *pascha* of Christ who leads from Egypt through the

---

15. Eph. 3:18–19. Bonaventure quotes Eph. 3:14–19 many times at crucial places of his work; for example, at the beginning of his prologue to the *Breviloquium,* where it summarizes the program of his entire theology. See also the *Comm. in Sent.,* prooemium; *Quest. de Scientia Christi VIII; Itin.* 4, 8; *Hex.* 8, 4; *Soliloquia,* prologue. The indices to the critical edition give 16 places.

Red Sea and the desert to paradise. At this point (*Itin.* 7, 2), it becomes clear how Bonaventure interprets the inherent negativity and the profound darkness *(caligo)* indicated by Dionysius' *Mystical Theology*, and quoted toward the end of the *Itinerary* (*Itin.* 7, 5). Reaching out to God leads through a desert of suffering with Christ into the peace of his grave. The certainty given by the Word of God that the very event of such a *pascha is* the presence *(hodie)* of paradise (Luke 23:43), is not only an article of faith, but a felt experience (*sentiens tantum, Itin.* 7, 2). The union with God in the dark cloud of ignorance, as thematized by Dionysius' *Mystical Theology*, is retrieved in a hermeneutics of an affective response to the sacrament of God's historical Passion. The ascent from affirmative names to negations and from negations to the obscure clarity of union is transformed into the passage from a theology of being and generosity to the dark splendor of a "more than" divine, namely, divinely human and historical, humiliated and mortified love. Sharing Christ's destiny in faith and love transforms a human being in God (*Itin.* 7, 4).

The best preparation for this summit, which is at the same time the deepest depth, lies in the desire that motivates all the stages of the journey, but even this is a gift of the Spirit with whom Christ inspired human history. The "natural desire" that rules all human ways is finally revealed to be the fire through which God's own spirit inflames the human heart. To understand this pertains to "the mystical wisdom" that is sought from the beginning. Darkness and peace, suffering and enjoyment, death and resurrection coincide in the human history of God's hidden presence. The rose in the cross is found neither in a dialectical explanation of the universe in light of a logical or superlogical Absolute, nor in an endless series of negations and supernegations; it reveals itself in an affectionate excess beyond all theoretical wrestlings with yes and no. "The Son of God, Jesus Christ [. . .] was not Yes and No; in Him it is always Yes. For all the promises of God find their Yes in Him. That is why we utter the Amen through Him, to the glory of God" (2 Cor. 1:19–20). According to Bonaventure, this Yes and Amen is not a logical one; it is a passionate loyalty to God as present in human history and to human history as revelation of God, a loyalty that knows how to endure the darkness of its mortality.

8

Life, Science, and Wisdom
According to Descartes

IF IT IS TRUE that "the supreme good" of human life is wisdom, then all human endeavors are grounded in the search for wisdom, and all our scientific ventures are oriented by this search.

In a letter sent to Elizabeth along with the *Principles of Philosophy*, René Descartes defines wisdom as the "firm and powerful resolve to use reason as well as one can and, in all actions, to do whatever one judges to be best."[1] Wisdom grounds and encompasses "all the virtues" insofar as it is the foundation of the other three cardinal virtues, justice, courage, and temperance (successors to the Platonic *dikaiosynē*, *andreia*, and *sophrosynē*). While this definition emphasizes the will, the preface to the French edition of the *Principles of Philosophy* stresses the intellect insofar as it defines wisdom as both "prudence in our affairs" and "a perfect knowledge of all things that mankind is capable of knowing, both for the conduct of life" (moral knowledge) "and for the preservation of health" (medicine) "and the discovery of all manner of skills" (mechanics).[2] Neither definition of wisdom accords with the view of Plato and Aristotle that the highest form of knowledge and the absolute end of human life is contemplation, the desirable *par excellence*: instead, wisdom here is defined as *useful* knowledge.

1. Charles Adam and Paul Tannery, eds., *Oeuvres de Descartes* (Paris: Cerf, 1897–1913, cited as *AT*) IX B, p. 21; for the English translation of Descartes, I have used John Cottingham, Robert Stoothoff, and Dugald Murdoch, trans., *The Philosophical Writings of Descartes* (Cambridge: Cambridge University Press, 1985, cited as *PW*), although I have sometimes modified their translations. Cf. *PW* I, p. 191.

2. *AT* IXB, p. 2; *PW* I, p. 179.

We search for the knowledge of the truth because it enables us to be happy. To lead a satisfactory life does not simply require virtuous behavior, but also the health of the body and a certain mastery or control over the world.

Philosophy, as the search for wisdom, is the most useful thing there is for the accomplishment of a successful life; it is therefore also "the greatest good that a state can enjoy." As "more necessary for the regulation of our morals and our conduct in this life than is the use of our eyes to guide our steps," "it is this philosophy alone which distinguishes us from the most savage and barbarous peoples; [. . .] a nation's civilization and refinement depends on the superiority of the philosophy which is practiced there."[3]

Without philosophizing it is still possible to "live" in a more or less human way (which implies a certain morality), but it "is exactly like having one's eyes closed without ever trying to open them." Proceeding blindly, without attention to any "why?" characterizes savages and barbarians, but genuine knowledge teaches one how to *"proceed with confidence in this life."*[4]

This chapter will consider how Descartes revives the ancient idea of philosophy and the pursuit of wisdom as a search for the highest good. His view of philosophy as the supreme element in a culture and as the most certain guide along the path to the good life invites a comparison between his way of "proceeding" and the itineraries that other men and women have employed in order to discover wisdom, goodness, and happiness. So many locutions in the Cartesian texts echo a long Greco-Christian tradition that understands the truly human or "spiritual" life as a journey, voyage, ascent. In keeping with that tradition, these passages evoke the image of "stages along a way" or "steps on a ladder," and they underscore the necessity of an initial conversion, without which we could neither find the right path nor discover the conditions of further progress. It seems worthwhile, therefore, to ask whether Descartes's philosophy can be understood as a modern version of Greco-Christian spirituality.

---

3. *AT* IXB, p. 3; *PW,* p. 180.
4. *AT* VI, p. 10; *PW,* p. 115.

I.

Let us start by focusing on the beginning of the Cartesian journey. It seems clear that the reason why Descartes risks a radical questioning of his convictions is his need for certainty. His desire for wisdom is grounded in the desire to "proceed with confidence in this life," and the wisdom he desires is characterized by a fundamental and absolute solidity so certain that it can never again be doubted. "My whole aim was to reach certainty—to cast aside the loose earth and sand so as to come upon rock or clay."[5] The starting point and direction of the path that must be followed, the character of the distance that must be crossed, and the way to proceed from stage to stage, must all be known in advance, at least in their general patterns and essential characteristics. If, for example, we do not know which direction is the right one, the journey will take us farther and farther away from our goal rather than taking us closer to it. For, "so long as we turn our back on the place we wish to get to, then the longer and faster we walk the further we get from our destination, so that even if we are subsequently set on the right road we cannot reach our goal as quickly as we would have done had we never walked in the wrong direction."[6] True, it is not always good to "keep walking as straight as [one] can in one direction" because it is not always true that they who never change direction "will at least end up in a place where they are likely to be better off."[7] But when it is a question of gaining true and certain knowledge, we can never be satisfied by these kinds of considerations, where probability and chance play a determining role.

The history of philosophy, which is a long repetition of false certainties unjustified and masked by the appearance of a series of probabilities, provides an example of the disaster to which perseverance in a wrong direction can lead.[8] As long as the question of certainty was the

---

5. *AT* VI, p. 29; *PW* I, p. 125.

6. From the preface to the French edition of the *Principles, AT* IXB, pp. 8–9; *PW* I, p. 183.

7. This is a well-known phrase, in which Descartes, in the *Discourse on the Method* tries to justify the probabilist character of his provisional morality. The fact that Descartes defends the indispensable role of probability in the realm of practical life while excluding all uncertainty in the realm of theory, shows the price he was willing to pay to satisfy his desire for theoretical certainty. (*AT* VI, pp. 24–25; *PW* I p. 123).

8. *AT* IXB, pp. 6–9; *PW* I, p. 181–83.

only issue that interested Descartes in his rapid glance at the two-thousand years separating him from Plato and Aristotle, he could see nothing in that history that could possibly augment the knowledge of a well-educated person of his own era. In fact, for Descartes, those who have followed the path of Plato and Aristotle—and especially their epigones—are the farthest from true knowledge, whereas "among those who have studied whatever has been called philosophy up till now, those who have learned the least" are exempt from the mistakes of the so-called philosophers and are thus "the most capable of learning true philosophy."[9]

Descartes is thus the first true philosopher because he knows where to find certainty. Before the discovery of a solid ground and an absolutely certain principle, there was only a false science of the uncertain and doubtful. However, bridging the distance between pseudo-philosophy and true, that is, scientific, philosophy demands a radical conversion of each person who wants to be initiated. We must separate ourselves from a lifestyle content with probabilities and plausibilities in order to enter into the kingdom of solidly established and certain truth. But how?

We must renounce the old way of living, which is characterized by Descartes as a life led by "commonplace and imperfect knowledge" (*connaissance vulgaire et imparfaite*) or an everyday "wisdom," generally possessed "in four degrees."[10] These "degrees" are elements of this one wisdom or "means" to it rather than different degrees or types of distinct kinds of wisdom. Together, they constitute a sort of knowledge that Plato would have characterized by the word *doxa*. "All the knowledge that we now possess"—that is, all knowledge that has not undergone the conversion to which Descartes exhorts his reader—is composed of the following:

1. Some "notions which are so clear in themselves that they can be acquired without meditation."

2. "Everything we are acquainted with through sensory experience."

3. "What we can learn by conversing with other people."

---

9. *AT* IXB, p. 9; *PW* I, p. 183.
10. *AT* IXB, pp. 4–7; *PW* I, pp. 181–82.

4.   "What is learned by reading books [. . .] which have been written
     by people who are capable of instructing us well."

Apart from self-evident notions, which Descartes accepts as standing on their own, and sensible experience, which he does not entirely
repudiate but feels must be critically examined, prephilosophical
knowledge is composed of that which is said and written in the society we live in. That is to say, it consists of the common opinions of the
culture in which we are educated. It is difficult to know what books
must be read and which authors might be "capable of giving good
instructions" if we can employ only the first two "means." If, on the
other hand, we rely on oral and written "conversation" to discover who
might be worthy of confidence, we enter into a hermeneutic circle.
Descartes, however, must exclude this because it entails criticizing
doubtful opinions by means of other opinions that are themselves
uncertain. The true philosopher raises himself above the opinions of
cultivated people and looks for wisdom "incomparably more elevated
and more sure." However, because he must begin thinking somewhere
and because he cannot begin with the three last moments of pseudo-
knowledge, his only support will be the "notions that are so clear in
themselves that they can be acquired without meditation." This does
not imply, however, that he can neglect meditation. On the contrary, he
must freely direct his attention to these notions and assume the responsibility of selecting particular phenomena that are revealing enough for
discovering the truth.

The principle for the discovery of truth is not something that comes
to us by chance or "good fortune."[11] It is not an event, drama, meeting,
or divine grace awakening us from sleep but rather a decision of our
will; not a call coming to us from outside but a reversal of consciousness that comes from this very consciousness, thought, or will itself.
Thus I reform myself by an autonomous decision that changes the
grounds of my thought.

But how can I change myself if I am held prisoner by the *doxa* of
my culture? It is my longing for certainty that pushes me to do so. If
I let this desire develop to the point where it becomes imperious, if I

---

11. Literally "a happy part," (*une part heureuse*), which almost sounds like a
translation of the *theia moira* which Plato discusses in *Politeia* 493 a 1; *Phaidros* 230
a 6 and 244 c 4; *Nomoi* 931 e 6 and 946 b 3.

allow it to become so tyrannous that nothing else matters, either in my life or in the history of cultures, I can only decide by an act of will that the supreme good that I need must be indubitable. And that is my resolution!

To the extent that I find it impossible to doubt, I will be saved: the foundations of my life will be secure once I have escaped the domain where nothing is perfectly secure. A hatred of the uncertain and the anguish of being lost in the quicksand of insecurity seems to have motivated Descartes to find a solid "rock or clay" in which we can root ourselves: from here, we can raise ourselves straight up into the sunlight, in full confidence of bearing our own badly-needed fruits. Instead of merely hoping, which only prolongs gratitude for, and amazement at, one's own existence, Descartes chose to save his life through the autonomy of a few initial decisions and a legislation for the ordering of his thoughts and actions.

Everything that allows even the least opportunity for doubt must be abolished in the name of the desire for certainty. Everything written or spoken must be ignored, all advisors and all traditions must be bracketed. Doubt must be radicalized, a methodical skepticism embraced, and the uncertainty with which all human life is confronted, especially at the end of a culture or tradition, must be exaggerated.

Will we then sink into complete nihilism? As long as we do not find a solid principle, there will be no response to this question. We must simply tolerate the consequences that spring from the initial decision and wager that something solid and sure will emerge from the sea of doubt that threatens to drown us. This initial decision obliges me to marginalize and even exclude all that is not obviously clear to me because, in order to find "the rock," I must ignore or repress everything that seems "doubtful." However, because the flow of life cannot be suspended until nihilism is conquered, life itself must be protected from the general doubt that I decreed as the only means of approaching certain truth—if it is even possible to attain this at all. Within pure philosophy, however, I must restrict the terrain of all that is said and written, in order to isolate a domain, a little space or even just a point of certainty that will allow me to establish myself once and for all.

The project that results from the initial decision not to trust anything but the unshakable relies on two truths that it simply takes for granted, two prejudices the truth of which have not been proved, which are neither evident nor convincing in themselves, and which Descartes neither thematized nor made explicit.

According to the first prejudice it is possible to separate the philosophical search for true principles from practical life. In the third section of his *Discourse on Method* Descartes goes so far as to claim that the philosopher must live in two dwelling places: one is the house that is destroyed by the initial decision to no longer believe in anything, in the hope, however, that this house will be replaced by another more well-founded and solidly constructed edifice. Alongside this theoretical site the philosopher has another home, one where he can "live comfortably" while the theoretical building is in progress. What is surprising is that this second abode—the abode without a solid foundation—gives the philosopher the opportunity to "live as happily as he could" on the sole condition that he formulate some rules of conduct and conform his actions to them.[12] If indeed he can live there, and can do so more or less happily, several questions arise. For example: if it is possible to live happily without having acquired the absolutely certain knowledge that is sought on the philosophical site, what then is the importance of certain and perfect wisdom? What does it add to happiness? Is it not true that we need philosophy to know how to conduct our lives? Is philosophizing then not an integral part of the life and happiness of the philosopher?

The dualism of the two dwelling places suggests that philosophy does not occupy the abode of life but that it belongs rather to the dimension of the most serious abstraction and death. On the other hand, we know that it is precisely the quicksand of uncertainty that Descartes hates and rejects as the sepulcher of all truths.

II.

The conversion to which Descartes invites all those who are afraid of being deceived by other people's opinions, by prejudices of culture, by probabilities and the merely "moral certainties" of common sense, does not involve the whole person, but only their theoretical part. The

---

12. *AT* VI, pp. 22–23; *PW* I, p. 122.

practice of life, from which philosophical reflection, in his opinion, can isolate itself, continues to let itself be guided by opinions, laws, morals, and the pseudo-wisdom of everyday traditions, or, in other words, by a culture that is formed according to historical contingency.

The decision to abandon all pseudo-certainties leads to a decision that—against all likelihood—creates a gulf between theoretical work and practical life. The necessity of carefully preparing a rationally founded method demands that we know which path to follow in the absence of true knowledge. To "walk" on this road "with assurance," we must, however, content ourselves with the semblance of certainty that we find in common sense and the merely probable opinions of the culture in which we share. This is why, as long as the philosopher has not attained the final goal of his project, as long as he cannot gather the fruits from the branches of the tree of Science, he needs a "provisional moral code."[13] This *morale par provision* is a code that, similar to "a provisional judgment that precedes the definitive sentence,"[14] contains the sketch of a definitive morality, though more complete consideration is necessary to ascertain its final content.

The second prejudice on which Descartes's initial decision rests assumes that the ethos of a specific epoch is sufficient to make a good life possible. The happy life of a philosopher who is converted to pure theory in its initial form of methodical skepticism fits the portrait of the gentleman of seventeenth century France. Good citizen, good Christian, moderate and avoiding all excess, he follows the moral code of those he considers "the most sensible men" (those who reflect his own tastes and thoughts). He conforms to the expectations of his compatriots, yet is so concerned about his independence that he avoids, as much as possible, tying himself to promises, vows and contracts. The *first maxim* of the provisional and scientifically unfounded morality which Descartes embraces is "to obey the laws and customs of my country, persevering in the religion in which, through God's grace, I have been educated from childhood, and ruling my behavior in everything else according to the most moderate and least extreme opinions that are generally accepted and practiced by the most sensible people

---

13. *AT* VI, p. 22; *PW* I, p. 122.
14. Cf. *Petit Robert* s.v. " provision" II, where a *jugement par provision* is explained as " un jugement préalable à la sentence définitive."

with whom I would have to live." This *decision* thus forces the philosopher to rely on a series of subordinate presuppositions. These can be classified as the laws and customs of France, the Catholic religion, the opinions commonly held by the most moderate and "most sensible people"—insofar as these opinions are put into practice and not merely spoken and believed—and a freedom that is as uncommitted as possible.[15]

What is the foundation of the rule upon which this model is built? A clear response is given throughout the text of the *Discourse on Method*, which abounds in turns of phrases similar to this one: "I thought it would be most useful," while also affirming that the most moderate opinions are "probably the best." The basis for a happy life is thus sought in Descartes's rather subjective evaluation and the most moderate of "accepted opinions." The result is the complete opposite of what he stipulated as an absolute condition of perfect wisdom, which, in its turn, is the absolute condition for conducting a philosophically guaranteed good life. True, it is not impossible that the rules, virtues, and mores of this provisional morality will be seen one day to be identical with the scientific morality envisaged as one of the fruits of the tree of science. However, Descartes could not know whether these two moralities are in fact identical and we will never know, because the projected tree has never flourished enough. Descartes himself developed mechanics, medicine, and scientific morality only in a very fragmentary way, and he admitted in 1647 that he was "ignorant of almost all" the parts of the universal science on which "the principal benefit of philosophy" depends.[16] The post-Cartesian history of the

---

15. *AT* VI, pp. 22–24; *PW* I, pp. 122–23. Cf. also what Descartes says about Seneca in his letter of August 18, 1645 to Elizabeth, in Ferdinand Alquié, ed., *Oeuvres philosophiques,* vol. III (Paris: Garnier, 1973), pp. 592–98.

16. *AT* IXB p. 15; *PW* I, p. 186 Although Descartes admits here that he is "ignorant of almost all of [the sciences]" that constitute the branches growing out of the trunk of physics (moral philosophy, incidentally, must also be based on physics), he contributed three fragments to these sciences. In 1637, along with the *Discourse on the Method,* which contains a scientific logic and nonscientific morals, he published the *Optics,* the *Meteorology,* and a treatise on *Geometry.* The fact that he did not publish the sections on scientific morals seems to be a clear confession of sorts. In his letter of June 15, 1646, to Chanut (*Oeuvres philosophiques* vol. III, p. 657), he indicates, however, that the *Passions of the Soul* involves an intimate relation—as presupposition or part?—with the science of morality. See also note 33.

tree of sciences, meanwhile, is the history of the surgical interventions that its roots and trunk continuously underwent until its recent death.

Even if a scientifically founded and executed morality did have the same content as the provisional morality, there would still be a radical difference between them. Definitive morality would be deduced from the principles of Cartesian metaphysics and physics, and thus both its structure and the rational necessity of its rules and virtues[17] would be known and understood, while doxastic morality would be built on the authority of a particular culture. Furthermore, according to Descartes, the latter morality cannot be a morality of the truly happy and good life, since it has not accomplished the principal task of finding the overall certainty that is inseparable from true wisdom. Morality by provision is the morality of a person still embroiled in anguish. Faced with the dilemma presented by practical living, one can make a virtue of necessity by choosing to conform to the rules of the particular culture in which, by chance, one was educated, but in a Cartesian context, such a decision is as irrational and unwise as the decision to abide by the traditional philosophy.

The Cartesian person is divided between the theoretical attempt to retreat into an absolutely certain position removed from practical life, and a life of action that renounces the exigencies of rigorously critical reason. This schism is indicative of the divorce in most modern philosophy between the theoretical disciplines, including metaphysics, physics, and philosophy of mind, on one hand, and practical philosophy on the other. Perhaps Kant and Fichte alone realized that if a true starting point or principle of philosophy is possible, it will necessarily be both theoretical and practical. The postponement of ethics until the building site of theoretical philosophy is transformed into a solid edifice is co-responsible for practical nihilism. The idea that we will soon complete the construction of a scientific totality has created the illusion that we can cross the desert of a moral quicksand (the "provisional," that is, unfounded, morality) supported only by the decided, but uncertain, expectation of being able one day to justify a true and indubitable

---

17. Cf. *AT* IXB, p. 2; *PW* I, p. 179: The knowledge which man needs "for the conduct of life" is put on the same level as knowledge concerned with "the preservation of health" (medicine) and "the discovery of all manner of skills" (mechanics). In order for this knowledge to be perfect enough to be a component of wisdom, "it must be deduced from first causes," that is, from the principles of metaphysics and physics.

Law that—on the basis of our mechanical and medical expertise—will deliver us from our moral anxieties. At the beginning of the journey, we cannot know if the future Law will legitimize the initial morality or if it will radically recast it. What is certain, however, is that it must be grafted onto the scientific corpus and, in order to show its utility, be immediately applied to all the questions of human life. In fact, the goal Descartes set for himself—the wisdom that enables us to enjoy the supreme good—remains an ideal from which philosophical reflection has grown more and more distant as it endlessly digs up the ground again and again in order to reestablish or emend the foundations.[18]

III.

This brings us to the *second maxim* of the provisional moral code.[19] The voluntarist character of the provisional morality is here even more evident than in the first maxim, which involved only the decision to "obey the laws and customs of my country." For the philosopher about to begin his journey, Descartes stipulates the further guiding rule that he be as firm and resolute as possible in his actions, and that he follow the most doubtful opinions, once they have been determined, no less constantly than if they were well secured. Since practical life so often

---

18. To what extent does the project of a "most perfect moral system, which presupposes a complete knowledge of the other sciences and is the ultimate degree of wisdom" (*AT* IXB, p. 14; *PW* I, p. 186) contain a comprehensive casuistry, as Martial Guéroult writes in *Descartes selon l'ordre des raisons,* vol. II (Paris: Aubier, 1968), pp. 219–71? The parallel with the other two branches of the physico-metaphysical tree, and especially the comparison with the fruit that Descartes expects mechanics to bring forth, seem to suggest that a scientific ethics would at least contain a body of rules concrete enough to be useful for those who hesitate between the ethical alternatives of human conduct. The fact that few of these alternatives allow for entirely certain judgements does not eliminate the possibility of determining degrees of probability. The scholastic morality of the time (of which we can glean an idea, though it is really a caricature, from Pascal's *Lettres Provinciales*) was dominated by the confrontation of probable opinions, and the search for a method to escape the uncertainty created by the divergence of these opinions. A comparison of probabilist ethics, which Descartes certainly knew, with the moral maxims that he gives in the *Discourse on the Method,* his letters to Elizabeth, and the preface to the *Principles,* would no doubt show that Descartes is rather unoriginal on this subject. Here again, he follows the opinions of the most moderate authors of his time.

19. *AT* VI, pp. 24–25; *PW* I, p. 123.

does not allow us sufficient time to attain certainty in our action, all we can do is take even doubtful opinions as if they were certain truths. It goes without saying that this taking as (*"tenir pour"*) which presupposes a decision of the will, cannot be justified scientifically. The logic of Cartesian theory formally condemns making merely probable opinion identical with true and certain theses. Was this not precisely the great reproach leveled against the Platonic and Aristotelian tradition? In relation to the active life, however, Descartes adopts a methodological rule drawn from the probabilist morality of his time, which he might have learned from the Jesuits at La Flèche. In practice, one has to act *as though* a merely probable—and thus doubtful—opinion were a well-founded and certain rule. One should *decide* to see it as a normative truth that is rationally derived from well-established scientific principles. Since, however, it is obviously not this, Descartes, without giving an analysis either of the concept or of degrees of probability, employs a rhetorical strategy rather than put forward a rational argument. He leads the reader to believe that the fundamental ethical questions can be clarified by the image of "travellers who, upon finding themselves lost in a forest, should not wander about turning this way and that, and still less stay in one place, but should keep walking as straight as they can in one direction, never changing it for slight reasons even if mere chance made them choose it in the first place; for in this way, even if they do not go exactly where they wish, they will at least end up in a place where they are likely to be better off than in the middle of a forest." In this way, scientific theory preserves its dominion over all that is uncertain: but the price of this is that the domain of practical life is abandoned to the uncertainties and wars of probability. In order to rid theoretical philosophy of doubt, Doubt had to be crowned king over moral territory.

Even in provisional morality, however, not everything is doubtful, because there is at least one "most certain truth" that is methodic in nature: "When it is not in our power to discern the truest opinions" and in situations where our actions do not permit any delay, "we must follow the most probable [opinions]. Even when no opinions appear more probable than others, we must still adopt some." This truth is grounded in another certainty, namely, that one must act in the best manner, or according to the best norm. In the absence of any indubitable rules that indicate which actions are good, it is still certain that one must choose the least uncertain, that is, the most probable, rule. Descartes did not enter into the moralist debates of his time about the question of whether we must always follow the most probable opinion *(sententia probabilior)* or also can legitimately follow a merely probable opinion *(sententia probabilis)* even if a more probable one exists. He seems to lean towards the second position, but in general makes very little effort to prove the presuppositions of the second moral maxim he chose at the beginning of his philosophical explorations. A comparison of his position with the manuals of sixteenth-century scholastic morality would no doubt show that even in this point, he did not drift far from the accepted doctrines of his civilized and moderate contemporaries. When he delimits the domain of morality as the field of the most reasonable choices that can be made between probable opinions, he continues a tradition that reserves a strictly scientific method for questions of theoretical philosophy, while abandoning most ethical questions to prudential wisdom. What is typically Cartesian is the voluntaristic style of decisions and resolutions that have to compensate for the lack of evidence and conclusive arguments.

In fact, the purpose of his maxims of provisional morality is to not "remain indecisive in my actions while reason obliges me to be so in my judgements"[20] and this resolution reappears in texts where Descartes discusses the foundations of morality. Thus, in a letter to Elizabeth, dated August 4, 1645, he defines the virtue that encompasses all particular virtues as the "firm and constant resolution to carry out whatever reason recommends," a resolution made "without being diverted by passion or appetite."[21]

In the preface to the *Principles*, Descartes generalizes the maxims of provisional morality that were presented merely as rules of personal conduct in the *Discourse on Method*. He writes that "a man who still possesses only the ordinary and imperfect knowledge" of prescientific wisdom "should try before anything else to devise for himself a code of morals which is sufficient to regulate the actions of his life. For this is something which permits no delay, since we should endeavor above

---

20. *AT* VI, p. 22; *PW* I, p. 122; Cf. *AT* VI, p. 24; *PW* I, p. 123: "My second maxim was to be as firm and decisive in my actions as I could. . . ."

21. *AT* IV, p. 262; Anthony Kenny, trans. and ed., English translation of Descartes' letters in *Philosophical Letters* (Oxford: Clarendon Press, 1970) (cited as *PL*), p. 164.

all else to live well."[22] The second maxim is there formulated as follows: "so long as we possess only the kind of knowledge that is acquired by the first four degrees of wisdom [that is, prescientific "knowledge"], we should not doubt what seems true with regard to the conduct of life, while at the same time we should not consider them to be so certain that we are incapable of changing our views when we are obliged to do so by some evident reason."[23]

In a letter written on November 20 of the same year (1647), Descartes repeats this doctrine, insisting again upon the role of the will: resolution should compensate for the imperfections of knowledge. Speaking about the goods of the soul, which are the true moral goods, he says that they

> can all be reduced to two heads, the one being to know, and the other to will, what is good. But knowledge is often beyond our powers, and so there remains only our will of which we can dispose outright. I do not see that it is possible to dispose it better than by a firm and constant resolution to carry out to the letter whatever one judges best [even if our judgment cannot surpass the level of probability] and to employ all the powers of one's mind in order to acquire adequate knowledge [that is, in practicing philosophy]. This by itself constitutes all the virtues; [. . .] it is this which constitutes the supreme good.[24]

Does the methodological rule as formulated here characterize only the nonscientific and provisional moral code that the *Discourse on Method* and the preface to the *Principles* speak of? Or is it also a part of the scientific morality that—as a branch of the philosophical tree—should be deduced from metaphysics and physics? Perhaps Descartes, after several years of reflection, realized that the domain of moral questions

---

22. *AT* IXB, p. 13; *PW* I, p. 186.

23. *AT* IXB, p. 7–8; *PW* I, p. 182. Cf. also at the same page: "Some of those [disciples of Plato and Aristotle] who were in favour of doubt extended it even to the actions of life, so that they neglected to employ common prudence in their behaviour."

24. *AT* V, p. 81; *PL,* pp. 226–27 (translation modified). Cf. also the letter to Elizabeth of September 15, 1645 (*AT* IV, p. 287; *PL,* p. 171), where we find a sort of synthesis of the first two rules of the provisional moral code of the *Discourse on the Method:* "one must also examine in detail all the customs of one's place of abode to see how far they should be followed. Though we cannot have certain proofs of everything, still we must take sides, and in matters of custom embrace the opinions that seem the most probable, so that we may never be irresolute when we need to act. For nothing causes regret and remorse except irresolution."

will never be entirely free of uncertainties, and that in the realm of concrete action one must remain satisfied with a knowledge that is only more or less probable. Risk is therefore essential to all human action; it cannot be abolished by any science or philosophy. But should not this discovery have compelled Descartes to radically recast his starting points? The concept of wisdom, for example, and the relation that it implies between science and life or between logic and a philosophically founded morality seem to demand another analysis than the one with which Descartes begins. But let's leave that for now, in order to ask whether the late work of Descartes contains a definitive morality or at least the basic outline of such a morality.

The reply has to be negative, if we agree with Descartes that the highest and most perfect moral code, presupposes "a complete knowledge of the other sciences" from which it should be deduced. Although the *Passions of the Soul* and the letters contain some material for such a science, the "ultimate degree of wisdom"[25] is not fully developed anywhere in his works. Thus in the letter of August 1641 to Hyperaspistes, Descartes describes the uncertainty that exists on the level of action not only as inevitable, but also as insurmountable. In response to an objection from his pseudonymous interlocutor, Descartes writes: "It would indeed be desirable to have as much certainty in matters of conduct as is needed for the acquisition of scientific knowledge; but it is easily proved that in such matters so much is not to be sought nor hoped for."[26] Then he sketches two possible ways of demonstrating this statement, one *a priori*, or from the principles of philosophy, the other *a posteriori*, or "by the consequences." Given the perspective of the scientific project, symbolized by the tree of the sciences,[27] we are interested especially in the first proof, which promises to be a true deduction.[28] The language in which this proof is articulated gives us only a starting point: "This can be shown *a priori*, to wit, from the fact that the human composite is naturally corruptible, while the mind is incorruptible and immortal." The reader can attempt to

---

25. *AT* IXB, p. 14; *PW* I, p. 186.
26. *AT* III, p. 422; *PL,* p. 110 (translation slightly modified).
27. *AT* IXB, p. 14; *PW* I, p. 186.
28. According to the same passage (*AT* IXB, p. 13; *PW* I, p. 185), the scientific character of a philosophical discipline consists in the fact that its truths are "deduced" "by very evident reasoning" from very clear and evident principles.

reconstruct the unspoken argument in this rather enigmatic clue. Descartes neither indicates how the notion of uncertainty is related to the notions of composition and corruptibility,[29] nor does he give us an explicit theory of moral phenomena and the ethical or meta-ethical rules by which these are governed. He himself recognizes that he knows almost nothing of the three sciences represented by the branches of the philosophical tree;[30] and both the preface and the conclusion of the *Principles of Philosophy* state clearly that the program of Cartesian theory has not yet reached the point where it can scientifically treat questions of medicine and morality. Even physics has not yet been completed. The only completed part is the realm of non-living material things, with the exception of minerals. If we accept Descartes's framework, how can we write a moral treatise if we have not even developed a philosophy of animals and of the human composite?

> But in order to bring the plan to its conclusion I should need to explain in the same manner the nature of all the particular bodies which exist on the earth, namely minerals, plants, animals and, most importantly, man. And then to conclude, I should have to give an exact account of medicine, morals and mechanics. This is what I should have to do in order to give to mankind a body of philosophy that is quite complete.

We still need a lot of time, money and work to accomplish this, however.[31]

By the word "exact" in the penultimate sentence of this text, Descartes seems to indicate the difference between the nonscientific consideration of morality, such as we find it in the account of provisional morality and

29. Compare this text to Descartes' letter of September 1, 1645 to Elizabeth. He distinguishes there between two sorts of pleasure and insists on the confusion that characterizes the pleasures of the spirit, inasmuch as it is joined to the body (*AT* IV, p. 262; *PL*, p. 168).

30. *AT* IXB, p. 14; *PW* I, p. 186.

31. *AT* IXB, p. 14; *PW* I, p. 188. The same self-criticism is found in the *Principles of Philosophy* IV, n.188 (*AT* IXB, p. 315; *PW* I, p. 279): "Up till now I have described this earth and indeed the whole visible universe as if it were only a machine of which one should consider nothing else than the shapes and movements of its parts." As a kind of appendix, Descartes then provides a rapid theory of the objects of our senses (nn.189–206), on the basis of which he claims "that there is no phenomenon in nature which I have omitted to consider in this treatise," and that he has "proved that the entire visible or sensible world contains nothing apart from the things I have given an account of here" (n.199, *AT* IXB, p. 317–18; *PW* I, p. 283–84). Even if we admit this, the fact remains that Descartes did not treat the human composite as such.

some epistolary arguments,[32] and "the most perfect morality" which should be a well-grounded, exact and evident science. The *Passions of the Soul* is his last effort to scientifically ground the most urgent thing in life,

---

32. Descartes' letter of September 15, 1645, written to Elizabeth (*AT* IV, pp. 287ff; *PL,* p. 171–74), gives several examples of moral prescriptions which should find a place in a scientific moral system, although they are not yet methodically grounded. A first norm commands us to love God and to "accept calmly all the things which happen to us as expressly sent by God." A second orders us to take care of our soul above all, and to scorn death and chance. Another norm, also very fundamental but neither obvious nor proved, says that "the interests of the whole, of which each of us is a part, must always be preferred to those of our individual personality—with measure, however, and discretion."

In his letter to Elizabeth of August 4, 1645, Descartes criticizes Seneca, not because Seneca was mistaken in the content of his normative ethic, but because he did not ground its principles sufficiently: "[. . .] it seems to me, Seneca should have taught us all the principal truths whose knowledge is necessary to facilitate the practice of virtue and to regulate our desires and passions, and thus to enjoy natural happiness. That would have made his book the finest and most useful that a pagan philosopher could have written" (*AT* IV, p. 262; *PL,* p. 166). By "pagan philosopher" Descartes means "a philosopher [. . .], unenlightened by faith, with only natural reason to guide him" (p. 164), a philosopher thus like Descartes himself, who claims that he can completely abstract from his faith and Christian theology.

Descartes' distinction between a correct but ungrounded morality and a scientifically grounded morality explains why, in the same letter, he distinguishes between "solid contentment," which springs from a real knowledge of the good, and the resulting contentment of a resolution grounded in the most probable judgement. Having reminded us of the rule that we must let ourselves be guided by that which seems true or probable to us at the moment of action, Descartes sketches the project of moral science and the goal of the whole Cartesian revolution as a condition of "the greatest happiness," and thus of perfect wisdom. "It is not necessary that our reason should be free from error; it is sufficient if our conscience testifies that we have never lacked resolution and virtue to carry out whatever we judge the best course. So virtue by itself is sufficient to make us content in this life. But virtue unenlightened by intellect can be false: that is to say, the will and resolution to do well can carry us to evil courses, if we think them good; and in such a case the contentment which virtue brings is not solid." On the contrary, "the right use of reason . . . by giving a true knowledge of good, prevents virtue from being false; by accommodating it to licit pleasures makes it easy to practice; and by making us know the condition of our nature sets bounds to our desires. So we must recognize that the greatest felicity of man depends on the right use of reason; and consequently that the study which leads to its acquisition is the most useful occupation one can take up" (p. 166).

In the same way, section 49 of *The Passions of the Soul* notes a "great difference between the resolutions which proceed from some false opinion and those which are based solely on knowledge of the truth" (*AT* XI, p. 368; *PW* I, p. 347). This distinction sheds light on the phrase already quoted from the *Principles,* where Descartes extols the utility of his philosophy, arguing that "the study of philosophy is more necessary

but it is only a fragment of what must be known in order to achieve the very wisdom that is the goal of the Cartesian undertaking.[33]

IV.

The *third maxim* shows that Descartes draws on the neo-Stoic morality of his time, which seems reasonable to him, since it teaches that we must not want or desire the impossible.[34] He admits that it is not always easy to will in accordance with reason. In order to accomplish this he recommends a spiritual method which he also inherits from the tradition: a more or less secularized version of meditation in the Ignatian style.

The *fourth maxim* formulates a condition of true philosophy:

> Finally, to conclude this moral code, I decided to review the various occupations which men have in this life, in order to try to choose the best. Without wishing to say anything about the occupations of others,

---

for the regulation of our morals and our conduct in this life than is the use of our eyes to guide our steps" (*AT* IXB, p. 3; *PW* I, p. 180). The same distinction appears in the context of the difference between the three levels of consciousness: 1. "Living without philosophizing," which is a way of "having one's eyes closed without ever trying to open them"; 2. Having one's eyes closed and following the conduct of someone else (if we think of the authority Descartes grants to the "laws and customs" of his country, this level seems to be that of provisional morality); 3) "Using one's own eyes to get about," which corresponds to moral conduct grounded in the certain, and hence scientific, knowledge of truth.

33. Cf. the letter of June 15, 1646 to Chanut: "what I have written is only distantly connected with moral philosophy . . . "; "the safest way to find out how we should live is to discover first what we are, what kind of world we live in, and who is the Creator of this world, or the Master of the house we live in. But . . . there is a very great distance between the general notion of heaven and earth, which I have tried to convey in my *Principles,* and the detailed knowledge of the nature of man, which I have not yet discussed. However, I must say in confidence that what little knowledge of physics I have tried to acquire has been a great help to me in establishing sure foundations in moral philosophy. . . . So that instead of finding ways to preserve life, I have found another, much easier and surer way, which is not to fear death, without, however, being depressed about it." "I am spending some time also on thinking about particular moral problems. Last winter, for instance, I sketched a little treatise on the nature of the Passions of the Soul. . . ." (*AT* IV, p. 440; *Oeuvres philosophiques,* vol. III, pp. 656–65). Cf. note 16.

34. *AT* VI, p. 25–27; *PW* I, p. 123–24. The same rule is given in letters to Elizabeth (*AT* IV, p. 262; *PL,* p. 165); and to Christine (*AT* V, p. 81; *PL,* p. 226); and in the *Passions of the Soul,* art. 146 (*AT* XI, p. 439; *PW* I, p. 380).

I thought I could do no better than to continue with the very one I was engaged in, and devote my whole life to cultivating my reason and advancing as far as I could in the knowledge of the truth, following the method I had prescribed for myself.[35]

Only those who choose to spend their lives cultivating their reason and progressing as much as possible in the knowledge of the truth can rely on the customs and opinions whose authority in moral matters has been stipulated in the first three maxims. The last maxim is not an appendix reserved for private use only. For, as Descartes specifically states, it formulates the pattern from which the first three borrow their indispensable foundation. None of the maxims would have any value if the path of the philosopher did not promise a personal knowledge that replaces the authorities on which he had depended with the autonomy of a self-justifying science. With regard to the first and second maxims, Descartes says that he would never have been able to rely on other people's opinions had he not already been convinced that he could arrive at better and more certain judgments by the use of his own reason, "in case there were any." The third maxim also presupposes the progress of autonomous knowledge, notably of the knowledge of all the true goods, both those that do not depend on us, and those that—like virtue—are in our power.[36]

According to the criteria of Cartesian science, provisional morality is based on the sands of a "moving earth," without being grounded on "rock or clay."[37] Inasmuch as we must live and act, we must be

---

35. *AT* VI, pp. 27–28; *PW* I, pp. 124–25.

36. Understood in this way, the fourth maxim of the *Discourse on the Method* bears a resemblance to the first rule of morality which Descartes gives in his letter of August 4, 1645 to Elizabeth (*AT* IV, p. 262; *PL,* p. 168): that one should "employ one's mind as well as one can, to know what should or should not be done in all the circumstances of life." In both cases, the distinction Descartes makes between the path of science and the conduct of one's life, poses difficulties. The third rule in the letter corresponds to the third maxim of the *Discourse;* but the maxim that, as second in the letter, insists on the autonomy of reason in relation to the passions and appetites, has no counterpart in the *Discourse.* We can only say that the second maxim in this latter work also regards firmness of resolution. The first maxim of the *Discourse* has no parallel in the letter cited, although the problem of a critique of common opinions and customs, which this maxim inevitably poses, is touched upon in the remarks that another letter offers, in the context of the first chapter of Seneca's *De Vita Beata.* Cf. also the letter to Elizabeth, August 18, 1645 (see note 15).

37. *AT* VI, p. 29; *PW* I, p. 125.

content with a ground and a path that lack certainty. Because the urgency of an exact and clear science involves delaying a scientific and certain ethics, a philosopher who is also an honest man, lets himself be guided by the impure reason concealed in the mores and opinions of his epoch. Pure and unmixed reason is found only in the domain of theory, which is separated from the concerns of practical conduct. The project of a secure ethics demands that we spend a long time concentrating on questions of pure theory, even if this means taking up the problems of practical life only after science has reached its completion.

The conversion to pure theory for the sake of constructing a fully justified science of morality stands in singular contrast to the itineraries drawn up by the European tradition of spiritual guidance. Whereas the latter emphasize a deepening of the desire for God and combine charitable practices with meditations on the meaning of charity, the Cartesian philosopher leaves practice to the mores and codes of a more or less civilized society and to the good sense of people who lack the vices of excess. He protects his concentration on pure theory against the intrusions of practical and social concerns. Instead of an asceticism modeled after the sufferings of a persecuted but just man who is willing to sacrifice himself for others, Descartes advocates a sober utilitarianism motivated by the desire to master the world, conserve health and regulate the conduct of individual and social life in a prudent and happy way.[38] The desert of nihilism and the nights of anguish that all spiritual travelers have to cross are replaced by the methodically regulated experience of a conversion to science. "*Semel in vita,*" one should put an end to all radical doubt in order to establish oneself on the unshakable rock of one's own conscience which functions as an absolute principle. In fact, the end of insecurity only comes with the discovery that everything that appears clear and distinct is guaranteed by the truth of an infinite God.[39] Once we are certain of this, we can concentrate on the path we have to follow according to a prearranged and fixed method in order to accomplish the

---

38. *AT* VI, p. 62; *PW* I, pp. 142–43: "and thus to make ourselves, as it were, lords and masters of nature." Research on the frequency of the words *power, to have, possession, certainty, assurance,* and so on, and on the power these words wield in Cartesian texts, would no doubt reveal the practico-theoretic motivation which is behind the Cartesian project.

39. *AT* VI, pp. 42–43.

proposed program. All the battles and experiences that the masters of spirituality since Plato and Origen have described or stylized, all the meetings, transformations, adventures, sufferings, and passions along the path to wisdom are annulled in one instant by the simple decision to trust only clear and distinct evidence in conjunction with an understanding that refuses to accept conjectures.

V.

Descartes's supposition that the philosopher can live two lives at the same time clears the way for theoretical opinions. Because I do not want to be deceived by anything, I must eliminate everything that can be put into doubt, conserving only that which is so certain that even the most distrusting person cannot doubt it. This involves narrowing the field of appearances until we hit upon something that is undeniable and thus resists the infinite capacity of the will to affirm or deny. To be completely rational, this narrowing should be regulated with a view to the decisive discovery of a place or a point where we can finally lay the foundations of a sure and lasting construction. This is why a *method* and a *logic* precede the search for a fundamental site. Before metaphysics, which Descartes takes to be the most radical part of science, there is thus a *logic* or doctrine of "the method of rightly conducting one's reason and seeking the truth in the sciences."

If we have learned anything from post-Hegelian philosophy, and especially from Nietzsche and Heidegger, it is that no logic is innocent, because it is always also an ontology (disguised or not), full of presuppositions that cannot be justified by this very same logic. In his examination of Cartesian logic, Heidegger tried to sketch the ontological position entailed by it, that is, its specific way of dealing with the world and one's own particular mode of practicing philosophy. But Heidegger himself follows the Cartesian and modern tradition of philosophy insofar as he, too, indefinitely postpones the philosophical consideration of ethical questions. Nevertheless, it should be clear that all ontology is necessarily also a fundamental ethics, inasmuch as every attempt to think the being of beings (which is always also a *taking up* and *acceptance* of a position) inevitably embraces a specific attitude and praxis on the basis of affectivity and passion. The "onto-logical" constellation of a specific theory, even if it is "only" a methodology or meta-theory, reflects the profound inspiration of a human life. Every philosophy, including the logic under which it operatives (which can, moreover, be considerably different from the logic made explicit in it) is inspired by a source that precedes the schism between theory and affectivity. The roots of science are also the roots of morality.

VI.

A diagnosis of modern philosophy would have to analyze the fundamental presuppositions of Descartes's logic, which are as much theoretical as affective and practical. In particular, we would have to discuss Heidegger's interpretation of the Cartesian corpus from a perspective more open to the original unity of ontology and fundamental ethics. Here, we can give only a few indications of the hidden morality that seems to have motivated the Cartesian undertaking.

If the fundamental anguish of all human life can be extinguished by a refusal of the insecurity that emerges from the social and cultural life of an epoch that we have neither chosen nor justified, we must count on a wholly private and pure knowledge as the only way of saving ourselves from the situation of "a man who walks alone in the dark."[40] However, neither the dualism of theory and practice involved in this choice, nor his radicalization of doubt prevented Descartes from devoting his scientific endeavor to the sole aim of enabling humanity to possess and master the earth. *Mastery* and *possession* thus constitute the meaning of wisdom's most precious fruit: *utility.* The highest good is understood according to a notion of welfare that begins with consciousness possessing itself as self-consciousness, and the ultimate good is the possession of the entire universe. This self-possession encompasses the mastery of a legislator governing oneself according to rules that assure the organization of all thoughts and actions. The will that rules this legislator is a will to independence. If such a will can be called a power, the profound wish of a Cartesian philosopher would generate an ethics of the will to power. Its wisdom is a combination of science and unfounded praxis.

---

40. *AT* VI, p. 17; *PW* I, p. 119.

VII.

One possible objection to the sketch presented in this chapter is that God plays too large a role in Descartes's emphasis on the difference between human finitude and God's infinity on which we depend at every moment for our existence and the truth of what appears to us.

In fact, the "thinking I" on which the edifice of knowledge must be constructed, includes not only a secure intuition of its own essence and existence, but also the indubitable certainty that God guarantees the truth of our clear and distinct ideas. Doesn't the third *Meditation* identify the idea of the infinite too quickly with "a substance that is infinite, independent, supremely intelligent, supremely powerful," and with the creator, the author, and the cause of "both myself and anything else that exists"? Is Descartes not too prejudiced, when he states that the presence of the Infinite in consciousness is indicated by an idea that contains so much objective reality that it can only have been placed there by the Infinite itself, and by concluding that God, by putting this idea in me, has imprinted his mark on his work?[41]

The quoted phrases abound in expressions Descartes inherited from the medieval philosophy that had developed within the Christian framework. He forwards them without feeling the need to fully justify them. What he preserves from the traditional doctrine is not so much a clarification of the original and preconscious relation that links man to God, but the certainty that we can trust in the evidence of phenomena and ideas that appear to us. Once in a lifetime, one must be certain that an infinite God is the guarantor of our clear and distinct thoughts. Then, having established this universal insurance company, we may forget the difficult task of formulating the proofs that were necessary to secure his existence: it is sufficient to recall the previous conclusion and its accompanying certainty; the path of metaphysics can be abandoned, and the seeker can dedicate himself entirely to the more concrete and useful sciences: physics and its application to mechanics, medicine, and scientific morality.[42] Our earthly tasks and the conduct of a decent life can be accomplished without turning to God in the

---

41. *AT* VII, pp. 45–46; *PW* II, p. 31.

42. Cf. Descartes' response to an objection to the sixth Meditation in Charles Adam, ed., *Entretien avec Burman* (Paris: Vrin, 1975), p. 74.

hope that he will save us from blindness and deception. From now on, humankind is adult and on its own.

And yet, the two last paragraphs of the third *Meditation* do not at all fit with the kind of deism just presented. True, Descartes presents them as a pause or *entr'acte*, that is, as a text on the edge of his philosophical discourse, but he also says that the contemplation and adoration of God, to which the text refers, gives us "the greatest joy of which we are capable in this life." Thus, almost in the exact middle of his six days lasting *exercitia metaphysica*, Descartes devotes some time to a "contemplation of this all-perfect God" that does not obey either the structure of representation or the method of theoretical research. Here Descartes is not studying the idea of God, but rather "pausing" and "dwelling" on the wonder of his attributes. He tells us in first person language that he "gazes" "with wonder and adoration" at "the beauty of this immense light, at least so far as the eye of my mind, which is somehow blinded by it, can bear it."[43]

We must scrutinize all the words that Descartes uses here in order to draw from them all their concentrated wealth. By showing the possibility of responding to that which is most perfect, his text points here at a very different way to wisdom than the scientific one, a way much closer to the precartesian philosophy for which he has shown his scorn. For the sake of brevity, however, I will restrict myself to make only a few remarks.

Descartes states that we should "believe through faith that the supreme happiness of the other life consists solely in the contemplation of the divine majesty," and that "experience tells us in this very moment that this same contemplation, albeit incomparably less perfect, grants us the greatest joy of which we are capable in this life." Thus he formulates the most fundamental thesis of ethics, to which all other theses must point as their source and apex.

The style of this contemplation is not at all similar to the methodical thought Descartes proposes as the right way to metaphysical truth. The passage cited continues the Augustinian tradition, according to which the realm of ideas is animated by another mode of intentionality than the scientific one: that of prayer and admiration, gratitude, hope

---

43. *AT* VII, p. 52; *PW* II, p. 36 (translation modified).

and adoration. The God of contemplation is not an "insurer" of propositional truth but a dazzling light that we can neither know nor understand. This does not at all prevent us from recognizing this light as coming from God, but such a recognition presupposes a kind of contemplation that grows out of adoration. In the *Confessions* of Saint Augustine the conceptual search for truth is integrated with ongoing prayer. In the *Proslogion* of Anselm, thinking begins to detach itself, becoming more studious, although it remains integrated in the praying context. The growing separation of prayer and thought has begun long before Descartes, but his "hexaemeron" still contains the residue of the twofold intentionality common to Augustine and Anselm. All three thus testify that the ultimate "usefulness" of demonstrative discourse is its capacity to direct human conduct towards a kind of happiness that goes beyond the capacities of an ego trapped in the finite consciousness of a finite world and itself.

Returning from the end of the third *Meditation* to its center, we recognize that the idea of the infinite cannot be a product—dream, projection or idol—of our thought. If it is true that the idea of God does not offer us an object of study, but rather dazzles us by its incomprehensibility,[44] then it follows that the cogito itself is and always remains obscure. The great clarity of the infinite is not captured by an idea that is found along side other ideas in consciousness, sharing with them a more or less similar status. It cannot be ranked in a totality according to an order of different levels, limits and degrees. The wonder of this so-called idea goes beyond our capacity to understand it, and thus shows us that we cannot fully possess our own consciousness. We find ourselves inhabited by an "idea" that is too big, too strange and too enigmatic to be an idea. This enigma bears a singular resemblance to the Platonic idea of the Good, which is not an idea either.[45] Being neither the sun nor the light, but rather something like the nonvisible and untouchable source from which all light and affection come, it is responsible for the fact that we can experience the wonders of the universe and recognize them for what they are.

---

44. Cf. *AT* VII, pp. 45–46, *PW* II, pp. 31–32; *AT* IX, p. 89, *PW* II, p. 61; *AT* IXB, p. 33; *PW* I, p. 236; *PL,* pp. 8–12; *PL,* pp. 171–74 and 208–18.

45. See my *Platonic Transformations: With and After Hegel, Heidegger, and Levinas* (Lanham: Rowman and Littlefield, 1997), pp. 32, 97–98.

In the light of this transcendence, consciousness cannot remain a gaze that thematizes the infinite, as if it were an object for a panoramic consciousness. The mind must change itself by bowing before that which is absolutely other than all objectifying thought. Surprised by the infinite Other, consciousness does not simply abandon its desire to master and possess the world, but, being delivered from anguish by recognition, it becomes respondent and responsible rather than obsessed by its own originality.

To contemplate God, a few meditations are not enough; the only serious way to recognize the obscure presence of the Infinite is involvement, filled with wonder, in the social and historical reality of the world. Not only natural and cultural phenomena then surprise us by their amazing incomprehensibility; my very own existence continually points to an Enigma than can neither assure nor be assured. More than insurance, we need the risky wisdom of decided travelers.

9

Philosophy and Christianity
(An Hour with Pascal)

For David Tracy

ANYONE WHO REFLECTS on the relations between Christianity and philosophy encounters a number of difficult questions, such as the following:

1. What do we mean by "Christianity?"

2. What is "philosophy?"

3. What relations have developed in the past between the different varieties of Christianity and philosophy?

4. How are the different versions of Christianity and philosophy currently related to each other?

5. What sorts of relations need to be developed between Christianity and philosophy, both now and in the future, and how can these relations contribute to a good and successful life?

This chapter will offer only a fragment of the reflection required to deal with these questions. Moreover, not all the assertions made here will be completely argued, but that is no exception for either philosophy or theology.

PHILOSOPHY

More than ever before, professional philosophers are debating what philosophy is and how it must be practiced. A neutral manner of determining, at least in a provisional way, what philosophy is and what it wants to be, avails itself of the words "experience" and "thinking" and represents philosophy as a unique combination of both. All philosophers base themselves on one or more sorts of experience and pursue reflective insight.

For a good grasp of this description, it is important from the outset that we not restrict experience to the sort of empirical material that is viewed by modern natural science as the only serious, objective, and "exact" basis for knowledge. All authentic experiences of an affective, moral, erotic, or religious nature are likewise components of the *empeiria* and the experiments in which philosophical thinking lives. Such experiences are described and celebrated in exemplary ways—long before and after the origin of the modern sciences—by poets, sages, prophets, mystics, and philosophers, who still form the most interesting part of Western literature. It is the great but still strongly underestimated significance of phenomenology, practiced by Husserl, Heidegger, Merleau-Ponty, Ricoeur, Levinas, and others, that it preserves the uniqueness of the many ways of experience through which people engage in an understanding of the reality about them and of themselves, and accepts them as the irreplaceable basis for its descriptions and analyses.[1]

The development of the phenomenological movement has made it clear that the idea of an evident givenness of things as they are in and from themselves, prior to all differences in language and culture, was too naïve. We realize now that all contact with reality-as-it-is is already marked by particular perspectives and schemas, which attach themselves to the manner in which we exist in the world and lead our lives. To the extent that the attitude and way of life of societies or individuals has a specific, particular character, things show themselves in a particular light conforming to the particularities of the dominant view and language. The original and immediate givenness of things themselves corresponds to a specific manner of relating with them. We cannot extricate what and how a reality is in itself, independent of a specific culture, language, character, and life-history. We cannot leap over our own rootedness in order to stand eye-to-eye with a not-yet-cultural reality.[2]

---

1. Cf. my "A la recherche de l'expérience vraie," in *Archives de Philosophie* 29 (1966), pp. 348–62, and "Pointers Toward a Dialogic," in *Man and World* 9 (1976), pp. 372–92.

2. In agreement with what is argued here, we must conceive of anyone's philosophizing as one's own way of participating in some cultural traditions and in the ways in which others have passed them on. It is unfeasible to cite all the "influences" thanks to which one has learned to speak in a philosophical manner. Hence, citing a few advisors always does injustice to those who are passed over. Because the first

Because the idea of truth inevitably directs and dominates our think-ing, I necessarily hold fast to the thought of "the thing as it is in itself" and affirm it as the fundamental moment of the phenomena with which we come into contact.[3] We thereby find and move ourselves in a dou-ble contact with reality: it gives itself to knowledge as staged by the peculiarities which make me into this person, a partner in a specific culture, language, and history, and someone who has lived this unique but to a great extent fortuitous life-history. All forms of experience are thus perspectival—and to that extent nonuniversal, contingent, and individual—illuminations of a reality that at the same time reveal and conceal, color and limit its truth.

All experience, even thinking itself, is a particular way of relating to reality. The scientific study of nature that has characterized modern culture is an example of such a particular relation to things. Previously it was not accepted as the obvious way of dealing with reality and presently we question more vehemently than ever its overall validity. The rage of making everything into the object of a problematizing and representational thought and to understand even humanity and culture from such a perspective is a manner of reflection on that which per-tains to a specific epoch with particular—and to a certain extent fortu-itous—tendencies, customs, and interests.

Even with regard to the 2,500-year-long tradition of Western phi-losophy, we must ask ourselves whether it is not colored by a partic-ular character. Has this history of amazing discoveries and refreshing interpretations of reality not restricted and bent the truth or even deformed and obscured it? Heidegger has given us an eye for the ambiguity of the ways in which Descartes and Leibniz, but also Plato and Nietzsche, have at the same time illuminated and concealed the truth of things. When he himself asks to which ruling of the truth we

version of this chapter was my inaugural address at the Catholic University of Nijmegen, I mention here only some of my academic mentors to whom I am particularly grateful: the Franciscans Dr. Adelard Epping, Dr. Clementius Schoonbrood, and Dr. André Schuwer; the Professors of the Institute of Philosophy in Leuven; Paul Ricoeur of the Sorbonne (Paris); and Emmanuel Levinas, who, after my university studies, became a beacon and a friend.

3. I have attempted to show this in the last chapter of my *System and History in Philosophy* (Albany: State University of New York Press, 1986).

owe our modes of relating to the world and history, no more than anyone else does he escape from the unique perspective that has been allotted to him, a perspective that simultaneously fosters and obstructs the truth.

Thinking itself is always attuned in a characteristic mode. Just like all other manners of experience, it is an historical event and not a timeless gaze *sub specie aeternitatis* that would be able to establish once and for all the truth. The progress of thought is not a cumulative process and there is no extrahistorical basis for knowledge on which we safely could build further. The presuppositions of thinking must be brought into discussion time and again, because they themselves simultaneously open up and close off truth. The idea of an objective, universal, unrestricted, true and neutral knowledge is not meaningless, since we thereby are in a position to distinguish the finitude of our finite possibilities of truth. Universality might be found in some sort of convergence or affinity that binds the many ways to truth together, but we do not have at our disposal a nonperspectival gaze that escapes the variability of history, so that we would be able to look down on the totality of particular standpoints and manners of thinking. An uninvolved standpoint is not possible, if it is to mean more than an abstractly conceivable "point" to which all serious and genuine approaches refer and perhaps converge. The only hope we have is that our philosophizing proceeds in the right direction, and that our manner of thinking offers us, in spite of and thanks to its limitations and obscurations, enough familiarity with the reality of world, persons, and history to lead a good life.

For that is the point of it all, is it not? A life that is worthwhile contains a certain measure of truth. For untruth, inauthenticity, and lying make life hollow and worthless. A good life is, in one way or another, "in the truth." It is not necessary to be engaged in science or philosophy, but *if* the professional practice of philosophy constitutes a great part of your life, then the truth your life needs cannot bypass your philosophizing. The thoughtful experiences and the experienced thought that constitute your philosophy do not, then, hover above the decisive experiment from which you must draw all the wisdom that can be gained in earthly existence: the unique and unrepeatable experiment of human life, which will once appear to have been more or less wise and experienced. The rigor of description, analysis, formalization, determination, and argumentation after which a professional philosopher strives is restricted by the experimental side of a lived life, which is the issue "on trial." The methodical techniques that one has appropriated owe not only their subject matter, but also their orientation to the thinker's affective, practical, and pragmatic involvement in an experimental history.

As we try to reconstruct from their writings what happened and still happens when great or small philosophers are serious about thinking, we cannot completely detach the theoretical elements from the affective and practical elements that constitute their life in a radical way. The thinking of philosophers for whom philosophy is more than an uncommitted game shows where their heart is. Philosophical texts bear witness not only to the brain from which they originate, but also to the most radical dimensions from which their author lives: the *erōs* that animates their advance and stance. "Logic" and the whole ensemble of techniques that characterize an expert in philosophy lose their gravity as soon as they are separated from the existential search for the meaning of a socially and historically situated life. If a serious philosophy is bound up by inner ties with experience and prudence, philosophy is much more than a discipline that can be learned in the university. *Theoria* does not succeed when it separates itself from its pretheoretical, emotional, experimental, and practical roots. The human whole—with its individual, social, historical, and religious articulations—is the reality on which an earnest philosophy reflects in order to discover how the nonlogical elements of meaning influence this very same reflection.

THEORY AND WISDOM

From Descartes to Hegel, modern philosophy has represented philosophy as an autonomous theory obligated to ground everything that is true and worthwhile on a neutral, "objective" experience and a noninvolved, distant logic. Philosophy was seen as a superscience of leadership for societies and individuals. Some went so far that they conceived of everything that was true and valuable as a direct or indirect expression of Thought itself—and for them, this Thought was a suprahistorical, eternal, and absolute Principle. However, even for them philosophizing was more than an a theoretical skill; it was inter-woven with their existential search for a good and successful life.[4]

In Greek and Hellenistic antiquity, a philosopher was someone who coupled logical and methodical thinking with a well-conducted behav-ior on the basis of a balanced affectivity. Thus, philosophy pointed to a way of life rather than to erudition or scholarship. The philosopher was not only the specialist of a particular discipline; he understood the art of life. He was well-versed in the main task of humans as humans (*to ergon tou anthrōpou*), which Aristotle analyzed in his *Ethics*.[5] The wisdom that expressed itself in an experienced *theoria* embraced the level-headedness that grows out of a prudent conduct of life; it was a conquest to which philosophical discipline and meditation were sup-posed to lead. For the enlightened Greek who no longer believed in the old myths, philosophy was a road to salvation.

It is obvious that the history of philosophy presents a very different character if it is seen as a sequence of purely theoretical systems or rather as a repeated attempt to answer the central questions of human life along the way of meditative experience. A fruitful recalling of ear-lier philosophies can retrieve for our own time the historical experi-ments in which thoughtful experience has played an exemplary role.

Not only the ancient Greeks, but also many Jews, Christians, and Muslims have defended the ideal of an integral *philosophia* that coin-cides with a well-conducted life. Saint Augustine, for example, sees "the love of wisdom" as a passionate mode of thought that looks forward to an encounter with the God of Jesus Christ,[6] because he believes that the *sophia* for which philosophy longs is none other than Christ, whom the apostle Paul calls the "wisdom and power of God" (1 Cor. 1:24).

---

4. If Plato, Anselm, Bonaventure, Descartes, Pascal, Leibniz, Hegel, and Levinas indeed illustrate this statement, modern metaphilosophy and methodology might be considered too abstract to do justice to the philosophical praxis, including its modern version. Has the philosophy of the last centuries then lived in an illusion? Has its preoccupation with consciousness and self-consciousness failed to fulfill the old imperative "know yourself!" from which it originated?

5. Aristotle, *Nicomachean Ethics*, 1097b22.

6. Cf. Etienne Gilson, *Introduction à l'étude de Saint Augustin* (Paris: Vrin, 1931), pp. 38–42 and the following quotes: *De moribus Ecclesiae*, I, 17, 31: "Nam si sapientia et veritas non totis animi viribus concupiscatur, inveniri nullo pacto potest"; *De Civitate Dei* XIX, 1: "nulla est homini causa philosophandi nisi beatus sit"; VIII, 1: "De theologia quippe, quam naturalem vocant [. . .] cum philosophis est habenda conlatio;

With this reference we have stepped over the border between philosophy and Christianity, but before I focus on the border or chasm or bridge between the two, I would like to dwell a moment on the question whether it is still possible for us to practice philosophy as a central concern of life itself—as more, thus, than a profession that one can engage in without at the same time caring about the ultimate meaning of a human life. The answer to this question will yield little benefit for the national economy; neither will it open new possibilities for technology or science; but it might shift the borders between academic philosophy and the rest of human culture. And perhaps such a correction of the borders is all the more important as training for professional philosophy results more and more in unemployment.

I risk here the hypothesis that the interest of genuine philosophers is less a desire to reconstruct the universe as an articulated system than the much more radical interest of life's experiment with itself. The egological postulate of the supreme Archimedean overview, in alliance with the ideal of human autarchy, has been worn out. The modern systems, which originated in such a view, are now in ruins; within the domain of philosophy, modernity lives on in the shape of most ambitious but irreparably unfinished monuments. The idea of total verifiability and an all-encompassing grasp is forsaken, although it retains its charm and even a certain necessity.[7] Experience and thinking are not the pure products of a self-determined activity, but specific manners of assimilating a received inheritance. Philosophy is more like a destiny or vocation than a work of production.

Without going into an analysis of prereflexive levels and motives from which our reflecting cannot entirely free itself, I want here only to point at the most radical foundation or relation by which a person's stance is ultimately determined. Let us call this root or ground "faith." This word, then, must not be heard as the sign for a true or untrue

---

quorum ipsum nomen, si Latine interpretemur, amorem sapientiae profitetur. Porro, si sapientia Deus est, per quem facta sunt omnia, sicut divina auctoritas veritasque monstravit, verus philosophus est amator Dei"; *Contra Julianum* IV, 14, 72: "Obsecro te, non sit honestior philosophia Gentium quam nostra christiana quae una est vera philosophia, quandoquidem studium vel amor sapientiae significatur hoc nomine."

7. The *attempt* to encompass and understand the universe (*ta panta* and *to pan*) should not be given up, because all the issues of philosophy refer to the universe as the context that co-determines their meaning and truth.

opinion or an intellectual "holding-as-true" (*Fürwahrhalten*) of particular pronouncements, facts, or dogmas, but rather as a radical position,
a stance and a movement of the heart (and therefore also of sense and
reason), a manner of relating to the ultimate meaning of "it all" such
as it "now actually" is. Each human life is animated and oriented by
some sort of faith concerning the meaning of existence; many varieties
of faith are possible and actual, as is shown in the different moods and
attitudes of contented and bitter, enthusiastic, nostalgic, distressed, and
resigned people. That faith is a universal and fundamental phenomenon, I cannot demonstrate in this chapter; but it does not seem an out-
rageous assumption that the thought of Christians, as an integral part
of their life, must be connected with their ultimate belief.

CHRISTIANITY

The word "Christianity" has perhaps even more meanings than "philosophy." It includes a whole series of historical phenomena involving a
group of people who declare their devotion to Jesus of Nazareth, in
whom they see the definitive revelation of God. Between "the pure
Gospel," such as it was practiced and preached by Jesus, and the history
of the Christian Churches, in which the proclamation and practice of the
Gospel compromised with power, violence, stupidity, phobias, and lies,
there are countless differences, but also a certain continuity to be further
determined. Purity and kitsch, authenticity and semblance, goodness and
degeneracy have become interwoven and it is a chief task of Christian
theology to distinguish the chaff from the grain in this tangle. Whether
they can completely be separated remains to be seen, since the kernel of
Christian belief cannot be obtained separately, but only in one of the concrete versions that it has assumed in the course of history.

With regard to the relations between Christianity and philosophy, I
will limit myself to a few characteristics of Christian existence while
emphasizing their cognitive aspects.

To begin with, faith means for a Christian that in everything the primary and ultimate issue is God. Radical and total devotion to God participates in the relations that connect Jesus with God and God with Jesus
and all other persons. Faith is not primarily the acceptance of theses or
statements, but the most radical form of trust and devotion. It expresses

itself in an unconditional receptivity and gratitude, and thus in a joyful experience of the earth, the body, intersubjectivity, and history. As participation in a collective history, faith is being at home in a specific tradition that is kept alive by speaking and practice and documented by canonic writings. Transmission and faithful transformation of the Same are the forces by which Christianity remains a living history.

Christians experience themselves as here and now belonging to a historical community, whose traditions heed God's alliance with humanity. Through their faith, they take part in a history of Compassion, the signs of which they perceive in the history of Israel and of the followers of Jesus, the Christ. One of the ways to summarize this history focuses on God's "incarnation," but other perspectives are possible, such as those of the "assumption," "liberation," "resurrection," or "deification" of humanity.

Many expressions and explanations of Christian faith are possible; grace has created a space wherein many variations of stance and advance are possible. But two fundamental lines are clear, outside of which no genuine Christianity is possible. Since it deals in everything with God as turned to humans and with humans as oriented toward God, faith stands or falls with a threefold relation that could be summarized by words such as "mercy," "love," "generosity," "goodness," and so on, if those words were not all too worn out. This threefold relation consists in benevolence of God toward the human world, of humanity toward God, and of human individuals toward each other. (To what extent and how a similar benevolence of human beings to nonhuman creatures must be added to these relations is another question I would like to reserve for another occasion.) The Scriptures in which Christians seek the guiding principle for their life express the indissoluble intertwining of these relations by representing the love of God and the mutual love of human individuals as moments of one single love.[8] Christians know themselves to be taken up in an historical constellation of relationships which make them coresponsible for the continuation of divine benevolence.

---

8. Lev. 19:18, 34; Deut. 6:4–13; 10:18–19; Exod. 22:20–26; 23:12; Mark 12:23–33; Gal. 5:6, 22; 6:2; Rom. 13:8–9; Col. 3:14; I John 4:20–21; 5:2; II John 5, and so on.

At the same time, Christians are children of their own age, with which they share a great number of ideological, political, and moral conceptions. They are not immune to the prevailing spirit of relativism and indifference and they do not escape the general ethos of present-day culture, not even when they explicitly try to turn away from these. Because all times and cultures possess their own possibilities and impossibilities, Christians always face the question of how far the concretization of the Gospel allows an engagement with the characteristic customs and conceptions of the society of which they want to be loyal members. This situation contains the danger that they might unjustly condemn specific aspects of their time, not because these would be opposed to the Gospel, but because they themselves stubbornly adhere to outworn elements of a former culture with which their beliefs had contracted an alliance. The history of Christian conservatism and fundamentalism provides sufficient examples of such superstitions. Perhaps we could reserve the term "progressivism" or "modernism" for the opposite position, which falsely presupposes that all that is actual, thereby alone is already true and good. The battle between conservative and progressive Christians and the attempt to incarnate faith in a timely version concentrates itself by its very nature on the most obvious changes between yesterday and today. Hence the center stage is often filled with controversies about new customs and viewpoints, such as those concerning the exercise of authority or the rituals of sexuality. Sometimes we let ourselves be diverted by the hottest topics from the main concerns around which the Gospel revolves. Incessant moralism, for example, is such a diversion from the main point, if it overwhelms the religious core of loyalty to one another in loyalty to God.

CHRISTIAN AND PHILOSOPHER

If Christianity no less than philosophy implies a particular way of life, the question arises whether one can be a Christian and a philosopher at the same time. Are their ways compatible?

Many answers have been given to this question. The father of modern philosophy, Descartes, testified to his unconditional devotion to the Catholic church, while trying to develop his philosophy independently from any appeal to his religious life. In the meantime, it has become clear that he in fact borrowed several of his prejudices from seventeenth century French Catholicism, even though he might not have been aware of this.

Heidegger likewise posits in his *Introduction to Metaphysics* a sharp division between faith and philosophy. According to him, Christians cannot philosophize; if they try, they deceive their interlocutors since they have already answered the essential questions in a dogmatic way. Consequently, the philosophizing of Christians is a mere semblance: an apologetic "proof" of the truth that they think they already have in hand.[9]

In his first letter to the Christians of Corinth, Paul, too, seems to express an irresolvable contrast between the Gospel and philosophy, when he opposes "the wisdom of the world," which he also calls "human wisdom" and "the wisdom of the wise," to "the wisdom of God," which is revealed on Jesus' cross, and therefore is viewed by "the people" as "foolishness" (1 Cor. 1:18–2:16). It is clear, however, that "the world," "the people," and "the wise" in Paul's thought do not allude to the essence of humanity, world, or philosophizing, but to the arrogance of those who are not open to "the spirit of God."[10] The arrogance of the self-proclaimed "wise" should not prevent more humble persons from making the spirit of truth philosophically fruitful. The difference between the two sorts of people resides not in a contrast between independent thinking and slavish obedience, but in their being open or closed to the ultimate mystery.

According to Saint Augustine, philosophy and the Gospel can very well be reconciled with each other. Like all the dimensions of a culture—from hygiene and sports to rhetoric, morality, and religion—a great philosophy is an admirable achievement, but it is inspired by a specific spirit, which is not necessarily divine. Pious as well as mean-spirited philosophies are possible, but even God-hating and misanthropic philosophies can be corrected and purified.[11]

---

9. Martin Heidegger, *Einführung in die Metaphysik* (1953) (Tübingen: Niemeyer, 1966), pp. 5–6; *GA* 40, pp. 8–9.

10. Cf. Rom. 3:27 and 4:2; 1 Cor. 1:29 and 4:7.

11. Cf. Rom. 1:18–32; Acts 17:22–29; 19:21; Heinrich Schlier, *Die Zeit der Kirche,* 2nd ed. (Freiburg: Herder, 1958), pp. 29–37.

How does the thoughtful experience of a modern person in search of independence relate to a Christian's commitment to the praxis of faith? Spinoza and Hegel thought that Christian faith contained the most important truths, but also that the philosopher comprehends them in a more adequate manner. They overestimated the reach of thought and underestimated the radicality of affective determinations that provide, with their own sort of precision, a deeper certainty and a more spacious housing than the clarity of concepts can offer. Christianity is not a doctrine, but a living familiarity with the deepest meaning of existence. Its cognitive elements can, but need not, be explicated in logical or sophical form.

Pascal's Mémorial

For an answer to the question of whether a Christian can also be a philosopher—and conversely, whether a philosopher can also be a Christian—we find inspiration in the often-quoted text known as the *mémorial* of Blaise Pascal, who was as much a fervent Christian as a philosopher. The first words of this text, "God of Abraham, God of Isaac, God of Jacob, not of the philosophers and scholars," introduce a strictly personal prayer that Pascal secretly carried with him until his death, but it can be recognized as a paradigm for Christians who seek God beyond philosophy. A concise commentary on this text may somewhat clarify to what God and how Pascal addressed himself in this prayer.

> The year of grace 1654
> Monday November 23 day of Saint Clement, pope and martyr and
> others according to the martyrologue,
> Eve of Saint Chrysogone martyr and others.
> Since about ten thirty at night until about twelve thirty
>
> FIRE
>
> God of Abraham, God of Isaac, God of Jacob, not of the philosophers
> and the learned
> Certainty, Certainty, Feeling, Joy, Peace.
> God of Jesus Christ.
> My God and your God

Your God shall be my God
Oblivion of the world and everything besides God.
He can only be found along the paths taught in the Gospel.
Grandeur of the human soul.
Just Father, the world has not known you, but I have known you.
Joy, Joy, Joy, Tears of Joy.
I have separated myself from him. _____
Derelequerunt me fontem aquae vivae.
My God, will you leave me? _____
That I may not be separated from him forever.

This is the eternal life that they know you, the only true God and him
    whom you have sent, J. C.
Jesus Christ _____
Jesus Christ _____
I have separated myself from him. I have fled, renounced, crucified him.
That I may never be separated from him! _____
He is kept only along the paths taught in the Gospel.
Total and tender surrender.

The first word, written in capital letters and by way of a title, "FIRE,"
summarizes the state of rapture in which Pascal found himself when
he wrote this text. Instead of an argument, we read an exclamation,
the expression of an overflowing joy; spiritual as well as bodily
peace. Pascal experiences an affective and rock-steady certainty.
Through feeling he knows that he is established on a *fundamentum
inconcussum*,[12] but the nature of this fundament is very different
from the foundation that Descartes saved from his methodical doubt
about all certainties.

Pascal's experience is not a vague feeling of happiness because it
intends, addresses, and communicates with someone: "God." God
addresses and touches him through certainty. God overwhelms him.

---

12. Though Descartes does not use this expression, it renders well his search for
an "unshakable" foundation. Cf. his *Meditationes Metaphysicae,* I, first section: "a
primis fundamentis denuo inchoandum . . ." (*AT* VII, p. 17) and II, first section:
"punctum petebat Archimedes quod esset firmum et immobile, . . . si vel minimum
quid invenero quod certum et inconcussum." (*AT* VII, p. 24) and fourth section: ". . .
illud tantum quod certum est et inconcussum." (*AT* VII, p. 25).

Like a lover who expresses his feelings in such unoriginal phrases as "I love you," Pascal uses Biblical quotes to express the unique experience in which he knows himself to be transformed.[13] The God who overwhelms him here and now in an unfamiliar manner is the God who called Abraham, who gave life to Isaac despite the age of his mother, and who wrestled with Jacob, attacking him so fiercely that Jacob limped for the rest of his life. It is also the God of Jesus of Nazareth, who fulfilled what was begun with Abraham and in whom Pascal sees the summation of God's dealings with humanity. Feeling himself united with God, he describes this commerce with the help of John's words: "This is eternal life, that they may know you, the only true God, and Jesus Christ whom you have sent," while the repetition of Jesus' name ("*Jésus-Christ . . . Jésus-Christ . . .*") summarizes his experience.

Pascal's felt certainty implies a new awareness of the significance of being human: "*grandeur de l'âme humaine.*" A human being is wide and deep enough to be filled by the Infinite. And to know this casts new light on the life of a believer who lives out what he believes and thus experiences the ultimate horizon. His past is characterized by withdrawal from the ultimate Meaning, but the future is welcomed as the possibility of a new experience. There is no guarantee that the certainty he feels is safe from erosion, but faith conquers dread.

Falling in love puts the whole of reality in the shadow of one central concern. This might explain why Pascal places the encounter with God over against the world and everything that is not God: "*Oubli du monde et de tout hormis Dieu.*" However, since God is neither an individual nor a being, he cannot be opposed to anything else; not, for example to the

---

13. Besides the literal or nearly literal quotes from Exod. 3:6 ("I am the God of your fathers, the God of Abraham, the God of Isaac, and the God of Jacob," cf. Matt. 22:32), the letter to the Eph. 1:16 ("the God of our Lord Jesus Christ"), John 20:17 ("my God and your God"), Ruth 1:16 ("your people will be my people and your God will be my God"), John 14:17 ("the world . . . neither sees nor knows Him"), Jer. 2:13 (according to the Vulgate translation: "me derelequerunt fontem aquae vivae"), John 17:3 ("This is eternal life, that they may know you, the only true God, and Jesus Christ whom you have sent"), and Ps. 119:16 ("I will not forget your word," also quoted from the Vulgate), many more words (such as *fire, joy, peace, my God, renounce, crucified, separated, the paths, taught by the Gospel*) allude to Biblical passages. Even the great scholar that Pascal was did not create a new language to put into words the most dramatic revolution of his life. Old phrases relentlessly repeated by millions of people, though always in danger of being worn out, can borrow a new life from genuine experiences.

totality of all beings. "Forgetting the world and all the rest" (*oubli du monde*) is thus not a flight from history. Through its affective anchoring in God, the earth is transformed into God's earthly revelation. That earthly and interhuman relations are implied in Pascal's proclamation "*Jésus-Christ*," might be indicated by the plural he uses in the sentence: "this is eternal life: that they know you . . ." Like many other mystics, however, Pascal is so intensely fascinated by God that he does not explicitly refer to the identity of theophily and philanthropy.

The Living God and the God of "Philosophy"

By opposing the "God of Abraham, Isaac, and Jacob" to "the God of the philosophers and the learned," Pascal seems to cut off his faith from philosophy. But is this impression correct?

As we have already observed, Pascal's text does not present us with an argument but with a prayer, which, at the same time, expresses an overwhelming experience. Pascal rejoices, because now finally—and in a certain sense for the first time—he has encountered the God of the Gospel. He had never experienced anything similar in the study of science and philosophy.

In order to precisely determine what Pascal meant by "the philosophers," a study of many other texts would be necessary, but on the basis of a small selection from his *Pensées* we can safely venture the following sketch. When Pascal, following Saint Paul, dismisses "the foolishness of human science," or when he calls Descartes' enterprise "useless and uncertain," declaring "that the entirety of philosophy is not worth a single hour's exertion,"[14] we must not forget that he sees human *grandeur* as a question of "thinking": "*Pensée fait la grandeur de l'homme*" (n. 346). Although man is only a reed, "he is a thinking reed." "The whole of our dignity exists [. . .] in thinking" (n. 347). "Spaciously the universe includes and engulfs me as a little dot, but through thinking I comprehend the universe" (n. 348). "Let us therefore apply ourselves to good thinking" (n. 347).

---

14. These quotes are found in numbers 74, 78, and 79 of the edition of Pascal's *Pensées et opuscules* by L. Brunschvicg in the *Classiques Hachette* (Paris: Hachette, n.d.), pp. 317–748. The following quotes are also taken from this edition. "La folie de la science humaine" (n.74) seems to be an allusion to Paul's first letter to the Corinthians 1:20.

Thinking is, however, not the same as the practice of reason (*raison*), since for Pascal this word has a more restricted meaning. The work of reason is primarily reasoning, of which mathematics gives the most shining examples. Over against reason stands "the heart" (*le coeur*), which is not only the seat of the affections, but also the organ that provides us with immediate certainty regarding principles on which all thinking relies: "The heart has its own reasons, which reason does not know" (n. 277). "We know the truth not only through reason, but also through the heart. In the latter manner we know the first principles; if reason has no part therein, it does not attain anything through its reasonings, if it tries to combat that knowledge of the heart." "Reason must rely on the knowledge of the heart and instinct and thereupon found its entire demonstration." Especially religious knowledge relies more on feelings than on reasonings: without the feeling of the heart, faith is inhuman and useless (n. 282). For "it is the heart, not reason, that senses God [*sent Dieu*]. This is faith: God [as] sensible to the heart, not to reason" (n. 278).

A reason that is founded only on itself—that is, on its "natural light" (n. 233)—is not in a position to attain the truth. *Either* it finds no genuine certainty in itself and falls into skepticism, such as a series of philosophers from Pyrrhus to Montaigne demonstrates, *or* it expresses itself from the Stoics to Descartes in a dogmatism that conceals its uncertainty with firm proclamations (n. 432, 434). True, a non-Christian philosopher, too, can discover that a mighty and eternal God exists, but if his conviction stops there, his deism remains almost as far removed from the true God as the atheist who denies God's existence (n. 556). The true God has compassion for those who without it would be confined to a miserable condition. Genuine knowledge of God presupposes, besides knowledge of the human misery, the knowledge that compassion is more characteristic of God than might or eternity. Whereas atheism sees only the misery, deism identifies God only as the highest Being. The truth exists in the union of God's compassion with a fallen but saved humanity.

> The God of the Christians is not the mere origin of geometric truths and the arrangement of the elements; that is the God of the heathens and the followers of Epicurus. He is more than a God who exercises his providence in concern for the life and the well-being of humans, in order to give to those who worship Him a blessed life [. . .]. The God of

Abraham, the God of Isaac, the God of Jacob, the God of the Christians is a God of love and comfort; it is a God who fills the heart and soul of those who belong to Him; it is a God who makes them feel how miserable they are on their own and how unlimited his compassion is. He unites himself with the ground of their souls, fills them with humility, joy, trust, and love, and makes them unable to have any other aim than Himself (n. 556).

With this we are back to the *mémorial*, and perhaps we now understand better why the words "Jesus Christ" are the summary of Pascal's "joy, trust, and love." They express precisely the unity of God and humans—a unity which the deists and atheists miss because they are fixed on one-sided interpretations of humanity. We now understand also why Pascal attaches little or no worth to rational proofs for the existence of God or the immortality of the soul. His reason is not so much that he doubts the stringency of such proofs, as the conviction that such knowledge is "useless and sterile" (n. 556). What counts in the end is not a theory about God, but a kind of knowledge that creates intimacy. To know that God is a God of "love and consolation" coincides with an acknowledgment that is itself the beginning of love. "How far is the knowledge of God still from love of God" (n. 280). Thus, "the philosophers" are not in a position to indicate the way that one must go, not even when, like Epictetus, they think very loftily about God (nn. 461, 466–67). However, once one has gone "the ways of the Gospel," the true God reveals himself everywhere—*without giving up his hiddenness*. The entirety of nature and history as revelation of grace, that is Pascal's last word on the significance of what exists. It is also the beginning of a philosophy that respects the experience of a genuinely Christian existence.

PHILOSOPHY AND BELIEF

Origen, Augustine, Anselm, Bonaventure, Thomas, Malebranche, Blondel, Ricoeur, Levinas, and so many other great thinkers have known that it is quite possible as a philosophizing person to remain in close contact with faith in the living God of the Jewish and Christian history. As elucidation of self-experienced phenomena, philosophy presupposes a sensibility that responds as adequately as possible to the manner in which the phenomena present themselves. Thinking about religious phenomena presupposes that one either has experienced them or, through imagination and empathy, revives what others, on the basis of their sensibility, have experienced and described. Whoever is insensitive to religion or holds that all religious experiences are only symptoms of something else, will deny that healthy and enlightened people have such experiences, but if they do not suppress the ultimate questions about meaning, they answer them through a belief of their own. Those philosophers, who think that human thinking indeed can thematize God, might try to continue the old endeavor of proving or postulating, on the basis of our existence in the world and its history, that God necessarily exists. Such an attempt cannot succeed, however, unless the transition from the finite to the Infinite is naturally oriented by a reference to that which transcends all finitude. For, in or between the finite realities connected by the so-called "proofs" of God's existence, no infinity can be found, not even in their totality. If the infinite that is sought is not present from the beginning in the finite reality of thoughtful experience—albeit hidden and only implicit—all endeavors to reason toward it are fruitless. All thinking beyond the borders of the finite expresses a radical longing or desire. In religious experience one undergoes this *erōs* as an unchosen determination that, with or without one's will, rules all thoughts and feelings. The reference that coincides with this desire indicates the "real thing" that, in the end and from the beginning, is *the* issue in philosophy, just as it is in human life.[15] If this ultimate rooting of thought in desire is not made explicit, the so-called "proofs of the existence of God" remain a bloodless display of abstract connections without orientation; they then lack the force to push our thinking forward beyond the finitude of nonabsolute beings and their totality. The desire that points beyond all representations and concepts can become aware of itself by peak experiences of beauty, love, innocence, or wonder, but the best—and certainly indispensable—manner of awaking occurs in the adequate perception of an other person. The other, who looks at me or speaks to me, draws me out of my narcissism. We do not need Socrates to drag us out of the cave of self-concern; a random other, any man, woman, or child provides me by his or

---

15. Cf. Adriaan Peperzak, *Der heutige Mensch und die Heilsfrage,* (Freiburg: Herder, 1972).

her mere presence with an infinite "horizon." A face or a voice is sufficient to disrupt the closed space of "the I." The obligation that thereby imposes itself upon me points simultaneously toward another human being—the "nearest"—and the infinite mystery that thus makes its invisibility strongly present.

If God, as hidden in the neighbor, is the desideratum of our desire—though not an entity (not even the highest one) among other entities—then it becomes doubtful whether one can make God the topic or theme for a demonstration. Can we speak about God without thereby immediately classifying our topic as one of many entities (e.g., the highest) and thus *ipso facto* making it finite? Does not the best manner of distorting or destroying the Ultimate consist in hiding it behind a host of theses? Or worse: by burying it under moralizing prejudices?

If we, by virtue of our humanity, are oriented toward a mystery that surpasses our reasons, this need not impede us to willingly address ourselves *to* it. Prayer reaches farther and is more natural than theology. Since believers, however, cannot simply stop reflecting about that which captivates them most, it is natural for them to pose the question of how their reflection can be integrated into their piety and devotion.

Augustine's *Confessions* and Anselm's *Proslogion* are attempts to solve this problem. In these texts, personal prayers alternate with argumentative passages. The elevation of the mind to God, to whom these authors refer all things and their totality, forms the framework within which their speech expounds. The ideal of a religious contemplation implies a kind of speech that is completely integrated in a passion that conducts not only "heart and soul" but also "understanding and will" toward the greatest possible simplicity.

CAN A CHRISTIAN BE A PHILOSOPHER?

The philosophy of a Christian who is also a philosopher takes part just as much in the history of Greeks and Romans as in the history of the Jewish and Christian traditions that constitute European culture. As an intelligent retrieval of the experiences, stories, rituals, customs, and wisdoms that belong to our inheritance, "postmodern" philosophy has turned away from the modern overestimation of its autonomy. This has made it possible to recognize that the philosophy of a Christian need not at all be second in critical judgment about the thinking that has unfolded itself inside and outside of Christianity. Self-criticism with regard to the superstitions with which the Christian community, like all others, gets blended constitutes part of its continual self-clarification. Spinoza, Hegel, Feuerbach, Marx, Nietzsche, and Freud can be of good service in the endeavor, but we find the most radical critics at home: more than anyone else, prophets, thinkers, and mystics have insisted on the necessity of going beyond all images, myths, and ideologies, and all conceptual shadows of God, in order to get in touch with the origin that does not fit in any horizon. The transcendence to which they point opens a space in which many ways of dwelling and going are possible. Thanks to an anchoring that lies deeper than any theory, a pluralism of interpretations and practices is to be expected. A Christian pluralism brings to light the affinity of believers who need not sacrifice their common reference to the one and only God in the name of their different participation in Jewish or Christian or Muslim history. Their difference-in-affinity has nothing to do with an arrogant individualism or a self-righteous democratism, but it is just as averse to a centrally regulated conformism.

The devotion of Christians to their hidden God does not mean that they have found a clear answer to all their questions. *All* the important questions of a philosophy that is close and true to life, remain questions, even if the philosophizing Christian believes that his community of faith has provided him enough certainty about the ultimate meaning of human life today. Dogmas, too, are mixtures of light and darkness and all social practices mingle good with bad elements. As a believer, a Christian lives in the awareness of the mystery; the answers of faith are thus themselves mysterious; though they invite a search for understanding, the sort of understanding they allow for, remains revisable. God is and remains incessantly "the Sought,"[16] and the familiarity with

---

16. Cf. Grégoire de Nysse, *La vie de Moïse* II (Paris: Cerf, 1968), nn.162–64: God appears in darkness, because he is invisible. "Herein stands the true knowledge and the true vision of the Sought: in the fact that one does not see him, because the Sought surpasses all knowledge, separated on all sides by his incomprehensibility as by a sort

it grows in direct proportion to the awareness of its incomprehensibility. Even mystics do not know more truths than other believers, but they know more intensely how unknowable God is. Although it causes them pain, they rejoice in this, since "the Sought" thus turns out to be much richer than a shallow mind can realize.

Heidegger's pronouncement, that Christians cannot philosophize because they assume to know the decisive answers, misunderstands the true relation between radical familiarity with an ultimate meaning and insight in a truth that can be expressed in descriptions and arguments. Through such a familiarity, one is "in the truth," but everything that is thus present must still be appropriated in practice, affection, and reflection. The philosophy of a Christian is not a tribunal from which the postulates of faith are condemned or acquitted, but a form of rigorous self-reflection on the way to a more genuine and mature kind of life.

---

of darkness [. . .] When Moses is advanced in knowledge (*gnosis*), he declares that he sees God in the darkness, that is to say, he knows then that the divine essentially is that which transcends all gnosis and all grasping [. . .] The world of God above all forbids persons from making the divine similar to something that they know; every thought that the understanding forms on the basis of imagination in order to touch and to capture produces nothing other than an idol of God and gives no knowledge of God." Cf. also n.231–39: "This is to actually see God: never to find the satisfaction [of seeing Him]" and nn.252–54. On the grounds of these and other texts of Gregory, H. de Lubac writes in *Sur le chemins de Dieu,* p. 191: "La mystique, 'intuition de Dieu'?—Oui, mais toujours dans la nuit. Car on ne Le trouve qu'en Le cherchant toujours; Dieu demeure toujours 'Le Cherché,' *ho zētoumenos.*"

10

Leibniz on God and Suffering

IN 1710 Leibniz presented his conception of the relation between God and the evil that disfigures his creation in his *Theodicy*.[1] This work does not present a systematic treatise on positive or natural theology but is rather a long series of polemical arguments, the whole of which constitutes a plea for the goodness of God: "it is the case of God that we plead."[2] Bayle is the principal prosecutor, and Leibniz takes the defense of the accused, in full confidence that "the assistance of God is not lacking to those who do not lack good will."

The issue that Leibniz is concerned with is the meaning of evil from the perspective of creation or—the other way around—he is concerned with the claim that the existing universe, despite its multitude of physical and moral evils, is created and maintained in existence by an all-powerful God who is infinitely wise and good. Indeed all of Leibniz's arguments are grounded on the firm conviction that the entire universe, including the human world, was created by God and that he is infinitely perfect, that is, supremely powerful, wise, and good. While Leibniz thinks that this can be philosophically demonstrated—something he does not attempt to do in the *Theodicy*—he assumes that this conviction is an integral and central part of Christian faith.[3] Moreover, through his revelation in Jesus Christ, God made himself known as a merciful God who wants to save all humans through his grace. This conviction seems, however, contrary to an evident fact of human experience that no one can deny: the existence of evil in the history of the

---

1. The citations from this work, although translated here, refer to the edition by J. Brunschwig of Gottfried Wilhelm Leibniz, *Essais de Théodicée. Sur la bonté de Dieu, la liberté de l'homme et l'origine du mal* (Paris: Garnier-Flammarion, 1969).

2. Leibniz, *Essais de Théodicée,* Préface, p. 39.

3. Cf. Préface, p. 27: "Jesus Christ accomplished the passage of natural religion to law, and gave it the authority of a public dogma. He did alone what so many philosophers had attempted in vain to do."

world and of humanity. How can evil exist if everything is always in the hands of an infinitely perfect creator? How, if evil exists, can this creator be powerful, wise, and good? Is he, although wise and good, too weak to prevent evil? Is he powerful and good, but not wise enough in his governance? Or worse yet: is he powerful and supremely intelligent but also a despot, given that he conspires with the forces of evil? One of the issues at stake in the polemic is the question of whether or not the unity of the three divine attributes—power, wisdom (or intelligence), and goodness (which includes justice and holiness)—can be preserved, despite the existence of evil. Or to put it another way: how can the existence of the world and of history, with all their crimes and disasters, attest to a God who not only hates evil, but is perfect in all aspects? In reflecting upon this question, it is well to remember that "the perfections of God" are described by Leibniz as "those of our souls," the only difference being that "he possesses them without limit."[4]

The existence of evil in a multiplicity of forms has not ceased to be the source of a major objection to the belief in a God who is the "creator of heaven and earth"; but because today this belief is not generally shared, the simultaneous existence of God and evil is no longer a widely debated *topos* of our philosophical culture. If the drama of evil, which has taken on enormous proportions, is still discussed, we relate it mostly to the historical actions and social structures of humanity, whereas the so-called interiority of individuals, almost as much as the religious dimension, is suppressed to the point of obscurity.

The enormity of evil can only be measured, however, by those who feel as affected by the certainty that the world is a given—in the most hyperbolic sense of the verb "to give"—as they do by the horror of recent and ancient evils. This is one of the reasons why I will follow Leibniz's example, and address myself in the following pages only to those who believe in the God of creation. Without trying to convince atheists, *and without ceasing to speak philosophically*, one can restrict oneself to other believers who feel torn between gratitude for the marvels of creation and abhorrence for the evils that seem to negate it. Their tornness is an affective version of a strong tension between two fundamental truths of their lives. However, in speaking thus to believers, we speak to ourselves at the same time. Thus, it is possible to

---

4. Préface, p. 27.

reread the discussion between Leibniz and Bayle as an account of what we might call an "inner" struggle. Although the Leibnizian discourse is characterized by a cerebral tone, its author, whose piety is beyond suspicion, clearly felt the pain of this struggle. Let us try to read his argumentation as the conceptual version of a lived drama.

Practiced as an element of an "inner" battle, rational reflection on the relation between God and evil is animated by the desire to adjust oneself to the hints that emerge from life itself, and to cautiously approach the generous origin that nonetheless does not abolish evil. The need to understand our involvement in a mixed history is encompassed and driven by a more profound dynamic. The type of clarification made possible by rational argument is helpful inasmuch as it resolves a more serious question: how can we tolerate evil without destroying our attachment to God? In other words, how can the relation that links human beings to God be unfolded and deepened, if we feel profoundly wounded by all the troubles afflicting us? Someone involved in these problems first of all asks two questions: (a) whether and how, in spite of evil, it is possible to be oriented to God by metaphors such as "creative power," "understanding," "goodness," and "justice"; and then, (b) what transformations must occur by way of accepting and understanding the evils and sorrows of life in order to achieve reconciliation with existence?

Suffering

To begin with the concrete reality of our historical existence, we might analyze the varieties of suffering and their formal structures in detail. If there is a general structure of suffering, we can venture to name the three following properties:

1. Suffering is the experience of something I feel *attacked* by. Even if there is no one who directly makes me suffer, as, for example, during a painful illness, I live my pain as wounded or pierced by an enemy. I cannot flee this enemy, because I feel him within myself. This experience is obvious if the enemy has implanted himself in my own body or soul, but it is no less true of injuries that arise from external causes. When my stomach hurts me, or I am eaten by remorse, the enemy attacks from within, but the wound of a bullet that pierces my skin is also felt as a part of myself that makes me suffer. Even injustices done

to another by someone other than myself can sicken me; although I am identical with neither party, not only do I find the humiliation of my neighbor painful, but my suffering attests to the fact that the violence done to her also pierces me. What attacks me in my suffering is not completely distinct from my own being. I experience a harmful conspiracy between my own being and the other who hates me.

I spontaneously avoid the attack. I try to flee or to make myself invulnerable, for example by adopting a posture of defense or by shrinking and withdrawing myself from the place where the pain delights itself in torturing me. If I cannot escape, I feel tense and divided like the field of an internal war. I am a living contradiction, and this is made even more painful by the fact that I cannot solve the contradiction.

2. Suffering harrows me to the point of suffocation. My heart can no longer expand; there is hardly any space to move freely, not even inside my own body. While time goes much too slowly, I am restricted to a place that is too narrow for me to relax.

3. Suffering is the declared enemy of my desire for free flourishing. Mocking my glorious independence, it is a kind of counter-autonomy. It makes me feel powerless in that it can neither be fought openly, nor suppressed as if it were a lesser power. Traitor that it is, suffering humiliates me by thwarting my initiative and rendering all my strategies ineffective.

To combat the heteronomy, anguish, and enmity that are revealed in suffering, I seek what gives me deliverance, harmony, concord, and peace. If my sufferings disappear, I will not have driven them away or overcome them, because I have no direct power over them—although sometimes I know how to facilitate their departure by indirect means.

The English language does not seem to have generic words to gather all of the different types of hedonistic or "lupistic" experiences. A good phenomenology of suffering and its contrary—and thus a cogent treatment of hedonism in ethics—would presuppose an analysis of all the hedonic varieties of experience such as joy, jubilation, delight, contentment, peace, satisfaction, pleasure, and so on, and of their opposites, such as sorrow, pain, dissatisfaction, displeasure, discontent, sadness, and so on. Such an analysis would show that human affectivity can be described on the basis of hedonic (or "lupic") differences that characterize the various experiences of human existence. We would thus draw up a plan of the pleasurable and painful possibilities of human affectivity. In this way, not only could we perhaps escape the persistent temptation of an anthropology that determines the essence of a human being as a spiritual soul linked to a sensible body, but we would also avoid becoming hung up on a distinction like the one Leibniz makes between physical and moral evil. In fact, although it is true that the pain of remorse or of structural injustice differs qualitatively from corporeal wounds or exhausting illnesses, there are other experiences that are neither "moral" nor simply "physical," such as the experience of an ugly piece of music, or that of the emptiness of radical nihilism.

SUFFERING AND EVIL

Have we in thus reflecting on *suffering*, comprehended *evil?* Inasmuch as it diminishes the well-being and freedom of human beings, suffering is spontaneously felt as an example of evil. Appearing as the opposite of our will to self-realization, it provokes an immediate resistance to its attacks. We flee from it and devote ourselves to a counter-attack. It seems impossible that we could ever welcome it, or even willingly allow it to settle in. According to the wisdom of spontaneous affectivity, pain is the opposite of what seems to be the meaning of human life. Does it not entirely contradict who we are, what we want and have to become? The conclusion seems to be that suffering should not exist; it is an evil.

For someone who believes in the goodness of the Creator, the paradox of evil arises from affective spontaneity itself; it takes the form of an ambiguous experience. How can I be affected by the phenomenon of evil and still believe that my existence and that of the universe are good? How can I live with an air of universal gratitude while at the same time feel in my very being that existence is corrupted by the contrary of its flourishing? In suffering, I feel diminished, divided, torn. If I believe in God, how can I affirm that his creation, myself included, is not altogether as it should be? If existent beings are not perfect, how can I maintain that God is good? In all suffering, there lurks the temptation of Manicheanism. Love of the Creator seems to be limited by the hatred of a considerable Adversary. The power of the Enemy who attacks us through his betrayals seems to paralyze the infinite goodness of the Origin.

A first step toward solving the paradox of suffering can be attempted by a reflection on the difference between *certain* forms or kinds of pain and *certain* forms of pleasure. The Kantian distinction between the Good (*das Gute*) that is found only in the good will, and the well-being of happiness (*das Wohl* or *Glückseligkeit*) and his parallel distinction between evil (*das Böse*) and unhappiness (*das Übel*) are doubtless too superficial. They do, however, have the merit of drawing our attention to the possibility that an experience of adversity is not necessarily the phenomenality of radical evil. Because he allowed himself to be guided by the traditional distinction of the spiritual and the sensible and thus understood 'happiness' in a much too trivial and empirical sense, Kant was not attentive enough to the obvious facts of human affectivity in relation to the difference between real and apparent forms of good and evil. The distinction between gastronomical pleasure, aesthetic joy, and inner peace, for example, is entirely affective and should be described first before asking traditional questions concerning the distinction between the soul and the body, and the essential differences between various bodies and souls. In all affection, even the most "spiritual" of the most sublime "spirituality," the heart, the brain, the mouth, the eyes, the ears, the fingers and all the members of the human body play an essential role; and no corporeal experience can be isolated from the behavior of a human being in relation to itself, others, and God. However, Kant was right when he said that *Glückseligkeit* (which in fact is a *particular* and rather trivial or mediocre form of happiness) does not coincide with the human good as such. As a particular good, happiness is relative, although no one can avoid desiring it. The absolute and ultimate good, which for Kant is identical with the moral good, may demand the sacrifice of happiness. In certain circumstances—notably if we pursue it at the price of moral purity—*Glückseligkeit* proves to be a subordinate good. Those who are well-schooled in affectivity have no need for long reflection to know this, since their feelings spontaneously grasp the qualitative difference between being happy and being good. *Glückseligkeit* becomes an evil if, in those circumstances, we refuse to give it up.

This example prompts the hypothesis that our joys and sufferings, and the spontaneous reactions they involve, do not necessarily determine the truth about good and evil. Affective spontaneity can lead us to err in fixing our loves and hates on certain goods and evils, which then become absolutes that obscure other more important goods and evils. Suffering can attack us precisely at the point where we have idolized a good that is merely superficial or relative. Thus, on the condition that we suffer in an appropriate way, such suffering can be favorable to us insofar as it delivers us from servitude. In this sense, suffering can be lived as a limitation that opens us to a truer good. The game of truth and appearance is played out in affective life itself. True evil is not everything that makes us suffer, but only what really diminishes or damages human life. An ethic of suffering must tend toward a wisdom that can distinguish between true and false appearances of evil, that is, between suffering that is good, and suffering that is bad. Suffering is not always a true evil, and a human being must learn to endure different sorts of suffering in such a way that they clear a path leading to a deeper truth. The ideal would be a life that rejoices, and that suffers only in full accord with what really counts—a mixture of joys and sorrows in which the truth of authentic goodness becomes phenomenal. A critique of affectivity presupposes the possibility of discovering the difference between truth and appearance. The identity of affectivity and being is played out in the experience of good and evil. In suffering we discover what we love. True evil is what *should* make us suffer. Merely apparent evil, on the other hand, should not make us really suffer; despite the sorrows that we cannot avoid feeling, we should sense their relativity and thus overcome them by the experience of a more profound and substantial joy. True suffering is a sign of human perfection. A hero or a god of affectivity would be someone whose enjoyment and suffering react in the most appropriate way to the goods and evils that make up human history. Such a saint could not be without suffering, because it seems clear enough that real abominations exist, such as hatred, despair, and other forms of hell.

Suffering is thus not a simple phenomenon that we can take or leave. True suffering must be learned, and the purification of the soul involves a purification of the way in which we rejoice or cry. Patience is not only the art of being able to endure; it is also the victory of profound joy over pain. To neither drug oneself with false consolations nor to make oneself indifferent, but to orient oneself by true pleasure . . . would that not be a respectable form of hedonism?

WHY IS THERE EVIL?

The very reality of evil that this analysis presupposes continues to pose a problem. Why is there evil and not only good? The myth of paradise lost and the image of a heaven where the saints rejoice in God with an eternal joy uncontaminated by pain suggests the possibility of a universe without evil or suffering. Was the Creator not able to create a world that would be a heaven? Why then didn't he do it? The traditional response exonerates God by explaining the existence of evil and suffering as an effect or punishment of human sin. "We" have allowed ourselves to be seduced by an enemy that is neither human nor divine. This response does not seem satisfactory, however, because it does not put an end to our questioning. First of all it is quite evident that many entirely innocent children have to suffer tremendous evils such as hunger, sickness, murder, and torture inflicted both by humans and natural causes. It is also very difficult to believe that pains and rewards are distributed proportionally.[5] It goes without saying that the myth of Adam's fall does not relate a story about some distant human ancestor, but represents what happens today, as it also did yesterday and has always throughout the course of human history. "All of us" are sinners. If this "us" has a meaning, can it be that each man, woman, and child—even if they are innocent of any personal crimes—has a share in the bad will of this community in addition to bearing the consequences of humanity's transgression? If we apply the rules of justice here, and especially that of punitive justice, the suffering of innocents is apparently unjust. According to the *ethos* of modern occidental civilization, no one seems ready to believe in a God who distributes pleasure and pains the way they are actually distributed in reality. Even if we recognize that the modern age, as an age of reason and freedom, is also an age in which "all of us" are somehow coresponsible for the worldwide crimes of starvation and mass murder, it is difficult, or rather impossible, to regard world history as a justly governed one. Why are we like this? Doesn't the universality of sin show that falling into it is almost

---

5. Cf. Leibniz, *Essais de Théodicée, Discours de la conformité de la foi avec la raison* (Discours), n.43 (p. 76) "[. . .] we cannot deny that there is in the world physical evil (that is, suffering) and moral evil (that is, crimes) nor even that physical evil is not always distributed here below in proportion to moral evil, as it would seem that justice demands."

inevitable? Is it just to call us to existence if this very existence involves such a destiny, if human history is simply a series of ambushes, betrayals, or irresistible seductions? Why are we so weak and stupid? What kind of demiurge could play such a cruel game?[6] Did God not want to create a benevolent and kind humanity who would have then lived an entirely different history or did he simply not know how? If God created Jesus, and if the communion of saints is not a fantasy, then he has demonstrated that he can and wants to create a perfect and holy humanity under certain conditions. Why is the world, if it is really his work, such a botched work? If we say that it is the fault of human beings, we exaggerate the power of human freedom. If we deny that we are guilty of a fault committed well before our births and if we discard the possibility of an evil genius, then we must admit that we, here and now, have caused our own unhappiness. But were we ever that free? Have we ever been in a neutral situation in the face of a clear alternative between good and evil? Before being able to choose or reflect, we were already integrated into multiple systems of violence and lies. The choice of innocence is something for which we must prepare well in advance, all the while being bogged down in a history where noble souls and the criminal ones are inextricably intertwined.

Some theologians think that all these questions, formulated here in a more or less Leibnizian style, are infantile because the people who ask them have not demythologized their presuppositions. However, by replacing the Creator and sin with the sequence of existence, being, history, violence, and inauthenticity, we are confronted with very similar questions concerning an historical world that is anguished, unjust, and in revolt. Of course, from an atheistic perspective we would no longer address ourselves to an ultimate Being nor would we revolt against Someone. This is perhaps one of the reasons why most atheists would prefer to stifle their inclination to revolt, rather than struggle with an Other whom they could accuse of having made such a deficient world.

---

6. Cf. Leibniz, *Essais de Théodicée, Deuxième Partie,* n.147 (p. 199): "God dupes, in a manner of speaking, the little gods that he saw good to produce, as we dupe children who take up professions that we favour or secretly prevent as it pleases us."

THE UTILITY OF EVIL

One of the ways that theology has tried to show that the existence of evil does not belie faith in a God who is "creator of heaven and earth" consists in heightening the usefulness of the evils that afflict us. Leibniz radicalized this practice by arguing not only that God knows how to use all evils to make them into elements of the good, but also that the actually created universe is the best of all possible universes, and that all actually existing evils are an inevitable element and a *conditio sine qua non* of this universe.[7]

It is clear that many trials and sufferings are either integral or opposed to a good that gives us a higher or more intense joy. Ascetic and educational difficulties, or the pain that alerts us to an illness can be useful evils, but I will not here dwell on those cases of evil that have an obvious utilitarian character. A utilitarian analysis of such cases is not enough to show that all useful suffering is necessary; even if we could show its necessity, this would not strip it of its evil character. If certain sufferings are unnecessary, then the question once more arises: why was the world not put together in a better way? Leibniz, however, aimed higher, and he did not make his own task any easier by concentrating on sins that deserve eternal damnation, while accepting—albeit reluctantly—the thesis of a particular theology, according to which the number of the damned is greater than the number of the chosen.[8] Faced with the possibility of a hell filled with

---

7. Cf. Leibniz, *Essais de Théodicée, Première Partie,* nn.8–9 (pp. 108–9): "Now this supreme wisdom, together with a goodness that is no less infinite, could not have done other than choose the best," and *Préface,* p. 47: "In saying that evil was permitted as a *sine qua non* condition of the good, I mean not following the principles of the necessary, but following the principles of the fitting." Cf. also n.10 (p. 109): "often an evil causes a good, to which we could not have come without this evil. Often two evils even have made a great good," and n.25 (p. 118): "But in relation to God nothing is doubtful, nothing can be opposed to the *rule of the best,* which suffers no exceptions or exemptions."

8. "In holding therefore the established doctrine that the number of the eternally damned is incomparably greater than that of the saved" (*Première Partie,* n.19, pp. 114–15). Cf. also n.4 p. 106: "his choice, which falls only on a very small number of people," and *Préface,* p. 36: "There are few saved or chosen, God does not therefore have the statutory will to choose many," and p. 47: "having explained, for example, [. . .] how it is possible that there is incomparably more good in the glory of all the saved than there is evil in the misery of all the damned, even though there are more of the latter."

millions of hating and hated beings in eternal despair—a concentration camp more horrible than all the historical ones—Leibniz dares to declare, and thinks it possible to demonstrate, that the universe, such as it actually exists, is the best that God could want, realize, and love. Without in any way condoning moral evil, God permits it in order to draw out a good that is greater than the good that would exist had he not permitted the evil that accompanies it.[9]

The existence of evil is an inevitable result of some metaphysical principles that express the essence of God. The first of these principles is the following: nonmoral evil often arises from a crossing of tendencies that—although good in themselves—produce an evil effect when they enter into conflict.[10] Here again we can ask ourselves why God did not realize an order in which there were only peaceful forms of cooperation. In secularized language, this is the question of how we can prove the *necessity* of unpleasant or painful consequences that follow the interaction of certain tendencies.

The second principle is that of divine respect for human freedom. The best of all possible universes includes human freedom despite all the crimes it commits because any other universe would lack the moral and other possibilities that presuppose freedom. The existence of freedom includes free will and therefore the capacity to choose—and most important, the capacity to choose between good and evil. In giving freedom to humans, God gives them the possibility of choosing evil by disobeying the law that he has placed in their conscience. It is part of the majesty and goodness of God to let a person decide freely whether she will be good or bad. If that person so wants, God will let her carry out what she decides. Through his infinite wisdom, God eternally knows what free beings, who belong to each of the possible universes, would choose to do. In comparing all possible universes, God chose to realize only one: the presently existing universe with its human history. Because God is infinitely wise, good, and powerful, he can choose only the best of all possible universes. Through an *a priori* deduction, we thus conclude that the presently existing universe is the best that is possible.

---

9. Cf. for example the phrases cited in note 7 and this one: "The allowance of evils comes from a sort of moral necessity; God is obliged by his wisdom and his goodness; this happy necessity [. . .]" (*Deuxième Partie*, n.128, p. 184).

10. Cf. *Première Partie*, nn.20–32 (pp. 116–23).

The third principle that Leibniz presupposes without justifying it, is the law that one who commits evil by freely transgressing the divine law must be punished. Justice, which is a moment of divine goodness, is retributive justice based on the model of criminal law. For Leibniz, this law seems self-evident, as it does for many other societies and thinkers before and after him. Retributive justice must therefore explain many of the evils of human history—and notably the damnation of all those who persevere in evil.

Despite the various misfortunes and crimes of a *massa damnata* more numerous than the number of the chosen, the presently existing universe is the best of all possible universes. It is neither a paradise nor a heaven, but a universe in which everything has its own place and function and reward—somewhat like the *Divine Comedy* of Dante Alighieri, but with a stronger accent on rational principles about order, power, knowledge, law, and justice. As we will see, beauty also plays an important role, namely in the form of *universal harmony*.

To those who are surprised by the assertion that our world is the outcome of God's choosing the best, Leibniz points out that the universe is much vaster than our world. He seems to want to suggest that the history of human crimes and the number of the damned is only a very limited evil, and that the mixture of historical goods and evils must be understood as a subordinate moment of the totality. Within this totality, the ensemble of light and darkness composes a glorious harmony. This cannot be empirically confirmed, but again must be deduced *a priori* from the unity of the divine perfections. If he wants to create, God can only realize what his wisdom and love represent to him as the most harmonious ensemble of things. The beauty of a harmonious universe thus becomes synonymous with supreme goodness.[11]

GOD AND FREEDOM

The image of God the Creator that Leibniz presents throughout the *Theodicy* is that of a planner, viewing, in the heaven of ideas, all the

---

11. On the beauty of the whole, which cannot be lessened by what is monstrous in the world, cf. especially *Troisième Partie,* nn.241–44 (pp. 262–64), and n.416 (p. 361): "Theodore [. . .] was in delighted ecstasy."

possible histories of all the possible universes, so as to decide which universe must and will be the only really existent one. This image presupposes that all possible universes can be surveyed by an infinite intelligence who remains distant, contemplating them in a uniquely atemporal here and now. But it also presupposes that each of these universes constitutes a closed totality, circumscribed therefore by a spatio-temporal beginning and end. How heaven and hell are supposed to be part of this universe is not clear, but let us not pursue this any further.

There are many *aporiae* inherent to the representative machine that Leibniz offers to our conceptual imagination, but I will here underline only a few.

The first involves the concept of divine permission. One of the key philosophers of the twentieth century wrote:

> The rigorous affirmation of human independence, of its intelligent presence to an intelligible reality, and the destruction of the *numinous* concept of the sacred comport the risk of atheism. This risk must be run. Only through it can man rise to the spiritual notion of the Transcendent. It is a great glory for the Creator to have fashioned a being who affirms the Transcendent after having contested and negated it in the glamour of myth and enthusiasm; it is a great glory for God to have created a being capable of seeking or hearing God from afar, from out of separation, from out of atheism.[12]

We can correlate this citation with Leibniz's conviction that God does not want to take away or restrict human freedom once he has created it. It seems difficult to reconcile the many freely committed crimes of human history with God's ongoing creation of all events and actions. God cannot be the author of criminal decisions or actions insofar as they are destructive, but can he cooperate with their positive aspects? Must we think of evil as a kind of nonbeing that in no way participates in the creativity of existence?[13] From the perspective of Leibnizian ontology, radical evil is pure desertion, a sort of fall without dynamism or energy of its own, self-exclusion from the process of generation that

---

12. Emmanuel Levinas, *Difficile liberté: Essais sur le Judaïsme* (Paris: Albin Michel, 1976), p. 31. Cf. Emmanuel Levinas, *Totalité et Infini: Essai sur l'extériorité* (The Hague: Nijhoff, 1961), pp. 57–62; 275–76.

13. Cf. *Première Partie,* n.29 (p. 120): "at this point we must consider the truth that has caused so much commotion in the schools since Saint Augustine pointed it out, that evil is a privation of being, instead of a positive action of God."

emerges from God's originary creativity. The nonbeing of evil is not even a negation—because this would again presuppose a sort of energy or activity—and certainly not a dialectical negation like the wickedness (*das Böse*) that Hegel thematized in his philosophy of morality and religion.[14] One could attempt to think this nothing by showing that a wicked action, since it creates no new product, is purely destructive insofar as it inverts order, hierarchy, and proportion; but it remains extremely difficult to remove all reality, energy or being from evil's "powers."

A second problem concerns the idea of divine permission. If God has so much respect for human free will that he does not want to interfere, even when someone decides to hate himself as much as he can, what then should we think of the impeccability of the heavenly saints? Why does traditional theology maintain that once in heaven, the saints no longer commit any sins? What explains their unwavering attachment to God? What else but grace, the free gift of God? Moreover, Leibniz insists on the fact that freedom as such is not identical with the capacity to choose both evil as well as good. The summit of virtue is the annihilation of any tendency to choose evil, whereas neutrality before evil is a sign of moral indifference.

A third question would ask why God did not give all free beings the grace he gave to the saints—so that the universe would be an eternally peaceful paradise. Leibniz replies that God must let himself be guided by general principles of wisdom instead of constantly interfering by means of miracles and particular grants of grace. However, he seems uncertain of his reply when he writes that "God could bring such order to bodies and souls on this globe of the earth, either by natural means, or by extraordinary grace, that it would be a perpetual paradise and a foretaste of the celestial state of the blessed; and there is even nothing to prevent there being happier worlds than ours; but God had good reasons for wanting ours to be such as it is."[15]

---

14. Cf. G. W. F. Hegel, *Grundlinien der Philosophie des Rechts* (1820), ed. Johannes Hoffmeister (Hamburg: Meiner, 1975) 4th ed., §§139–40, and *Encyclopädie der Philosophischen Wissenschaften im Grundrisse zum Gebrauch seiner Vorlesungen* (1830), §§568–69.

15. *Troisième Partie*, n.353 (p. 325). Cf. *Deuxième Partie*, n.120 (p. 175), n.207 (p. 242), n.211 (pp. 245–46) and *Troisième Partie*, n.337 (p. 316).

THE GOD OF LEIBNIZ

The Leibnizian image of God as a fabricator of the universe is a modernization of the Platonic model of the demiurge looking up toward the ideas, where he finds the exemplar for all his "poietic" works. Along with Plotinus and the Neoplatonic tradition, Leibniz incorporated the ideas into the divine intelligence, but the framework of the *poiēsis* stays the same. God is a grand architect or engineer[16] who compares and calculates the possible outcomes of his various plans. The criterion that guides his choices is the principle of teleology: everything that poses a potential problem is overcome when it can be shown that it is an integral part with a positive function within the totality. The universe is comparable to a machine or organism, or even a big game, as Leibniz seems to suggest when he writes that "God dupes, in a manner of speaking, those little gods that he saw good to make, as we dupe children who take up professions that we favour or secretly prevent as it pleases us."[17]

In the table of the divine "poietic," all the elements of the representative system are present. The world and its history are conceived as parts of a totality from which God remains distant; he can thus observe all the possibilities and judge the value of this world in comparison with other imaginable worlds. What is the horizon within which God makes his comparisons? How can he or we think the universe of all universes? If the reply to this question must be sought in the infinity of God, what then is the sense of the word "infinite" in this context?

In reading Leibniz, it seems that the infinity of God indicates only an ultimate degree or an extreme quantity of power, intelligence,

---

16. *Préface*, p. 41, and *Troisième Partie*, n.247 (p. 265): "God has the quality of the best monarch no less than that of the greatest architect." God is also called the "author" (*passim*), "the cause" of everything (*Première Partie*, n.30, p. 122) and "the good principle" (*Préface*, p. 35). The architectural metaphor is maintained in this passage: "We can say that people are chosen and ordered not so much according to their excellence as according to their suitability for God's plan; as it may be that we use a stone of lesser quality in a building or in a collection, because it happens to fill a certain void" (*Première Partie*, n.105, p. 163).

17. Cf. *Deuxième Partie*, n.147 (p. 199). Cf. *Première Partie*, nn.7–9 (p. 107–9) and n.22 (p. 117).

love, and so on, without a radical difference between the qualities of created beings ever seriously being considered. How can we otherwise explain the phrase that has already been cited: "The perfections of God are those of our souls, but he possesses them without limit" and the passage that follows: "He is an ocean, from which we have received only drops: there is in us some power, some knowledge, some goodness, but these are complete in God."[18] God is thus the being who possesses all perfections to the highest *degree*, but he is at the same time the *totality* of all the perfections that we humans possess only in part and to an inferior degree.

Leibniz represents God through yet another image: that of a great monarch who must be defended against the accusation of being a tyrant or a despot. "God has the quality of the best monarch no less than that of the greatest architect."[19] Leibniz's defense makes of him rather the best of all economists: despite the fact that his subordinates do not behave very well, he knows the art of using their faults and errors (*O felix culpa!*) to fashion the most glorious harmony of all. The universe as he wants it is "the state of a perfect government [. . .], where evil itself serves the greatest good."[20]

> If we knew the city of God such as it is, we would see that it is the most perfect state that could be invented; that virtue and happiness rule there, as much as possible, following the laws of the best; that sin and unhappiness (which reasons of the supreme order did not permit to be entirely excluded from the nature of things) are almost nothing in comparison to the good, and even serve as greater goods.[21]

Everything in the existing universe is effective and useful; the law of universal teleology best expresses the power, wisdom and goodness of the divine perfection. Universal harmony justifies even sin by putting it to good use; we could almost say that it needs it. The "combination, that makes up the whole universe, is the best: God therefore cannot avoid choosing it without creating a deficiency; [. . .] he allows the deficiency or the sin of man, that is encompassed in this

---

18. *Préface*, p. 27.
19. *Troisième Partie*, n.247 (p. 265); cf. *Première Partie*, n.6 (p. 107).
20. *Deuxième Partie*, n.125 (p. 182).
21. *Deuxième Partie*, n.123 (pp. 179–80).

combination."[22] "God, who can do everything that is possible, allows sin only because it is absolutely impossible for anyone to do better." He is incapable of having regrets "and does not find any subject [for regret] either; he feels infinitely his own perfection, and we could even say that the imperfection in detached creatures for him becomes perfection in relation to everything, and that it is an additional glory for the Creator."[23]

A total economy—or a totality thought from the perspective of an economy ruled by utility and calculation—is possible only if everything is interchangeable, that is, if everything has a price or a relative value. This is why the beauty of universal harmony that Leibniz deduced from his representation of an infinitely perfect Creator must allow arguments such as the following:

> I agree [with Bayle] that the happiness of intelligent creatures is the principal part of God's plans, for they resemble him the most: but I do not see at all how we can prove that it is his only aim. [. . .] Each perfection or imperfection in creation has its price; but there are no creatures that have an infinite price. Thus the moral or physical good and evil of reasonable creatures does not infinitely exceed the good and evil that is only metaphysical (that is, the good and evil that consists in the perfection of the other creatures) [. . .] No substance is absolutely contemptible or precious before God. [. . .] It is certain that God appreciates a man more than a lion; however, I do not know if we may assert that God prefers one man in all respects to the whole species of lions; but if this were the case, it would not follow that the concern for a certain number of human beings would be more important than the prevention of a general disorder spread over an infinite number of creatures.[24]

In response to this rather disconcerting text, we could refer to Kant's remark on the difference between relative values and the absolute value of human dignity. The latter has no price, because, being an end in itself, it can and must not be used for anything. The nonutility of the human subject, which is infinite, makes it incapable of functioning in

---

22. *Deuxième Partie*, n.159 (p. 206); cf. *Troisième Partie*, n.335 (p. 314): "God [. . .] permitted evil, because it is encompassed in the best plan that is found in the region of the possible, which his supreme wisdom could not fail to choose."

23. *Deuxième Partie*, n.165 (p. 210).

24. *Première Partie*, n.118 (pp. 170–71).

a framework of economic calculation. If such a framework is essential to all generalized teleology, this does not help us in any way to elucidate the meaning of human good or evil.[25]

What the economy of universal harmony does not do, is to reconcile a soul that is sick with pains and wrongdoing with its God, in whom it trusts despite everything. This deficiency is apparent in the framework in which the Leibnizian discourse unfolds, and in the ambiguity of the functions that are performed in it by different individuals.

Leibniz's polemic with Bayle was staged as an apology for the great Accused, and against the prosecutor's closing speech. In announcing that "it is God's case we are pleading,"[26] Leibniz, in his preface, sketched the framework of a trial; but who called upon him to take up the defense of God? Does the Creator of heaven and earth need lawyers to explain his conception of justice? Where are the people on behalf of whom Leibniz, the philosopher who knows the principles of the universe, renders God and faith invulnerable? In any case, it is not God who is the accused, but a very human, all too human, conception that is in danger. Or is it Leibniz himself who fights his own temptations of discontent by a discourse that tries to be as lucid as possible, in the hope of suppressing once and for all the objections by which he also feels a little shaken? Before what tribunal can this case be pleaded, and who is the judge?

Leibniz would no doubt respond that it is first and foremost reason itself that is the judge here, including the reason of natural theology that can demonstrate the implications of divine wisdom. For "we have no need of revealed faith to know that there is such a principle unique to all things, perfectly good and wise." We can therefore reply with a rational argument to "this question of natural theology, of how a unique principle, all good, all wise and all powerful can admit evil, how it could have allowed sin, and how it could decide to so often

---

25. The point to which a totalization of the economic point of view can bring an intelligent and pious spirit like Leibniz may be seen in a phrase like this one: "God has more than one design in his projects. The happiness of all reasonable creatures is one of the ends for which he aims; but it is not his whole aim, nor even his final aim. This is why the unhappiness of some of these creatures can happen by concomitance, and as a result of other greater ones" (*Deuxième Partie,* n.119, p. 171).

26. *Préface,* p. 39.

make the wicked happy and the good unhappy. "Reason teaches us by infallible demonstrations."[27]

This reply makes the judge identical with the Law in whose name the verdict must be pronounced. But when and how was it pronounced? Not only have we not yet heard the reply of Bayle, but many other thinkers, such as Voltaire, Kant, and Hegel, have demanded the right to speak in the name of reason or, like Marx and Nietzsche, have challenged this judge and proceeded to profound transformations of the judiciary setting.

In his "little methodical summary in Latin," published in the same year (1710) as the *Theodicy*, Leibniz had the courage—or the arrogance—to identify his defense plea with the work of God himself, when he gives it the following title: *The Case of God, Pleaded by his Justice, Itself Reconciled with all his Other Perfections and the Totality of his Actions*.[28] Leibniz seems a little too certain that he can speak in the name of the God of justice, which is also the God of rational power, wisdom, and goodness. And yet neither his rhetoric, nor the content of his discourse are prophetic.

The framework of the rational polemic, in which Leibniz situates the drama of the co-existence of God with evil, lends itself to a conceptual struggle between scholars, with God as the stake. God is a bit like the king in a game of chess, in which the world, humanity, history, evil, heaven, and hell figure as the other pieces that move according to the general principles of Reason. A theological discussion thus emerges, removed from the only battle where God can reveal himself without immediately destroying this revelation itself: the existential struggle of concrete individuals who, while attached to God, are amazed by the ways he is revealed in the events of their personal history and the history of the world. In order to be serious, this struggle should aim not at a representation or a concept of God, but at God himself. It is a question of piercing everything that is interposed between "God and the soul." A genuine theology is composed of discursive fragments issuing from such a struggle, which is first and foremost an affective process.

---

27. *Discours*, nn.44, 43 (p. 76).

28. *Causa Dei asserta per justitiam ejus cum caeteris ejus perfectionibus cunctisque actionibus conciliatam*. I have used the French translation presented in the above quoted edition of the *Essais de Theodicée*, pp. 425–52.

Toward the end of his *Theodicy*, Leibniz offers us a piece of fiction in the style of Lorenzo Valla's *Dialogue on the Free will*. He does it, as he writes, "much less to liven up the material than to explain myself, at the end of my discourse, in the most clear and most popular way possible for me."[29] To explain the paradox of evil in a world created by the God of love—a paradox that he sums up in mentioning Judas' betrayal of Jesus—Leibniz tells us an allegory concerning another criminal. By means of the story of Sextus Tarquinius, he explains the reasons why justice demands that this man had to be punished. Apollo, Jupiter, Pallas Athena, and the Fates here represent different aspects of what Leibniz takes as the God of the Christian religion. Whereas Jupiter holds the supreme and just power, Apollo and Pallas represent two moments of the divine science. The fact that Leibniz thinks he can explain the mystery of God and evil "in the most clear and most popular way" by using the language and images of a dead and anthropomorphically polytheist mythology, shows which God is made possible by his conception of life. Although the Leibnizian system very much resembles certain theologies of the seventeenth and twentieth centuries, it is quite rare that a supposedly Christian text so ingenuously exposes the non-Christian character of its God. In fact, the God of the Gospels is very different from a pantheon of Roman or Greek Gods. In relation to these divine super-humans, Christians are surely atheist. Despite Leibniz's protests against the anthropomorphism of his adversaries, which he criticizes particularly because of its too-finite concept of God,[30] his Creator too closely resembles a human being whose good qualities are magnified to the extreme.[31] When Leibniz tries to make his concept of God more concrete, he presents him as an architect, an engineer, a Jupiter, an Apollo, an Athena, a monarch, and at times as a good sculptor.[32]

---

29. *Troisième Partie*, n.405 (p. 355).

30. Cf. *Deuxième Partie*, n.122 (p. 179): "It is to scoff at God with perpetual anthropomorphisms; it is to represent him as a man who [. . .]," and n.125 (p. 182): "It is always the same thing, it is pure anthropomorphism."

31. Cf. *Préface*, p. 27: "God's perfections are those of our souls, but he possesses them without limit."

32. *Deuxième Partie*, n.130 (p. 184): "he is like a good sculptor, who only wants to make from his block of marble what he judges to be best, and who judges well. God makes the most beautiful of all possible machines from matter; he makes the most beautiful of all conceivable governments from spirits; and on top of all that, for their union he establishes the most perfect of all harmonies, following the system that I have proposed."

THE BATTLE WITH GOD

It may well be that the only scenario in which God's justice can become, in a certain way, authentic, is in the battle of one who has confronted his God through a profound suffering. This scenario is characterized by the duality of a radical confidence in God and a form of accusation that can go as far as rebellion and hatred. "How long will you assail me?" "Why do you continue to strike me?!" "Why have you abandoned me?!" "Why do you want to kill me?!" Before being questions, these complaints invoke an authority whose Name we dare not pronounce, yet we still address ourselves uniquely to him, and *not* to human society or the gods. Such a complaint is also a demand for justice: "Grant me justice against my enemy!" This enemy is the violence that destroys my honor and my flesh, but it is also the killer of others! As long as the battle continues—and even if it has every appearance of an atheistic rejection—it confirms an initial alliance without which it would immediately vanish. The most radical suffering is perhaps not torture or slow agony, nor even the pain caused by the injustice done to others. It is the living contradiction between a basic fidelity to and discord with God as he manifests himself here and now in the pains of this human body and this human heart. It is the very suffering of suffering itself that was the drama of Job, as it is also the drama of all those who are confronted with the human reality such as it is, splendid and unhappy, divine and diabolical. To approach the heart of existence without being intoxicated by all too reasonable words—is that not what Job had to learn?

The engagement in a battle with the God who causes suffering, *begins* with an accusation in the name of a certain conception of justice, coupled with a specific interpretation of the joys and pains of human existence. Various utopias and paradises play a role in our interpretations of suffering, evil, and justice and much narcissism is often invested in such representations. By imposing our standards on the reality, we might attempt to preserve our central and superior position, and by demanding that God justify the pain he inflicts, we submit him to our idea of justice. At the same time, however, our invocation recognizes in principle that all justification must come from God and that the meaning of our battle lies in the purification of our attitude. The battle can fail, for example because the end of suffering ends all interest in continuing the fight. If it succeeds, it involves a purification during which all the elements of the initial constellation are transformed. God is then revealed progressively by throwing off our all too human conceptions of justice, evil, and God.

A traditional manner of pleading "God's case"—Leibniz's *Theodicy* being only one illustrious example—can have the meaning of a stage along the way of a lifelong process. The quest for God must pass through such a process in order to free itself of all idolatry and completely concord with the alliance that preceded it.

IGNORANCE AND ACCEPTANCE

Despite their economic and calculative aspects, the essays of the *Theodicy* comprise an overture to such a transformation. Notwithstanding everything that Leibniz claims to know about the wisdom of God's will, his plea for the defense is ultimately founded on a clear awareness of his own ignorance. The force of the *a priori* deduction through which he concludes that the existing world must be the best possible, given that its Creator is perfect, also affirms that we are incapable of explaining why this world must contain so many evils. Leibniz's final word lies in a particular union of ignorance and confidence—not in clear and distinct justification.

His confession of fundamental ignorance is intimately linked to an oft-repeated argument he uses to pass from the actual existence of the world to its optimal goodness: if the existing world was created, it *must* be the best possible; because the Creator exists, the being of the world implies its necessity and its goodness. However, some passages clearly express this argument together with a confession of ignorance as to the internal necessity of the world's facticity.

To the question of whether God is able to give happiness to all, Leibniz replies that yes, "he could give it promptly and easily and without the least inconvenience to himself, for he can do anything. But should he? Since he does not do it, this is a sign that he had to do it entirely otherwise."[33] The certainty that God does what is best is sufficient for us to approve the totality of what exists. There is thus no

---

33. *Deuxième Partie*, n.122 (p. 179).

need to prove the goodness of the world by showing to what extent everything in it is ruled by a teleological economy. Would it be just to compare the Leibnizian response with the word of Job that "Yahweh had given, Yahweh has taken back, may the name of Yahweh be blessed?"[34] Or should we suspect all religious words in which there is no resonance of the lived drama from which they arise?

The same argument as above is repeated in relation to moral evil when Leibniz writes, "because he permitted vice, it must be that the order of the universe, found preferable to all other plans, required it."[35] But the ignorance in which we are immersed is expressed even more clearly in this passage: "We must judge that God had reasons for allowing sin, reasons more worthy of him, and more profound in relation to us";[36] and also in the following:

> God's object [the universe that he takes care of] has something of the infinite, his concerns embrace the universe; we know almost nothing, and we want to measure his wisdom and his goodness by our knowledge: what rashness, or rather what absurdity! [. . .] it is ridiculous to judge the law when we do not know the fact. To say with Saint Paul: *O altitudo divitiarum et sapientiae* [Rom. 11:33], is not to renounce reason, it is rather to use the reasons that we know, for they teach us this immensity of God of which the apostle speaks; it is to confess our ignorance of the facts, it is to recognize nonetheless, before seeing, that God makes everything the best possible, following the infinite wisdom that rules his actions.[37]

Leibniz finds a use even for this ignorance when he writes about the choice by which God saves the chosen but lets others go to their damnation: "so that we do not have reason to glorify ourselves, it is necessary that we not know the reasons for God's choice."[38]

The text in which Leibniz comes closest to the book of Job seems to be this one, however:

> If some people put forward experience to prove that God could have done better, they set themselves up as ridiculous censors of his works,

---

34. Job 1:21.
35. *Deuxième Partie*, n.124 (p. 180). Cf. also n.218 (p. 249), where the argument is reduced to its essence by the words "because they are there *[puisqu'ils y sont]*."
36. *Deuxième Partie*, n.166 (p. 210).
37. *Deuxième Partie*, n.134 (pp. 189–90).
38. *Première Partie*, n.104 (p. 162).

and we would tell them that we reply to all those who criticize the pro-
cedure of God: You have only known the world for three days, you
hardly see further than your nose, and you find fault with it. Wait to
know it better, and especially consider those parts that present an entirety (as do organic bodies); and you will find an artifice or a beauty that
goes beyond the imagination.[39]

TOWARD PEACE

Theology in the Leibnizian style seems to be motivated by a desire of
reaching peace between God and the soul—a peace that reconciles suffering, without abolishing it, with gratitude and hope.

To conclude, I would like to venture some remarks on the possibility of such a peace. Without diminishing the importance of the collective and individual struggle against all forms of corporeal, psychic,
aesthetic, moral, and religious evil, a certain apology for certain evils
seem to be possible. If it is illusory to believe that evil and suffering
can ever completely disappear from human history, then it must be
possible to meaningfully integrate them in our commerce with God,
others, and the world. Like Behemoth and Leviathan, the hippopota-
mus and the crocodile,[40] evils belong to the world, which, if created,
can only be experienced as a gift. If suffering and crime are "normal"
ingredients of history, they *must* have a positive meaning.

The God of the Gospels identifies with one who suffers, that is, with
all men, women, and children who come into this world, as long as
they do not close their minds to the creative inspiration that grants
existence and peace. This does not mean that poverty, persecution, or
torture automatically guarantee their victims the status of God's servants, but even such experiences might open their mind to the God of
compassion and grace. To participate in the Passion until the end of the
world, it is necessary that we undergo, more or less willingly and without spiritual or other drugs, the hostility characteristic of suffering.

As hostile toward an autonomous self that believes itself the center
of the world and its history, suffering undermines the arrogant attempt

---

39. *Deuxième Partie,* n.194 (p. 233). Cf. Also *Discourse,* n.44 (pp. 76–77).
40. Job: 40:15–24 and 41:1–34.

to conquer absolute independence, which is the source of idolatry. It can bend the will toward God's initial dispensation, to which we owe our freedom. Such a reversal cannot be accomplished by self-righteous choices; the initiative must be taken by the Origin that wishes me well. An overly concentrated ego is ignorant of the good. It is the least self-possessed and most useless suffering, then, that is particularly able to deliver the human heart from its obsessions. If the revolt against evil has been transformed into an acceptance without need for explanation, suspicions about an unjust Creator turn into silence. Having reached such silence, the soul is no longer inclined to find everywhere an economy of teleologically well-ordered possibilities. Filled with wonder at the possibility of a peace that hurts, the soul can freely love the real reality, such as it is here and now.

11

Hegel and Modern Culture

For Jean-Louis Vieillard-Baron

ALTHOUGH WE MAY AGREE that we are living through a decisive crisis in our culture, we are not all of the same opinion about the meaning of this crisis. Are we in agony? Are we just passing through one of the many difficult passages that punctuate Western history? What from our past is strong enough to be worthy of survival and what future possibilities are open to us?

We belong to the great tradition that is rooted in classical Greece, the Judeo-Christian faith, the Roman empire, and Germanic languages, but we may no longer swear by it. While following traditional schemas in our thinking and behavior, we might experience an inner distance that prevents us from feeling completely at home in them.

Geographical and historical knowledge has changed our world into a gigantic museum, where numerous languages, religions, histories, styles of art, and ways of life are arrayed as alternative possibilities: ours is only one among them. Although European science and technology have conquered the entire world we are not sure whether they are a blessing or a disaster. What most worries us, however, is the nihilism that Europe seems to have exported to all other continents. In these circumstances, a bothersome and sometimes depressing question arises: what chance do we have of passing the wealth of our traditions to other generations? Are we condemned to die with the treasures of our past, unable to participate in a new history? How can we prevent a final failure of the grandiose adventure that issued from Israel and Greece, Rome, Christianity, Arabia, and the Germanic tribes?

Whatever the case may be, to forget our historical roots would be a big mistake. Unable to start human history again, we live in our own culture with the knowledge of its particular contingency and without clinging to many dogmas of past times. Imperialist monologues give way to dialogues with other cultures; we have become modest, even poor: all that we still possess seems borrowed and provisional; rather than being a fixed legacy, our heritage invites us to reuse it for experimental transformations. A rather skeptical relationship to our own culture confronts us with what is most essential—more essential even than established civilizations.

Various diagnoses of our culture, sometimes accompanied by proposals for the future, have emerged from our crisis.

In all the critical epochs of Western history, moralism has tried to reduce the main question to a combat between devotion to the Good, on the one hand, and the multiple tendencies toward the pride, injustice, greed, and sensual pleasures, on the other. However, not only the inefficiency of endless sermonizing, but also the social sciences and philosophical critique have undermined our faith in moralistic approaches.

Martin Heidegger has interpreted the monstrosity (*das Entsetzliche*) of our situation as the outcome of a position that we inherited from the Greeks. Our dealing with beings expresses a stance (including a look and a standard) that does not allow them to play out their essence. Our acting and speaking is dominated by a radical insensitivity to the self-revealing nature of the phenomena. Scientism, the atomism of human rights, the desacralization of the universe, our inability to build real homes, modern nihilism's drive for panoramic and absolute autonomy—all this is only an outgrowth of an underlying relationship that links us to a mystery without name that we might evoke by calling it *Alētheia*, or *Ereignis* in order to distinguish it from any specific being, including God and the gods.

In sharp contrast to Heidegger's indifference about the moral aspects of our crisis, Emmanuel Levinas has interpreted our history as a combat between Israel and Greece. Western egology has suppressed the "humanism" of the human other that was our biblical heritage. By defining our essence as autarchic freedom, our civilization has suppressed the receptivity of our "being-for-the-other." Radical meaning is found in proximity and substitution, and history borrows its meaning from our responsibility.[1]

---

1. Cf. for example Emmanuel Levinas' *Humanism de l'autre homme,* (Montpellier, France: Fata Morgana, 1972).

In the traces of Nietzsche, we could attempt another interpretation. A will to power seems to hide in the practical and theoretical codes of our tradition, while disguising itself as a desire for peace and generosity. Pity and pardon are façades behind which a sick and fickle culture abandons itself to a contagious nihilism. We need courageous lucidity to sustain and bless the tragic reality of human existence with its insoluble antinomies.

Schopenhauer, Marx, Freud, Bergson, and others have proposed still other diagnoses. The critique of the Western crisis has become a central part of philosophy and meta-philosophy; it is already studied in a meta-critique of the critics and their theories. Conflicting interpretations of our situation might illustrate the uncertainty of our self-awareness. Are we capable of knowing where and how we are? If not, could an appeal to past philosophers clarify our predicament? All the authors mentioned above were conscious of the crisis in which we still find ourselves. What, however, can we learn from a modern classic, such as Hegel? Even if Hegel is a kind of Janus between modernity and post-modernity,[2] he at least represents a summary of the past, in which we, notwithstanding our wavering between loyalty and disbelief, are steeped. If his philosophy is a mirror in which we can recognize a part of our past and presence, this might provide us with the distance needed for a judgment about our situation.

HEGEL'S FRAMEWORK

To show how Hegel conceived of modern Western culture, I will refer particularly to the only work in which he attempted to summarize

---

2. As I have argued in my *Modern Freedom: Hegel's Legal, Moral, and Political Philosophy* (Boston: Kluwer, 2001), pp. 71–73, Hegel's philosophy can be understood as *one* possible summary of Western philosophy from Parmenides to Hegel. This summary is deficient, because (a) Hegel's reading of predecessors is often inaccurate, (b) he leaps from Proclus to Bacon, Hobbes, and Descartes without having any acquaintance with a millennium of philosophy separating Greek and modern philosophy, and (c) he presses the course of history into his own dialectical schema. However, this deficiency does not prevent him from representing, in some sense, the end of an epoch, and even the beginning of a postmodern philosophy. For the scholarly justification of the present essay, see also my *Selbsterkenntnis des Absoluten: Grundlinien der Hegelschen Philosophie des Geistes* (Stuttgart-Bad Cannstatt: Fromman-Holzboog, 1987), and *Hegels Praktische Philosophie* (Stuttgart-Bad Cannstatt: Fromman-Holzboog, 1991).

the *whole* of truth as he saw it: his *Encyclopedia of the Philosophical Sciences.*[3]

The project of encompassing the totality of beings and thoughts in a systematic and definitive text that allocates their places, relations, and functions, expresses a specific manner of holding oneself inside—or rather, above—the world and history. This project involves a particular assessment of all that is merely individual. The individual or the singular *(das Einzelne)* has no ultimate truth and value apart from its functioning inside the whole of which it is an element. As elements integrated in the ethical life of the State and the contemplative self-awareness of the Absolute, human individuals realize their contingent destinies. Insofar as they are only isolated singularities, they are not interesting: philosophy does not concern itself with the endless multiplicity of beings and events unless they can be understood as illustrations of necessary essences and structures. Immediate, that is, nonmediated, singularity has meaning only as a condition for the possibility of the spirit's exteriorization: without individuation, spiritual life would not have any concrete existence. In separating itself from the totality ("the concrete universal"), the singular loses its true being and becomes evil. While the essence of evil consists precisely in this movement of isolation, the Good is nothing other than the circular movement of the Absolute, which is structured as the totality of all totalities. Through multiple layers of subordinate mediation, the Absolute gathers all the natural and spiritual atoms of the world and its history into one supreme unity. Those who attempt to withdraw from this radical subordination destroy their lives. The primordial task of human individuals, their first duty, is to actualize their union with the historically existing universe, insofar as this is the empirical manifestation of the Absolute itself. If philosophy succeeds in laying out the structure and rhythm of the Absolute's life, on the one hand, and the essential possibilities of human beings, on the other, it automatically gives rise to a moral philosophy. In analyzing the diverse moments of the soul, consciousness, and spirit in his philosophy of subjective spirit, Hegel shows how the human spirit is differentiated

---

3. I will use here only the last version of this work, *Encyclopädie der Philosophischen Wissenschaften im Grundrisse zum Gebrauch seiner Vorlesungen,* *GW* vol. 20 (Hamburg: Meiner, 1992).

in a variety of capacities for self-realization. The theory of objective and absolute spirit shows the structure according to which the infinite but humanized Spirit realizes its rational freedom. If individual autonomy conforms to these structures and contents, the actualization of its capacities is good, because it is in order; if not, the individual is false and evil, because it has fallen away from the life of the Absolute.[4]

Hegel's ethics spiritualizes the principles of Aristotelian ethics by offering a new version of the imperative "become what you are," which Aristotle had thematized in terms of *dynamis* and *energeia*.[5] In conceiving of the Absolute on the model of a finite and corporeal spirit tending toward the actualization of its most essential possibility, Hegel presents the realization of the human task (*ergon*) as a finite aspect of the Infinite's own self-actualization. The absolute Spirit needs the actions and reflections of individual lives and particular cultures in order to fulfill its own virtualities.

A clear expression of Hegel's contempt for all individuals who isolate themselves from the social and religious totality is found in a remark appended to §549 of the *Encyclopedia*. Here he clarifies the concept of world history (*Weltgeschichte*), which is primarily the history of organized peoples or nations. Neither "the savage nations" (*wilde Nationen*), nor individual particularities are the subject matter of history. Human individuals are interesting only inasmuch as they represent certain nations, for example in the role of a prince, a founder or a legislator. "The many singularities" that do not play any particular role with regard to their epoch, nation, or culture "are a superfluous mass." Concentrating on the contingencies of their existence distracts us from the truly memorable subjects that are worthy of history. The essential characteristic of the spirit and its epoch is always contained in great events (*in den großen Begebenheiten*). Everything that has only a particular and individual interest is inessential for Hegel. The small facts "without importance" can be told in novels, where nobody cares whether their facticity is well-documented or just fantasy. It is a sign of bad taste to mix private interests and subjective passions with the universal interests of the spirit's substance.

---

4. Cf. *Encyclopädie* §§469–82, and 503–12 and my explanations in *Hegels praktische Philosophie,* pp. 26–108 and 186–236; see also my "The Foundations of Ethics According to Hegel," in *International Philosophical Quarterly* 23 (1983), pp. 349–65.

5. Aristotle, *Nicomachean Ethics,* 1097b22–1098a17.

In contrast with the historical irrelevance of average individuals, the significance of *all* individuals without exception is recognized on the level of religion. However, even there a distinction must be made between those people who are worthy of consideration and those whom we can treat as "a mass of singularities" with no particular importance. Religious individuals who have made history are even rarer than politicians whose glorious deeds are worth remembering. It is above all the great founders of particular religions who count in religious history. True, according to Christian doctrine, all humans are called to union with the Infinite, but this union does not constitute any particular history; in a sense, it is an "eternal history."

FREEDOM

Though the preceding résumé of Hegel's understanding of the relation between the universal and the singular might suggest a massive disregard for individual autonomy, we should not forget that from his youth onwards, the thrust of his thought was aimed at a reconciliation of the encompassing totality with individual subjectivity, such that this latter would lose nothing of its freedom and essential rights. From the very beginning of his reflections, Hegel tried to reconcile the Greek principle of concrete and harmonious totality with the principle of independent and free subjectivity. Hegel solved what at first appeared as an antinomy by positing a supra-individual spirit that differentiates its own freedom in particular cultures and individual instances of its overarching autonomy. It remains true, however, that his synthesis grants the principle of totality prevalence over the inalienable rights of individuality.

The Greece of young Hegel's dreams was the idealized image of a free and beautiful people, contrasted with the fragmented, despotic and decadent Germany in which he lived.[6] After 1815, when Hegel had finally become a university professor, he mainly dealt with the struggle of modern nations to establish constitutions that would assure a rational balance between individual and collective rights. In his interpretation

---

6. Cf. my *Le jeune Hegel et la vision morale du monde,* 2nd ed. (The Hague: M. Nijhoff, 1969), pp. 11–28.

of the world, Hegel is aware that the ideal image of a sentimentally and culturally united people is no longer a sufficient basis for politics. The ideal of his youth now was seen as inadequate with regard to the (relative) autonomy of individual citizens in their private and contractual relations. In recognition of their freedom within the framework of civil society, the traditional institutions were replaced by new ones and Hegel took great interest in this process; he even hoped to play a political role in it.[7] As an organization perfectly unified through the hierarchy of its institutions and the virtues of its members, the modern state would ideally accomplish and achieve the political history begun in Greece. As the first collective configuration that takes the subjectivity of its individual members seriously, it is the beginning of a new history, in which Hegel sees the final objectification of the principles of Christianity. Nonetheless, the subordination of the principle of individual subjectivity to the principle of the nation as a whole, without this latter being subordinated to a superior political dimension, constitutes a structure that we could call more Greek than Christian.

CULTURE

Although Hegel himself does not use the word "culture," the philosophy of spirit developed in the *Encyclopedia* can be read as a theory of culture, insofar as it considers the world and its history as specifically human and spiritual. Hegel thinks about human civilization in light of the opposition and union of nature and spirit. Civilization is the progressive spiritualization of nature, which itself is the expression of the abstract spirit that pre-exists in the Idea. The horizon in which Hegel understands culture is, thus, the concrete existence and movement of the infinite spirit itself.

"Nature" is the name of the universe insofar as this is given immediately, before any human presence has made contact with it. As immediately given parts of nature, human bodies are not (yet) civilized, but they are in fact oriented by a spiritual soul, which cultivates the naturally given phenomena. A human individual is thus the synthesis of

---

7. Cf. my *Philosophy and Politics: A Commentary on the Preface of Hegel's Philosophy of Spirit* (Boston: Kluwer, 1987), pp. 20–28 and 75ff.

three dimensions that cannot be isolated from one another because the spirit permeates all of them. The "natural"—corporeal and quasi-animal—dimension forms the "anthropological" aspect of human being; the "phenomenological" aspect lies in human consciousness and self-consciousness; while the spiritual dimension, studied in Hegel's "pneumatology" or "psychology," encompasses the former aspects and grants them their typically human character. Spirit and self-consciousness clearly characterize us, while our anthropological moments root us in the materiality of nature. For Hegel, nature is perhaps less animated than it is for Aristotle, but it certainly is more spiritualized than modern physicists believe. The essence of matter is exteriority pure and simple, even in relation to itself, but the various figures of the natural realm show, in different degrees, a certain interiority, which must be attributed to the spirit's presence in them. Having no cohesion by itself, nature requires a principle to assemble its dispersion in order to escape the chaos that has no meaning. All natural entities are syntheses that owe their meaning to spirit. Not only human cultivation but already its unfolding in higher forms of material cohesion and organized life shows the realm of nature as a progressive spiritualization.

The question of culture comes up in the course of Hegel's psychology. The human spirit, as finite expression of the absolute spirit, realizes itself in nature, that is, not only in its own body and consciousness, but also in its natural surrounding and time. Through human imagination and activity, the spirit transforms the natural universe into a humanly spiritualized world. The latter can be called "second nature," because it shows, on an all-encompassing level, a parallel to the "second nature" that, according to the Aristotelian tradition, designates the virtues into which human individuals transform their innate givenness. In a culture, the given nature is transformed into a human world that supports and forms us. As a world that depends on human activity, culture changes more rapidly than (the "first") nature, but it, too, is ruled by laws and other necessities.[8]

The necessary elements and structures of the human world are analyzed by Hegel in his philosophy of objective and absolute spirit. It is not necessary to dwell here on the details of Hegel's theory of culture,

---

8 Cf. my "'Second Nature': Place and Significance of the Objective Spirit in Hegel's *Encylopedia*," in *The Owl of Minerva* 27 (1995), pp. 51–66.

but some of its features must be remembered if we want to discover to what extent Hegel's conception of modern culture can help us to understand and evaluate our own.[9]

Human domination of the earth is part of the modern project, a project that in Hegel's time was seen as a task for powerful, Western nations. Each of these nations has a character and history of its own, which determine the citizens' lives and customs within its boarders. The individuals must respect each other as persons who have fundamental and inalienable rights: "Be a person and respect others as persons!" However, this principle threatens to divide a people into as many sovereign islands as there are individuals. The model of a fundamental contract is not sufficient to unite them because all contracts depend on the contingent and changeable willing of the contractors, whereas the political cohesion of a united people demands a more essential and radical union. The national union is found in the combination of institutions and objective powers, on the one hand, and the nation's *ethos* (*Sitte*) on the other. The latter involves, among other things, a patriotic disposition of the citizens. Only a synthesis of objective and subjective elements— only a union of powerful institutions with a moral culture—can create a framework in which mutual respect and civil collaboration, satisfaction of needs, and sovereignty of the national domain are guaranteed. Only such a synthesis can respond to the question of how an individual must behave in order to be honest. Individuals are morally good insofar as they accomplish their proper functions within the political, economic and familial ensemble to which they belong. Honesty (*Rechtschaffenheit*) is the Hegelian version of "justice" as defined by Plato's famous imperative "to do one's own."[10] We can also locate the other cardinal virtues in Hegel's conception of *Sittlichkeit* by showing that *courage* is equivalent to patriotism in times of war, that *temperance*

9. For details and references, see the studies indicated in notes 2 and 8, and "Hegel Contra Hegel in His Philosophy of Right: the Contradictions of International Politics," in *Journal of the History of Philosophy* 32 (1994), pp. 241–64; "Logic and History in Hegel's Philosophy of Spirit," in *Hans Friedrich Fulda and Rolf-Peter Horstmann,* eds., *Vernunftbegriffe in der Moderne* (Stuttgart: Klett-Cotta, 1994), pp. 607–22; and "Religion et politique dans la philosophie de Hegel," in G. Planty-Bonjour, ed., *Hegel et la Religion* (Paris: Presses Universitaires de France, 1982), pp. 37–76.

10. Cf. Plato, *Republic* 433a-e and my "Hegels Pflichten und Tugendlehre" in *Hegel-Studien* 17 (1982), pp. 97–117 or in Ludwig Siep, ed., *G. W. F. Hegel, Grundlinien der Philosophie des Rechts* (Berlin, Akademie Verlag, 1997), pp. 167–91.

is at play in civil society to the extent that the satisfaction of personal needs is limited by private law, and that *wisdom* is necessary for the leaders of political institutions and families.

Familial *piety* should be added to this list, as it is fundamental to the well-being and peace of families, while *solidarity* and a certain form of *compassion* are necessary for the good functioning of Hegel's "corporations." The morality of individuals is thus concretized by their belonging to "ethical" communities. It can also be realized through *"philanthropic"* dedication (Grl. §337), which is not confined to national boundaries, or through the *fraternal love* that unites Christians, but the latter virtues cannot be organized politically.[11] As far as I know, however, Hegel never offers a theory of the supranational aspects of morality. The predominant impression that emerges from his treatment of human praxis is that there are little or no differences between being a good person and being a good citizen.[12] However, this coincidence implies that it is also a duty of civic morality to ensure that the State functions well and to correct its failures if it does not. Faulty structures or customs must be reformed, and if anarchy arises, order must be reestablished or a new order must be imposed. The founding heroes of states are the clearest examples of ethical grandeur in a not-yet or no-longer ethically viable situation. Though their action can scarcely avoid violence, it is justified insofar as it creates the conditions for the possibility of a decent social life. In their case as well, moral goodness depends on individual devotion to the common good.

If morality is only a function of the common well-being, there are no supranational duties for individuals, for humanity as such does not form a community; the international order is in a state of nature, dominated by national sovereignty and violence. Moral behavior among nations cannot be enforced; nationalism remains the supreme principle of world politics.[13]

As sovereign individualities, nations are in a situation very similar to that described in the chapter on "abstract right," where men and

---

11. Cf. G. W. F. Hegel, *Philosophie der Religion,* in Hermann Glockner, ed., *Werke* XII (Stuttgart: Frommann, 1927), pp. 292–93.

12. Cf. Aristotle, *Politics* 1276b16ff.

13. Cf. G. W. F. Hegel, *Grundlinien der Philosophie des Rechts,* Johannes Hoffmeister, ed., 4th ed. (Hamburg: Meiner, 1955), §§330–39 and *Encyclopedia,* §§545–47.

women are considered solely as singular persons. Individual persons ought to respect each other, but will they do so effectively? Because a community presupposes at least a minimum of mutually respectful behavior, Hegel deduces the concept of a singular moral will (represented by the figure of the judge) that sanctions the laws by punishing offenders (Grl §103). At the international level, however, there is no place for a *"praetor"* who judges the crimes committed by one state in its dealing with other states (Grl. §333 Remark). As supreme actualizations of objective freedom, the nations certainly ought to respect one another, allowing each other to develop their own well-being according to their own insights and decision, but, on the international level, the law of mutual respect remains a completely abstract *Sollen*: no power in the world can legitimately sanction it, because each nation is "judge in its own affairs." International law suffers from an inevitable duality: an abstract exigency is opposed to the factual play of collective wills that follow their own decisions. Under these circumstances, peace is just one possibility among others, whereas war is always imminent. World history shows us what this signifies: it is a slaughterhouse (*ein Schlachtbank*).[14] Through a historical mixture of justice and injustice the Spirit of the world, Providence, is revealed to be the highest power that originates and accompanies the rivalry of empires and kingdoms, electing and rejecting one after the other. No nation escapes its destiny; every earthly power has its time of disappearance or submission. The supreme necessity that rules the entire practical dimension is *Moira, Fortune, Fatum,* or Destiny. *"Alles soll verzehrt werden"* (everything must be consumed) is the law that dominates freedom's objective reality.

According to Hegel, it is impossible for nations to form an international political community. This is precisely the reason why he thinks that politics (including its integral components, morality and right) must be opened up to a higher dimension: the dimension of absolute spirit, including art, religion, and philosophy. Yet, it would have been easier and more in accord with Hegel's logic to overcome the contradictions of the international scene by deducing the necessity of a worldwide unity on the level of objective spirit. The entire movement

---

14. Cf. G. W. F. Hegel, *Die Vernunft in der Geschichte,* 5th ed., Johannes Hoffmeister, ed. (Hamburg: Meiner, 1955), p. 261; cf. pp. 34–35.

of Hegel's philosophy of right orients the reader toward a final synthesis that should reunite all human individuals and nations in a universal "family" or "fraternity." Such a deduction would have realized the structure of a perfect concept: the whole of humanity as an original and ultimate unity that is differentiated into peoples and individualized into singular human beings. The particular institutions and mores of the nations would then form the variegated life of one historical community. However, there are at least two reasons why Hegel did not follow this logic: 1) the current political reality of his time seemed to contradict the orientation implied in such a deduction; and 2) Hegel *needed* the political impasse to introduce the highest, contemplative dimension of the spiritual universe. An elucidation of the first reason would engage us in a discussion of Hegel's identification of the real with the reasonable and his avoidance of philosophical prophecies;[15] the second leads to the heart of Hegel's interpretation of modern culture.

ABSOLUTE SPIRIT

The atomism of the many sovereign States, which through their natural tendency toward singularization enter into wars, cannot consummate the self-unfolding process of the Spirit. If history was merely that, then Spirit, like nature, would in the end expire in failure: it would not be able to accomplish concrete universality and unity. Civilization would in the end founder in endless conflicts between egoistic nations intent on mutual destruction. The death of nature has a positive meaning because it is the condition for the emergence of the spirit (Enc. §§375–76); but what meaning can we find in the death of practical spirit, this "slaughterhouse" of history? If the history of spirit ends with the death of one nation or empire after the other, what is its fruit? Is there a reconciliation for these deaths? Can we hope for a final victory despite the mortality of the entire objective spirit?

Hegel's response to this question is formulated in semi-Christian, semi-philosophical terminology, but it has a certain affinity with the response of Greek tragedy. For him, as for Aeschylus, supreme wisdom springs from the deepest suffering. The impasse of objective liberty

---

15. Cf. my *Philosophy and Politics*, pp. 92–103.

leads, through violence and misery, to a religion that, despite everything, recognizes in the history of the world the plan of an absolute Providence. Through the empirical history of finite lives and deaths, the Spirit reveals its superiority over its objective realization in politics. The truest name of religion is "philosophical knowledge of the Absolute," or "absolute knowledge" as unfolded in the finite universe. The truth is, in the end, effected and revealed in the knowledge of the infinite Spirit (or the Absolute) that is achieved by finite thinkers who recognize it as the source and completion of the universe. The ensemble of these thinkers constitutes the new spiritual Republic that embraces the whole of humanity. Their temple is the temple of Reason, where Reason is venerated through the artistic and philosophical rituals that celebrate its thoughts and decrees. The history of philosophy is the most divine aspect of world history and the supreme revelation of the meaning that justifies all suffering and evil. Political history is a necessary but subordinate dimension, needed by the Absolute to concretize its superiority over all the powers of isolation, pain, and evil.

Before proclaiming that philosophical truth reveals the ultimate meaning of the universe, Hegel presents religious reconciliation as its second highest and most universal realization. Hegel uses the word "religion" in a broad sense for the three dimensions of absolute spirit in general, (1) art; (2) religion in the current sense of the positive religions and the common essence they share; and (3) philosophical and scientific knowledge. The way in which he describes these dimensions shows that he considers art a deficient form of religion, whereas religion *represents* the truth, which is *comprehended* (or understood conceptually) in philosophy.

Greek art, the realization of absolute truth in the form of *beauty*, shows how the Spirit admires itself in the flourishing of successful peoples, and especially in the most beautiful of all: the Greek polis. However, even Greece was not free enough to fully respect the individuals' subjectivity and their inherent rights. Therefore, the spiritual ideal expressed in its art had to give way to the universal religion revealed by Jesus, in which the autonomy of all human individuals imposes itself on humanity. The Christian religion was the soil from which the modern idea of the State emerged. As we have seen, there is no objective universe beyond the nation-states, but the Christian religion realizes the Absolute's concrete universality by making itself felt

and represented in the images of a most intimate union of human individuals with God. Thus no longer limited to a particular people,
revealed religion contains within itself a disposition that suggests an
objective world organization, although Hegel does not say as much
and even avoids this conclusion. Christianity relativizes the importance of the nations; its fundamental virtue cannot lie in patriotism,
because it unifies all finite spirits in the Absolute, while thereby also
unifying them among themselves. It is strange that no trace of any
objective world union can be found in Hegel's philosophy of religion.
In speaking of brotherly love among Christians he seems to treat it as
a kind of solidarity characteristic of the association of Christian (especially Lutheran) believers. The factual absence of supranational organ-
izations seems to have prevented him from drawing the logical
conclusions from the basic theses of his practical philosophy. Whereas
he neglects universal fraternity, Hegel insists on the union of individual believers with the Absolute. In order to turn toward the Infinite, the
soul distances itself from politics and world history. Hegel repeats here
the gesture of Saint Augustine's "redi in te ipsum" (enter into yourself), but his picture of the ultimate dimension is much less communitarian than Augustine's "City of God." The intimacy of the believer
with the Absolute, repeatable as many times as there are individuals,
does not constitute a human universe. All individuals participate alike
in the light that reveals the Absolute. To bathe in this light and *comprehend* it is the highest stage of a fully human life: the supreme wisdom
that is promised to those who think.

Hegel Now?

The Hegelian thematization of modern culture reveals one of the most
fundamental contradictions of Western culture. The nationalism of
modern States cannot be reconciled with the ideal of fraternal humanity inherited from Christian humanism. Hegel tried to show the rationality and overcoming of this contradiction by subordinating the
objectivity of practical freedom to the freedom of thought. Human
beings fulfill their destiny through knowledge. The end of the
Encyclopedia explains why the philosophy of spirit does not begin
with the imperative *"Become* what you are!" (which could have been

developed into a theory of both practical and theoretical freedom that would have emphasized the communitarian aspect of theory and the universal aspect of praxis), but with a reminder of the Apollonian "commandment": "*Know* yourself!" (Enc. §377).

Hegel's interpretation of religion and philosophy sustains the principle of universality on all levels of culture. Faith and knowledge demand that individuals behave as singularizations of their absolute Origin, which gathers them as moments of one all-encompassing life. Their union is not restricted to the cerebral activity of cold reason; it takes possession of all the layers of human life, but thought is more ultimate than action and history. Union with the Spirit through theory penetrates the heart in which it is felt, the eye that sees the Spirit in all the phenomena, the imagination and memory, for which it manifests itself as a history, while art and religion express and celebrate its truth, which is comprehended by thought. Nothing is more natural than that a profound devotion to the entire humanity gushes forth from the Spirit into the interiority of all individuals. A singular being's acceptance of its own destiny naturally includes acquiescence to the rational necessities that rule the universe. Evil, on the other hand, realizes itself through attempts to isolate singular beings from the universe of which they are only moments, a separation that tends to change the universal harmony into anarchic atomism. What threatens modern culture most of all is its individualism. The ravages of privatization we see today seem to prove Hegel right, but the history of modern nationalism with its massive wars and holocausts have made us aware that the patriotic arrogance of sovereign states is even worse than the violence that originates from personal privacy. Plato, in the *Politeia*, responded to the individualistic threats with the tragicomic image of a polis in which a host of private rights were repressed. Hegel, who recognized the autonomy of human individuals and thought that he had found the means to integrate it into the totality of modern nations, subordinated the individuals' praxis to the absolute sovereignty of the state, but he could not repress completely the human tendency to surpass all national, cultural, and religious limits in the direction of a religiously and philosophically united humanity. His theory of the absolute spirit presupposes that there is nothing more rational in humankind than such a universality, but he repressed his own insight that true concepts *must* realize themselves in the objective reality of human history.

Epilogue

The discrepancy between Hegel's theoretical ideal (the perfectly coherent encyclopedia of all that is) and his practical prophecy (the unconquerable particularization of sovereign kingdoms) expresses the tragedy of Western history. Since the end of World War II, we see a glimmer of universal fraternity, but the practice of international politics is still dominated by particular powers and empires, and the fear that universal centralization will produce one dictatorial supersystem cannot be dismissed.

According to Hegel, justice is realized when citizens (who do not need to be heroes) accomplish their familial, civil, and political duties, without bothering about human life outside their own country. As for the spiritual education of the citizens, art is recommendable because it makes the "spirit" of the time and one's nation visible and thus consolidates the citizens' sense of being at home in their world. But even without engagement in art, one can be a good citizen if one shares in the religious feelings, symbols, and narratives that are accepted as the public mythology of one's nation. Philosophers can explain the truth that is contained in that mythology, but for most people it is sufficient that they adhere to the religious expressions of that truth.

Hegel's synthesis, however admirable and grandiose, is, in the end, too nationalistic, too bourgeois, and too intellectual to inspire us in a time where imperialistic will to power, capitalistic greed, and universal corruption are threatening our hope that universalization would foster justice. When concern for justice is monopolized by arrogant empires (among which "business" might be one of the most powerful), what can we, citizens of one world, do? Contemplation is certainly not enough, although it might break the spell of devilish ideologies. Dedication to the practice of justice demands a devotion as wide as the world and as open as the Spirit who creates and inspires the universe. Hegel's own proclamation of the respect that is due to each free will should not have been confined to the horizon of sovereign peoples. His insight that the moral freedom of individuals cannot be separated from their ethical communities should not have stopped at the family and the state. If, following Hegel's own logic, respect for singular persons and the entire human community can be shown to condition one another, we would have a better point of departure for further discussions.

Whether Hegel's logic and the totality to which it refers is, in the end, a satisfactory grid for understanding a culture of fraternity and peace, can neither be affirmed nor denied without a thorough discussion of the relations between individuality, universality (or totality), and infinity; but even if Infinity and unicity suffer under the pressure of Hegel's universality, we can transform his precious indications about the unbreakable identity of individuals with their community into pointers toward a more concrete but eschatological universality.

12

The Significance of Levinas
for Christian Thought

For Marco M. Olivetti

IT IS A FACT that gives one pause for consideration that in Holland, Belgium, France, Italy, South America, and the United States the work of Emmanuel Levinas has found its greatest readership among Christian philosophers and theologians. Although this work is supported by a long Jewish tradition—even in its strictly philosophical elements—it has impressed many Christians by its orientation, which, despite its great originality, seems familiar to them.[1]

Levinas's work rings with the voice of a master, not only in the sense of a teacher who translates a common heritage, but also in the sense of a critic who poses questions of conscience and who exposes the pseudo-answers and dishonest modes of conduct to which we are inclined. When we enter into his writings, they force us to a discussion through which our own thought and action can be renewed.

Despite the title of this chapter, I will be selective by focusing here only on some elements of Levinas's work from the perspective of my own understanding of Christian life and thought. In doing so, I will attempt both to heed the voice of a master and to link that voice with an interpretation of Christianity that I hope is not erroneous, though it is certainly fragmentary.

---

1. An earlier version of this text was written for a colloquium with Emmanuel Levinas on his work, which took place in Aachen and Simpelveld from May 31 through June 2, 1982. The title was given to me by the organizer. For more on Levinas, one can consult my *To the Other: An Introduction to the Philosophy of Emmanuel Levinas* (West Lafayette, Ind.: Purdue University Press, 1993) and *Beyond: The Philosophy of Emmanuel Levinas* (Evanston: Northwestern University Press, 1997).

Before beginning, however, I would like to make a remark about the expression "Christian thought." As the earliest Christian writings already show, there are not only several versions of a Christian interpretation of nature, the world, and history, but also different levels upon which one may speak of "thought." Not every thought expressed by a Christian is "Christian," and not every Christian is "a thinker," but every authentic believer at the least practices a naïve and implicit type of Christian-oriented thinking. One might possibly even consider dogmatic proclamations a type of thought, but here I will primarily concentrate on naïve religious convictions and some theological and philosophical elaborations in which Christian faith has expressed itself—albeit incompletely. It is not my intention to systematically compare Levinas's chief ideas with the theses of an orthodox dogmatic and moral theology; rather, I will attempt to partially answer the following questions: Why is Levinas's work so important for contemporary Christians, and how can it become fruitful for them?

To begin with, Levinas's critique of totality may be read as an invitation to criticize the idea that Christian faith is adequately summarized by presenting it as a doctrinal system. The wish to gather the evangelical message into a theological encyclopedia or *summa* issues in an attempt to represent the truth by identifying it in the theses and syntheses of a surveyable whole. The panorama of a complete dogmatics glorifies an "onto-theological" ego, which through knowledge has secured itself against the shocking character of the unexpected. The critique of egological totalitarianism can be carried out in a strictly philosophical critique of the universal reduction of all otherness to the Same, but the magnificent tautologies that result from such a reduction may be too rich and powerful to be Christian. They may be too powerful to agree with the spirit of poverty extolled by the prophets and the beatitudes.

Systematic syntheses and handbooks have a catechetical and didactic use, they may even be indispensable, but they are certainly secondary. Living tradition is a continuous awakening to authenticity through continually new interpretations that always critically test, purify, and deepen what has already been said and interpreted. Handbooks and *summae* belong to levels of administration that have expanded greatly since the churches began to organize the Kingdom of God in accord with the political models of profane society. The theoretical systematization of Christian belief, the organization of Christian practice

through a juridical codex, the subjugation of fraternal life and discourse to the structures of a quasi-political regime seem to show a certain affinity with the totalizing tendencies that characterize Western
science, technology, and philosophy. Are they typically Greek? Greco-
Roman? European? Do they betray a universal tendency toward domination and monopolization? Without answering the preliminary
questions formulated here, I will immediately focus on the question
that seems the most essential: the question of God.

GOD

In proceeding this way, I do not mean to suggest that the philosophy of
Levinas is only or primarily a philosophy of religion. Some commentators have said that Levinas has the great merit of having enriched
phenomenology through an ethics and philosophy of religion, but that
seems to me only a small—and not the most important—part of the
truth. The statement would even be false when taken to mean that one
could separate ethics and the philosophy of religion from the remain-
der of philosophy. The Levinasian philosophy is a *prima philosophia*,
a "first philosophy," which is at least as radical or fundamental as the
dialectic of Plato, the logic of Hegel, or Heidegger's "thought of
Being." Not only is it unthinkable that thinking about God and the
Good could stand alone, they unavoidably influence as much as they
presuppose all other thoughts one might have. However, one cannot
radically thematize the basic questions of philosophy—such as, What
is thinking? or, What is the significance of desire for thought?—if one
abstains from ethical and religious conceptuality.

In attempting to speak about God, we might begin with some meanings that "God" can *not* have in philosophy and theology. Thanks to
excellent exegetes of the last centuries, we again understand epic,
mythic, and poetic narratives about God as they are meant, in contrast
with scientific, philosophical, or theological theories about the universe. Yet, we might still be tempted to imagine the Kingdom of God
as a second, ideal, utopian world behind, before, or after our finite,
guilty, and sorrowful world. Behind, before, or after this mortal life,
the real life would take place in an ongoing history untouched by misery or sin. However, does such belief in a *Hinterwelt* not degrade

God's Kingdom to an improved version of this finite and mortal world, in which God would be the ruler of a paradise?

Modern man has attempted to take on the role of an absolute ruler; scientific and technological planning aim at universal domination through human will. But revolutionary atheisms and human autarchy seem to be losing their appeal. The monotheism of Judaism, Christianity, and Islam presupposes mature and alert individuals who reject all gods, including a supreme one, who could impress us by miraculous tricks or utopian liberations. We do not count on a quick abolition of injustice; instead of feeling consoled by the promise of a "life after death," we accept our own and others' death as a sad moment of human fate. We stand rather helpless when confronted with great suffering, especially when we cannot understand it as the consequence of our own mistakes or as sacrifice for others. Salvation should be given soon and prayer has become conditional because we no longer know what is good for us. What we desire most of all is a meaning that does not pale as soon as it arrives.

SALVATION AND LAW

Levinas has often intimated that the desire for personal salvation can contain a great deal of narcissism. A radical distinction separates the satisfaction of vital, aesthetic, theoretical, and "religious" needs from the desire that is oriented toward the absolute. Only this desire can deliver us from the disgust of isolated self-enjoyment. It reveals itself to me as an unchosen responsibility for and service of the Other. As I am "for the Other" prior to any possible choice of my own, I transcend my death by spending my life for the Other's existence, which does not belong to me. As a substitute, a hostage, or a victim, I am already dead inasmuch as a radical "being-for-the-Other" implies that my life no longer is my own.[2] Although I independently own and enjoy my world, I have already sacrificed it by welcoming the Other into my house.

---

2. The idea that I am not for-myself but for-the-Other lies at the heart of *Autrement qu' Être ou Au-delà de l'Essence* (The Hague: Nijhoff, 1974), especially chapter 4, "Substitution." It is, however, anticipated to a considerable extent by what Levinas, in *Totalité et Infini: Essai sur l'Extériorité* (The Hague: Nijhoff, 1961), calls the structure of "separation."

The fundamental law and the *normative* tenets that are constitutive of my existence translate into a philosophical interpretation of the prophetic texts about the Servant of *Jahweh*. If Christians consider the man Jesus to be the fulfillment (*plērōma*) of the Law, they believe that his life for others can be understood as exemplary obedience in the form of substitution, and that his death is the consequence of that obedience. To be delivered over to the Other is a break with hedonism. All suffering is a test, as it presses us to accept the authentic script of our destiny by giving away what belongs to us. When a subject accepts his passivity, he refutes the ideal of appropriation by preferring the poverty that the Bible terms "blessed." Such poverty is a passion through which innumerable Jews and non-Jews have died. How was it possible that many executioners of this passion were Christians? Was there a hidden paganism in their "Christian" interpretation of the Bible?

MYSTICISM AND LOVE

Enthusiasm, fusion, participation in the truth, and magical forces are typical forms of the nonmonotheistic religiosity that is condemned by the prophetic but sober inspiration of ethical responsibility.[3] Does Christianity contain similar seeds, or do these belong, if and when they appear, to its falsification?

Through his critique of mysticism and sacramentality, Levinas calls us to a radical purification of religious practices and convictions. If, as Paul says, all powers and authorities are subjugated to the Servant of God, who has sacrificed his life for all, then magic is finished. The Christian celebration of the sacraments cannot be represented as a form of magical overwhelming. The eucharistic remembrance of Christ's passion, for instance, cannot contain any trace of infantile thaumaturgy. The responsibility of each individual, touched and inspired by the celebrated event, is neither weakened nor violated by the influence of a higher will. Every hope for a secret mechanism of grace that operates independently of the participants' devotion is to be rejected. The core

---

3. For a definitive statement of Levinas's position on these matters, and for clear evidence that the word "participation" refers not to Plato but to Lévy-Bruhl, see his essay "Lévy-Bruhl et la philosophie contemporaine" (1957), republished in Emmanuel Levinas, *Entre Nous: Essais sur le penser-à-l'autre* (Paris: Grasset, 1991), pp. 53–67.

of sacramental prayer consists in gratitude for an existence that successfully embodies ultimate meaning, and in the hope that it may live and die for others. However, such prayer does not cancel the thought that this form of life and death has been and will be given to us. "Everything is grace" *(tout est grâce)*, not only the creation that constitutes us—even before all acceptance—as responsible subjects, but also the justice that is realized through our responsibility. The heteronomy of the law that orients us develops into a second heteronomy—or into a second phase of the same radical heteronomy: the grace of law-abiding loyalty to our original passivity. The free conduct that follows the call of human conscience, the human good through which God reveals the way, presupposes the sanctifying Spirit that motivates creation. The meaning of creation is revealed through the inspiration of Spirit-guided servants.

Is human autonomy, without which a religion for adults seems unthinkable, denied by the thought that grace not only determines our central task but also grants us the very capacity to be good? Does a Christian theology of grace, like Christian mysticism and the belief in a hypostatic union of God and humanity, exhibit a magical conception of God's work? The criterion on which Levinas insists holds that all religious relations in which one forgets one's fellow are inauthentic. In a discussion with some Christian philosophers and theologians on the concept of "revelation,"[4] his key references included not only Jer. 22:16 "He did justice to the poor and unhappy, and that benefited him. This is surely what is called to know me, says the Eternal" but also Matt. 25:40: "And the King will answer, 'Truly I say to you: What you did to one of the least of my brethren, you did to me'"; and 25:45: "Truly, I say to you, what you did not to the least of these, you did not to me" and the first letter of John, in which we read: "If someone says that he loves God, but hates his brother, he is a liar. For he cannot love God, whom he has not seen, if he does not love his brother, whom he has seen" (1 John 4:20); "Whoever does not love abides in death. . . . If

---

4. Cf. Levinas's intervention in the discussion recorded in *La Révélation* (Bruxelles: Publications des Facultés Saint-Louis, 1977), pp. 224–25. The discussion itself was preceded by Levinas's contribution: "La révélation dans la tradition juive," pp. 55–77, which was republished in his *L'au-delà du verset: Lectures et discours talmudiques* (Paris: Minuit, 1982).

one has this world's good, and sees his brother in need, yet closes his heart from him, how does the love of God abide in him?" (1 John 3:14–17); and "No one has ever seen God; if we love one another, God abides in us, and his love is perfected in us. By this we know that we abide in him, and he in us, because he has given us of his own Spirit" (1 John 4:8–9,12–13).

The inseparability of God's love of us, our love of God, and the love of each person for the other is so constantly and strongly proclaimed in the books of the New Testament that Christians must be fully in agreement with Levinas on this point. However, there remain some questions and doubts concerning the meaning we should attribute to the union of humans with God. Can we defend the notion that the Christian conception of the mystical is radically distinct from magical enthusiasm, and that it does not contradict the prophetic reading of responsibility for one's neighbor, but rather demands and presupposes it, possibly even coincides with it?

The mystical moment of the Christian religion shows itself in the writings of the great mystics who have come forth in all periods of Christian history. They have assumed no independent authority in relation to Christian life and practice, but have emphatically experienced and brought to expression what the Church always has believed concerning the possibility of the most intimate intimacy between God and humans.

At times, it is said that the mystics have experienced God and their union with him, but that is an inaccurate and misleading expression. The presence of God which they write about—they write considerably more about God's absence,[5] incidentally—is in their own words not a presence of God "as He is," "since the condition of this life does not admit of that."[6] God does not allow himself to be seen (cf. 1 John 4:20,

---

5. The following citations are all taken from the commentary of John of the Cross on his own *Cántico Espiritual,* Version B. In the following notes, the Spanish citations are repeated immediately in English, as taken from *The Collected Works of St. John of the Cross,* trans. K. Kavanaugh, O.C.D., and O. Rodriguez, O.C.D. (Washington, D.C.: Institute of Carmelite Studies, 1979) and occasionally slightly modified.

6. *Canción* 11a, n.3: "todas [estas presencias espirituales] son encubiertas, porque no se muestra Dios en ellas como es, porque no lo sufre la condición de esta vida" (p. 449: "all are hidden, for in them God does not reveal Himself as He is, since the conditions of this life do not allow such a manifestation").

as cited above); the vision of God kills; it demands the self-sacrifice of an entire life in the service of the transcendent, an obedience that gives away and consumes. God is near when the mystics ponder his actions and desire union with him, whose hiddenness, through their advancement, does not diminish but grows.[7] The acts of God through which Christians trust themselves to be carried, are the creation which calls them to servitude, the passing by of God in Jewish and Christian history, the unfolding of life in the Spirit of God for one's neighbors. Gratitude is the appropriate answer to these acts, a gratitude that knows of itself that it is a gift. "Gratitude for giving thanks" (*rendre grâce de rendre grâce*), to owe one's very thankfulness to the initiative of the Other, is the opposite of an attempt to consider oneself the origin. The mystic experiences the essentially veiled presence of God as the tension between the past of a having passed and a coming that is continually deferred (it is always still to come). But "desire for God's presence"—does this not sound like a sublimated need, a kind of hunger that should be satisfied by God as the supreme good? If that were mystical desire, the ultimate meaning of life would lie in a highest autarchy or self-sufficiency. Does not such a hedonism destroy the absolute demands of morality?

What is the content of the presence that mystics have experienced? What is the aim of the love through which the saints characterize God? The texts from Jeremiah, Matthew, and John cited above illuminate Saint John of the Cross's answer: to say that the love of God is a desire for his presence means that love desires yet more love (*está clamando por más amor*).[8] The "fulfillment" or completion for which love yearns is a greater love. Love wants no stilling of its hunger, but rather its radicalization. The "perfect grace which I desire"—expressed by Moses with the words "Show me your Face, so that I may know you and find

---

7. Ibid., n.4: "sintió estar allí un inmenso ser encubierto, del cual le communica Dios ciertos visos entreoscuros de su divina hermosura. . . . en deseo de aquello que siente encubierto allí en aquella presencia. . . . con deseo de engolfarse en aquel sumo bien que siente presente y encubierto, porque, aunque está encubierto, muy notablemente siente el bien y deleite que allí hay" (p. 449: "the soul feels an immense hidden being is there from which God communicates to her some semi-clear glimpses of His divine beauty . . . desire for what she feels hidden there in that presence . . . longing to be engulfed in that supreme good she feels present and hidden, for although it is hidden she has a noticeable experience of the good and delight present there").

8. *Canción,* n.10 (pp. 451–52 passim).

the perfect grace in your sight, which I desire" (Exod. 33:13)—is understood by John of the Cross as "the perfect love of God's glory."[9] John knows that not even Moses could see the face of God, since no soul in this weak life can bear the enjoyment of seeing the face of God."[10] Love itself is the healing and health of the soul,[11] for which it gladly gives its life, because "the soul lives more where it loves than there where it gives life."[12] The soul remains ill so long as its love is not perfect, that is, so long as it is not unified with the presence and shape or figure (*presencia y figura*) of the beloved and so is "reshaped" or "transfigured."[13] This transfiguration is in no way a submerging of the independent subject into an ocean of divine energy and feeling, but a completely different sort of transformation. In praying that God may "take possession" of it,[14] the soul expresses its desire that the "sketch" (*cierto dibujo*) of love which it has become through radical passivity be transformed into an actual figure of perfect love. This happens, John says, when in grace, that is, through the Spirit, the soul shows the *figura* (the form and appearance) of the one who is the definitive word of God, or, drawing on another metaphor, the Son of God, or again, using a third metaphor, the splendor of God's glory.[15] The suffering of love (*dolencia de amor*), far from expressing a narcissistic nostalgia for the

---

9. Ibid., n.5: "la gracia complida que deseo, lo cual es llegar al perfecto amor de la gloria de Dios" (p. 450; "the full grace which I desire [Exod. 33:12–13], that is, to reach the perfect love of the glory of God").

10. Ibid., n.5: "es tanta la hermosura de mi cara y el deleite de la vista de mi ser, que no la podrá sufrir tu alma en esa suerte de vida tan flaca" (p. 450: "such is the beauty of My face and the delight derived from the sight of my being, that your soul will be unable to withstand it in a life as weak as this"). Levinas refers frequently to the immediately subsequent passage from Exodus, according to which Moses must remain in a cleft in the rocks as God "passes by." Cf, e.g., Emmanuel Levinas, *En découvrant l'existence avec Husserl et Heidegger,* 3rd ed., (Paris: Vrin, 1974), p. 202.

11. Ibid., n.11: "la salud del alma es el amor de Dios" (p. 452: "love of God is the soul's health").

12. Ibid., n.10: "porque más vive el alma adonde ama que donde anima, y así tiene en poco esta vida temporal" (p. 452: "for the soul lives where it loves more than where it gives life, and thus has but little esteem for this temporal life").

13. Ibid., n.12: "el amor nunca llega a estar perfecto hasta que emparejan tan en uno los amantes, que se transfiguran el uno en el otro, y entonces está el amor todo sano" (pp. 452–53: "love never reaches perfection until the lovers are so united that one is transfigured in the other, and then the love is in full health").

14. Ibid., n.2: "Deseando, pues, el alma verse poseída ya de este gran Dios . . ." (p. 448: "The soul, desiring to be possessed by this immense God . . .").

15. Ibid., n.12 (references occur on p. 453).

mother's lap, is the pain that lies in not being-for-the-Other in a perfect mode. Authentic suffering consists in the imperfection of love (*falta de amor*). It shows that the soul has a lack of love—though not a complete lack—since it is only through the love it does have that it can discover what it lacks.[16]

DEATH

Unity with God is reached as a likeness with the Son, that is, through uniformity with the perfect image of the Good. This correspondence can be indicated by the words cites above from Jer. 22:16. Since the goodness toward one's neighbor includes giving one's own life and thus also one's own death for the Other, it can be clarified through Christian metaphors in which the cross has become the central image. The God of whom it is said that he is *semper major*, greater than every reality that can be thought, reveals himself as *semper minor*: as a man humiliated unto death because he did not refuse service, but rather became completely one with it.

In our history, we have been confronted with the terrible fact that Christians, whose election implies the suffering and death of Christ—a suffering and death which they likewise had to fulfill—again and again imposed suffering and death on Jews. How is it possible that we have not recognized the Passion in the persecution of God's people, and why is it so difficult for Jews to recognize the same Passion in Jesus?

The encounter with Christ is an encounter with the poor, the leprous, the foreign, the oppressed, the persecuted, the humiliated, and the marginal. The presence of Christ is, as the presence of God, essentially hidden. The encounter with a neighbor is at the same time a memory of the Lord's passing by and an anticipation of his coming. Between the events we memorialize and the ever-deferred coming, Christ does not reveal himself through appearances, but in the figure of the needy. The poor come "in the name of the Lord." Christ therefore comes as the always present exception that disturbs the order of powers and authorities. Recognition of this presence shows understanding of the Spirit and obedience to God's Word.

---

16. Ibid., n.14 (p. 453).

RESURRECTION AND FORGIVENESS

Some people have suggested that belief in the resurrection is an unbiblical version of the apotheoses through which Greeks and Romans have deified some of their heroes. Such deifications were easy because their gods were human, all too human. Christians who celebrate the death of Christ testify to the indestructible meaning and posthumous fecundity of a life that has exhausted itself in obedience. The Christian overcoming of death does not lie in the promise of a second, paradisal life; it does not point to a repetition of this earthly life on a happier plane; instead, it announces the possibility of perfect intimacy with the spirit of God, a spirit that is love. In the death of the righteous, the Torah has revealed itself to be invincible. The peace which the resurrected preaches to his disciples and the blessedness of the Sermon on the Mount are not forms of compensation, but "consolation": one will be completely united with the task to which one has been called. And yet, perfect obedience to the law of love seems to surpass our capacity.

How can one really and truly live for all others? When Christians speak of forgiveness, do they not awaken the suspicion that they take neither human crime nor the divine commandments seriously? Do we not say that the passion of Christ has expunged sins, repaying them on our behalf? Do we not trust that God's mercy clothes us in a justice given from on high? We represent salvation as the participation in a drama performed "for us" by Christ. Do we do so in order to free ourselves from the hard demands of the Law, the responsibilities of justice and justly deserved punishments? Do we prefer the pathos of tragedy to the prosaic and boring everydayness of a morality that is always unsatisfied?

Intimacy with God cannot mean that the law of love is abolished in the Kingdom of God. There is no place in heaven for the criminal. On the other hand, we are also convinced that life and hope have the same duration. Christian hope is always hope for a still greater capacity for love, never a hope that love can be mixed with injustice, or God with the devil. Sometimes hope for greater love means that we should begin to love. Conversion to the practice of being-for-the-Other presupposes grace, however. The Spirit of the Good is older than human freedom. Grace reveals itself as mercy, which grants us the ability to act. The law that links us to each other does not oblige us to choose between two alliances. The claim that grace takes up the law as an element of itself does not relativize or degrade the law of justice and love; instead, it emphasizes the spirit through which the law is God's way of making us spiritual.

AUTONOMY AND HETERONOMY

The heteronomous orientation of original passivity confirms and strengthens the autonomy of a subject who is at home in the world and enjoys life. Autonomy and heteronomy go together, once love of life develops through a conversion of spontaneous egoism into hospitality and gratitude. However, gratitude—and the same is true of hope—does not primarily concern the enjoyment of life, but rather the capacity for hospitality, sufferance, gratitude, and hope themselves. Patristic and medieval theologians have employed Greek categories in their attempt to think the unity of human autonomy and God's sovereignty. Revelation was interpreted with the help of concepts such as "participation" and "analogy." Wishing to expand on the central place of the will, late medieval and modern theologians have favored other categories, and interpreted revelation in juridical metaphors. Judgments, decisions, decrees, laws, rewards and punishments were preferred over the language of Greek ontology, which later was criticized for polluting the biblical message. Was this critique a return to a genuinely Judaic understanding of the tradition? Can the Greek elements within Christian theology be defended as *logoi spermatikoi* of the Christian faith? Or must we begin by freeing ourselves of all Greek influence in order that we might hear the pure voice of the one God who kills all gods?

Levinas's critique of ontology is certainly not a plea for the eradication of the Greek components from our culture. He has frequently pointed to the greatness of Greek rationality, metaphysics, science, and politics. Judaism does not aim at a destruction of Greek, Roman, German, or any other culture. Indeed, it is essentially universalistic. Does not the Judaic people stand for the whole of humanity?

Modern individuals cannot sever their Greek roots. Those who nonetheless attempt to do so most often fall themselves into caricatures of Greek thought. However, it is obvious that the spirit of Christianity is neither Greek nor Judaic. Are we children, brothers and sisters, or distant relatives of Israel? Many Jews standing at the beginning of

Christian history, Jesus in the first place, attempted to renew the heritage of Israel. Through their interpretation of the Mosaic and prophetic traditions, they wished to radicalize them. In Levinas's
understanding, the law of universal love is as old as the revelation
through which God assembled his people; it is the *plērōma*, the perfection and fulfillment of the Thora.

It is a world-historical tragedy that Judaism and Christianity so
quickly separated from one another. What was meant as a Judaic return
to the source became an extra-Judaic movement that sometimes turned
anti-Judaic. Since the break between the Jews who rejected Jesus and
those who acknowledged him as the greatest prophet, the two families
have never ceased searching in the Bible for traces and instructions of
God. Currents of interpretation confronted one another for two thousand years. On one side we find the long history of Talmudic and post-
Talmudic commentaries, on the other side the Christian Bible and a
multiplicity of Christian theologies. Thus the faith of Abraham is presented to us in a broken form which contradicts the universalistic claim
of Judaism and the desire of Christianity to gather all Jews and
Gentiles to itself. Was it necessary to leave the synagogue in order to
welcome the Gentiles? Did we sin by impatience? Was the lack of a
dialogue a necessary detour toward an eschatological universalism?
Through the division, Christians have lost a part of their heritage,
including certain parts of the Talmudic and later Jewish developments
that went unnoticed by Christians. No Christian church can say that it
fully understands the Bible as long as it has not patiently opened itself
to the long wisdom of Jewish interpreters. We cannot fully understand
the *plērōma* of the Law so long as we have not worked through the
questions that separate us from older brothers and sisters. Does the
Spirit of God reveal itself now, in our efforts of mutual understanding
and discussion?

EPILOGUE

—Though this is the "next meeting" for which you set me a task in our first discussion, I will not yet offer you a systematic theory of the basic definitions and connections between human life, reason, opinion, faith, knowledge, perception, intuition, science, argumentation, philosophy, theology, and so on, but rather invite you to reflect with me on the ways in which the master-thinkers presented here tried to make sense of human destiny.

—To tell you the truth, most of them struck me—and regularly irritated me—by their pious attitude. You seem to prefer religious minds over rigorous scholars who refrain from bothering their readers with private musings on God and religion.

—If it is true—as some thinkers have maintained—that a human being is not only a *living* being that is *rational* and *free*, but also a *praying* being (an *animal orans*), it would be odd to believe that religion is something so private that one should keep it out of the public domain. I agree with you that our most intimate feelings should not be trumpeted lightly and that authenticity in doing so is difficult and rare, but there are circumstances that demand it. Could we, for example, avoid talking about piety in a conversation on the ultimate meaning of our lives? It is revealing that scholarly language about (for example) love, trust, anxiety, despair, art, religion, and so on, neither irritates nor embarrasses us, as long as we confine ourselves to an academic treatment, while the objectifying reduction that is inherent to such treatment cannot but scandalize those who are involved in love, poetry, religious celebrations, and so on. Is the academy incapable of taking the lived reality for what it is? Has it narrowed its scope by deciding that objectivity excludes being touched by emotional phenomena? If so, could this fact be an indication of its lack in profundity? Is modern scholarship not thorough enough to welcome the most important questions of life and destiny?

—Even if that were true, it would not imply that believing scholars should mix the results of their research with effusions about their religious emotions. I find it outright indecent that certain professors do not respect the well-established code that preserves the University from contamination by Church affairs.

—Does not the separation between University and Church (or between research and religion) reveal the academic inability or unwillingness to seriously deal with questions of ultimate meaning?

—That separation rather manifests the contrast between the objectivity of the scientific enterprise and the subjectivity of metaphysical and theological questions. Even many Catholic philosophers keep their professional work apart from their religious convictions.

—If this is a fact, they might be mistaken. How can persons for whom God is the creative, redemptive, and all-embracing presence, exclude their deepest conviction from a discipline that claims to seek the most originary and universal principles and perspectives of the human world and history?

—Many of your theologians seem to disagree with you, when they state that philosophers cannot surpass the limits of "natural reason," and that the difference between philosophers and theologians lies exactly in the fact that the former abstract from any faith and revelation. For atheists the distinction between natural reason and faith-guided reason is of course futile, but atheist and Christian philosophers share the same point of departure: their search for truth and meaning is autonomous. Whether, in fact, philosophizing Christians do not in some secret or unrecognized way appeal to their faith is not clear, however. Heidegger might be right in stating that Christians cannot be authentic philosophers because their faith has provided them with the answers to the most fundamental questions even before they can ask them. The (re)search of Christians who philosophize is neither serious, nor authentic: they play a game.

—If "natural" experiences and assumptions from which atheist and Christian philosophers start were identical, their agreement would show in the ethical and theoretical practice that follow from their shared perspective. The difference would then lie in some additions for which a certain faith or belief would be responsible. How important could such additions be for the life and thought of the philosopher who accepts that belief or faith? If, for instance, a Christian interprets the Revelation in which she believes as a "super-natural" addition to the (partial) truth that can be discovered through the "natural" reason she shares with all other philosophers, what then is the impact of this super-structure on her life? Would faith and revelation not rather permeate and transform the presupposed "nature" (including its reason) that was the (putatively) common point of departure? If "nature" and "super-nature" remain two neatly distinct and theoretically separable parts of the truth without influencing one another, what then does it mean that the one God is the infinite, omnipresent, and all-embracing Creator and Lover of humanity, as Christians believe? In fact, the idea of two layers—one of which ("nature") Christians share with non-Christians, while the other (grace) is reserved for the former alone—does not do justice to the basic experiences on which they build their philosophies. Certainly, the theological distinction between "nature" (or creation) and "grace" has a useful meaning, but it does not run parallel with, on the one hand, a non-Christian ("natural" or "pagan") existence, and on the other hand, a "supernatural" supplement that belongs to those who have not only reason, but also faith. If the Creator is gracious, grace is operative in everybody everywhere ("*tout est grâce*"); no "nature" or "reason" escapes this influence. If the Good exists, it must be real and experienced. A theology that separates the concrete reasonability of historical persons from God's self-revelation is as outdated as the idea of a faithless autonomy.

—Are you attacking the very principle of all philosophical principles?!

—Are you defending that any modern thinker has produced a presuppositionless philosophy? Or are you prepared to recognize that not only theologies but even all philosophies are rooted in some kind of faith?

—Even if a historian of philosophy could prove that none of the proposed systems was independent with regard to some faith, this would not destroy the principle on which the entire modern philosophy was based. We might still lack the intelligence to realize the ideal of intellectual autonomy, but we must uphold it as an *ideal*, lest we fall back on the arbitrariness of a fideistic subjectivism.

—Is there no middle way? The fact that none of the historically exist-ing philosophies have been successful in fully meeting the modern standard of autonomously proved truth certainly does not demonstrate that such an endeavor is impossible. But can we even imagine the con-tours of its successful realization after all we have learned about the importance of contexts, traditions, and history? In any case, the claim that the ideal must be maintained, even if it might turn out to be a utopian dream, is a clear example of faith. As one version of modern humanism, it competes with other forms of trust and piety. If it is affirmed or practiced as the radical and ultimate truth for humans or as the all-encompassing framework of all truth, then it is a religion with-out God (though it might revere its own god or gods).

—I like neither the trick you are playing on me in reducing my posi-tion to one of the many religions, nor the suggestion that I would adore lower gods than the God of Christianity. You must recognize that mod-ern humanism has liberated the world from a superhuman Power that threatens us by diminishing the grandeur of human freedom and cre-ativity. Your God flattens our drama, whereas our courage has opened space and time for as yet unsuspected adventures without end.

—If the Infinite indeed endangered human freedom, growth, and grandeur, I would adopt your kind of humanism; as a Christian, how-ever, I believe that infinite Goodness can only be manifested and expe-rienced as a generous promise of utmost width and unsurpassable joy. If admirable thinkers—whether they are Christians or not—show me signs and traces of such a Goodness, it makes me happy; wouldn't you be delighted to ruminate the food such thinkers have prepared for our souls?

WORKS CITED AND EDITIONS USED

Anselmus of Canterbury. *Fides Quaerens Intellectum, id est Proslogion; Liber Gaunilonis pro insipiente, atque Liber Apologeticus contra Gaunilonem.* Ed. Alexandre Koyré. Paris: J. Vrin, 1930.

Aristotle. *Aristoteles, Graece ex recensione Immanuelis Bekkeri,* 2 vols. Ed. Academia Regia Borussica. Berlin, 1831.

Augustinus, Aurelius. *De Moribus Ecclesiae.* In *Obras de San Augustín,* vol. 4. Madrid: Biblioteca de Autores Cristianos, 1956.

_____. *De Civitate Dei.* In *Oeuvres de Saint Augustine,* vols. 33–37. Paris: Desclée de Brouwer, 1959–60.

Bonaventura. *Commentaria in IV Libros Sententiarum.* vols. 1–4 of *Opera Theologica Selecta.* Quaracchi-Firenze, Italy: Collegio de San Bonaventura, 1934–49.

_____. *Itinerarium Mentis in Deum.* Trans. and ed. Philotheus Boehner. St. Bonaventure, N.Y.: The Franciscan Institute, 1956.

_____. *Breviloquium.* In *Obras de San Buenaventura,* vol. 1. Madrid: Biblioteca de Autores Cristianos, 1957.

_____. *Collationes in Hexaemeron.* In *Obras de San Buenaventura,* vol. 3. Madrid: Biblioteca de Autores Cristianos, 1957.

_____. *Soliloquium.* In *Obras de San Buenaventura,* vol. 4. Madrid: Biblioteca de Autores Cristianos, 1957.

_____. *Disputed Questions on the Mystery of the Trinity.* Trans. and ed. Zachary Hayes. St. Bonaventure, N.Y.: The Franciscan Institute, 1979.

Bougerol, Jacques Guy. *Saint Bonaventure: Études sur les sources de sa pensée.* Northampton, England: Variorum Reprints, 1989.

Buckley, Michael. *The Origins of Modern Atheism.* New Haven, Conn.: Yale University Press, 1987.

Catechism of the Catholic Church. New York: Paulist Press, 1994.

Courcelle, Pierre. *Connais-toi toi-même de Socrate à Saint Bernard.* Paris: Etudes Augustiniennes, 1975.

De Lubac, Henri. *Surnaturel: Études historiques.* Paris: Aubier, 1946.

_____. *Sur les chemins de Dieu.* Paris: Aubier, 1956.

Descartes, René. *Oeuvres de Descartes.* Ed. Charles Adam and Paul Tannery, 13 vols. Paris: Cerf, 1897–1913, cited as *AT.*

_____. *Oeuvres Philosophiques.* Ed. Ferdinand Alquié. Paris: Garnier, 1963–73.

_____. *Philosophical Letters.* Trans. and ed. Anthony Kenny. Oxford: Clarendon, 1970.

_____. *Entretien avec Burman.* Ed. Charles Adam. Paris: J. Vrin, 1975.

_____. *The Philosophical Writings of Descartes.* Trans. John Cottingham, Robert Stoothoff, and Dagald Murdoch. Cambridge: Cambridge University Press, 1985, cited as *PW.*

Dionysius. *The Divine Names and Mystical Theology.* Ed. and trans. John D. Jones. Milwaukee: Marquette University Press, 1980.

_____. *Corpus Dionysiacum,* 2 vols. Ed. Beata Regina Suchla, Günter Heil, and Adolf Martin Ritter. Berlin: Walter de Gruyter, 1990–91.

Dupré, Louis. *Passage to Modernity: An Essay in Hermeneutics of Nature and Culture.* New Haven, Conn.: Yale University Press, 1993.

Gilson, Etienne. *Introduction à l'étude de Saint Augustin.* Paris: J. Vrin, 1931.

Grégoire de Nysse. *La vie de Moïse.* Paris: Cerf, 1968.

Guéroult, Martial. *Descartes selon l'ordre des raisons,* 2nd ed. 2 vols. Paris: Aubier, 1968.

Hegel, Georg Wilhelm Friedrich. *Gesammelte Werke.* Hamburg: Meiner, 1968ff, cited as *GW.*

_____. *Werke* (Jubiläumsausgabe), ed. Hermann Glockner, 20 vols. Stuttgart: Frommann, 1927ff.

_____. *Vorlesungen über die Geschichte der Philosophie,* ed. Glockner 19 (XV).

_____. *Vorlesungen über die Philosophie der Religion,* ed. Glockner 16 (XII).

_____. *Die Vernunft in der Geschichte,* 5th ed. Ed. Johannes Hoffmeister. Hamburg: Meiner, 1955.

_____. *Grundlinien der Philosophie des Rechts,* 4th ed. Ed. Johannes Hoffmeister. Hamburg: Meiner, 1955.

_____. *Berliner Schriften 1818–1831*. Hamburg: Meiner, 1956.

_____. *Encyclopädie der Philosophischen Wissenschaften im Grundrisse zum Gebrauch seiner Vorlesungen. GW* vol. 20. Hamburg: Meiner, 1992.

Heidegger, Martin. *Einführung in die Metaphysik*. Tübingen: Niemeyer, 1966.

Historisches Wörterbuch der Philosophie, Joachim Ritter and Karlfried Gründer, eds., Basel: Schwabe, 1971ff.

Juan de la Cruz. *Obras Completas*. Ed. Simeon de la Sagrada Familia. Burgos, Spain: El Monte Carmelo, 1959.

_____. *The Collected Works of St. John of the Cross*. Trans. K. Kavanaugh and O. Rodriguez. Washington, D.C.: Institute of Carmelite Studies, 1979.

Leibniz, Gottfried Wilhelm. *Essais de Théodicée: Sur la bonté de Dieu, la liberté de l'homme et l'origine du mal*. Ed. J. Brunschwig. Paris: Garnier-Flammarion, 1969.

Levinas, Emmanuel. *Totalité et Infini: Essai sur l'extériorité*. The Hague: Nijhoff, 1961.

_____. *Humanisme de l'autre homme*. Montpellier, France: Fata Morgana, 1972.

_____. *En découvrant l'existence avec Husserl et Heidegger*, 3rd ed. Paris: J. Vrin, 1974.

_____. *Autrement qu'être ou au-delà de l'essence*. The Hague: Nijhoff, 1974.

_____. *Difficile liberté: Essais sur le Judaïsme* (deuxième édition refondue et complétée). Paris: Albin Michel, 1976.

_____. *L'Au-delà du verset: Lectures et Discours Talmudiques*. Paris: Minuit, 1982.

_____. *Entre nous: Essais sur le penser-à-l'autre*. Paris: Grasset, 1991.

Pascal, Blaise. *Pensées et opuscules*. Ed. Léon Brunschvicg. Paris: Hachette, n.d.

Peperzak, Adriaan Theodoor. "A la recherche de l'expérience vraie." in *Archives de Philosophie* 29 (1966), pp. 348–62.

_____. *Le jeune Hegel et la vision morale du Monde*, 2nd ed. The Hague: Nijhoff, 1969.

_____. *Der heutige Mensch und die Heilsfrage*. Freiburg, Germany: Herder, 1972.

_____. "Pointers toward a Dialogue" in *Man and World* 9 (1976), pp. 372–92.

_____. "Religion et politique dans la philosophie de Hegel," in *Hegel et la religion*. Ed. G. Planty-Bonjour. Paris: Presses Universitaires de France, 1982.

_____. "The Foundations of Ethics According to Hegel." in *International Philosophical Quarterly* 23 (1983), pp. 349–65.

_____. *System and History in Philosophy*. Albany: State University of New York Press, 1986.

_____. "Hegel et la culture moderne." in *Revue Philosophique de Louvain* 84 (1986), 5–24.

_____. *Selbsterkenntnis des Absoluten: Grundlinien der Hegelschen Philosophie des Geistes*. Stuttgart-Bad Cannstatt: Frommann-Holzboog, 1987.

_____. *Philosophy and Politics: A Commentary on the Preface of Hegel's Philosophy of Spirit*. Boston: Kluwer, 1987.

_____. *Hegels praktische Philosophie:* Stuttgart-Bad Cannstatt: Frommann-Holzboog, 1991.

_____. *To the Other: An Introduction to the Philosophy of Emmanuel Levinas*. West Lafayette, Ind.: Purdue University Press, 1993.

_____. "Logic and History in Hegel's Philosophy of Spirit" in *Vernunftbegriffe in der Moderne*. Ed. Hans-Friedrich Fulda and Rolf-Peter Horstmann. Stuttgart: Klett-Cotta, 1994.

_____. "Hegel Contra Hegel in His Philosophy of Right: The Contradictions of International Politics" in *Journal of the History of Philosophy* 32 (1994), pp. 241–64.

_____. "Second Nature: Place and Significance of the Objective Spirit in Hegel's Encyclopedia" in *The Owl of Minerva* 27 (1995), pp. 51–66.

_____. *Platonic Transformations: With and After Hegel, Heidegger and Levinas*. Lanham. Md.: Rowman and Littlefield, 1997.

_____. "Hegel's Pflichten und Tugendlehre." in *G. W. F. Hegel: Grundlinien der Philosophie des Rechts*. Ed. Ludwig Siep. Berlin: Akademie Verlag, 1997.

_____. *Beyond: the Philosophy of Emmanuel Levinas*. Evanston, Ill.: Northwestern University Press, 1997.

_____. *Modern Freedom: Hegel's Legal, Moral, and Political Philosophy*. Boston: Kluwer, 2001.

_____. *Elements of Ethics.* Stanford, Calif.: Stanford University Press, 2003.

Plato. *Oeuvres Complètes.* 13 vols. Paris: Les Belles Lettres, 1925–30.

Plotinus. *Plotins Schriften.* 5 vols. Trans. Richard Harder. Hamburg: Meiner, 1956–58.

Schlier, Heinrich. *Die Zeit der Kirche.* 2nd ed. Freiburg, Germany: Herder, 1958.

Schlosser, Marianne. "Lux inaccessibilis. Zur Negativen Theologie bei Bonaventura" in *Franziskanische Studien* 68 (1968).

_____. *Cognitio et Amor: zum kognitiven und voluntativen Grund der Gottes-erfahrung nach Bonaventura,* Paderborn, Germany: Schöningh, 1990.

Siep, Ludwig, ed., *G. W. F. Hegel, Grundlinien der Philosophie des Rechts,* Berlin: Akademie Verlag, 1997.

Tennemann, Wilhelm Gottlieb. *Geschichte der Philosophie,* 11 vols., Leipzig, 1798–1819.

INDEX